Theory of Mind

How Children Understand Others' Thoughts and Feelings

- Martin J. Doherty

Psychology Press
Taylor & Francis Group

HOVE AND NEW YORK

1005711061

First published 2009
by Psychology Press
27 Church Road, Hove, East Sussex BN3 2FA

Simultaneously published in the USA and
Canada
by Psychology Press
270 Madison Avenue, New York, NY 10016

*Psychology Press is an imprint of the Taylor &
Francis Group, an informa business*

Copyright © 2009 Psychology Press

Typeset in Sabon by RefineCatch Limited,
Bungay, Suffolk
Printed and bound in Great Britain by
TJ International Ltd, Padstow, Cornwall
Cover design by Aubergine Creative Design

*British Library Cataloguing in Publication
Data*
A catalogue record for this book is available
from the British Library

*Library of Congress Cataloging-in-
Publication Data*
Doherty, Martin J., 1968–
   Theory of mind : how children understand
others' thoughts and feelings / Martin J.
Doherty.
      p. cm.
   Includes bibliographical references and
index.
   ISBN 978–1–84169–570–9 –
ISBN 978–1–84169–571–6   1. Philosophy of
mind in children.   I. Title.
   BF723.P48D64 2008
   155.4′13 – dc22
                                        2008006823

ISBN: 978–1–84169–570–9 (hbk)
ISBN: 978–1–84169–571–6 (pbk)

Dedication

To Mattie Agnes Doherty, 1940–2007.

Contents

List of figures

FIGURES

Acknowledgements

General gratitude is due to my undergraduate and PhD supervisors. Norman Freeman's infectious enthusiasm strongly influenced my choice of career. Josef Perner led me through the difficult process of becoming a competent scientist. A number of people have helped me to write this book, especially through discussion and comments on early drafts. Thanks are particularly due to James Anderson, Steve Butterfill, Robin Campbell, Mickey Yu Chi Huang, Daniela Kloo, Debbie Riby, Josephine Ross, Ted Ruffman and Marina Wimmer. Josephine Ross drew Figure 2.1. Hannah Buchanan-Smith, Michelle Klailova and Louise Lock kindly supplied pictures of three of the primate species in Figure 7.1. Catriona Bruce and Bob Lavery were very helpful with the illustrations. Ian Apperly and Claire Hughes reviewed the first draft and made numerous helpful suggestions. Roger Watt, my former head of department, advised me to stop writing this book—sage advice that would have given me back 2 years of evenings and weekends. Phyllis Lee, my current head of department, has been very supportive as the effort drew to a close.

Milne extract in Chapter 1 used with permission: text by A. A. Milne, copyright © The Trustees of the Pooh Properties included with permission of Curtis Brown Group Ltd, London.

While writing this I was obsessive about consulting primary sources. Using other people's accounts of others' research findings or theories can save a lot of time. However, secondary sources are often inaccurate, and occasionally plain wrong. I have consulted virtually everything cited in the book, except where otherwise stated. Any mistakes are therefore my own.

This book is dedicated to my mom, who would have given it pride of place on her bookshelf.

Chapter 1

Introduction to theory of mind

Introduction

TELLING PEOPLE YOU ARE a psychologist rarely goes down well. The usual response is, "Oh, you must be analysing everything I say". Well, yes and no. The truth is that despite years studying their subject, psychologists are little or no better than everyone else at working out what is going on in the minds of those around them. This is because human beings are natural psychologists. We have an insatiable interest in people. Even in casual meetings we make constant inferences about the psychological states of others. Consider the following excerpt from Jane Austen's *Pride and Prejudice* (1813, volume 1, chapter 10):

> ... Elizabeth could not help observing ... how frequently Mr. Darcy's eyes were fixed on her. She hardly knew how to suppose that she could be an object of admiration to so great a man; and yet that he should look at her because he disliked her, was still more strange. She could only imagine, however, at last that she drew his notice because there was a something about her more wrong and reprehensible, according to his ideas of right, than in any other

1

person present. The supposition did not pain her. She liked him too little to care for his approbation.

Elizabeth notices Darcy's *attention*, and tries to infer his *attitude* and *intention*. She uses her opinion about his peculiar *beliefs* of what is good and bad in other people. Her conclusions do not cause her negative *emotions*, because she is indifferent to his *attitudes*. Elizabeth is doing some subtle psychology here, and the reader is doing more by considering Elizabeth's thoughts about Darcy's mental states. We find this effortless—adults are great natural psychologists.

This everyday psychology is what is meant by theory of mind. Arguably it is a defining characteristic of human beings, distinguishing us from other animals. Nick Humphrey (1983) has suggested we might more appropriately be called *Homo psychologicus* rather than *Homo sapiens*. The nature of our theory of mind is therefore an important issue. Long-standing debates concern whether this ability is unique to humans, or shared with any other species, whether it requires language, and whether or to what extent it is an innate ability. To address these questions requires the study of children as their theory of mind develops.

Children are no less fascinated by other people than adults. This is reflected in children's literature. Consider this excerpt from the classic, *Winnie-the-Pooh* (Milne, 1926). Rabbit has a plan to get Kanga and Roo to leave the forest. The plan is motivated by jealousy of the attention Christopher Robin is giving the new arrivals:

> "The best way," said Rabbit, "would be this. The best way would be to steal Baby Roo and hide him, and then when Kanga says, 'Where's Baby Roo?' we say, '*Aha!*' "
> "*Aha!*" said Pooh practising. "*Aha! Aha!* ... Of course," he went on, "we could say '*Aha!*' even if we hadn't stolen Baby Roo."
> "Pooh," said Rabbit kindly, "you haven't any brain."
> "I know," said Pooh humbly.
> "We say '*Aha!*' so that Kanga knows that *we* know where Baby Roo is. '*Aha!*' means 'We'll tell you where Baby Roo is, if you promise to go away from the forest and never come back,' ...." (p. 91)

To understand this passage, amongst other things children need to understand Rabbit's *jealousy*, and that Rabbit *thinks* that, when they say "Aha!", Kanga will *know* that the conspirators *know* where Baby Roo is. This kind of sophisticated mental state reasoning may be available to children by the age of about 7 years (so Milne perhaps overestimated his readership). Whether or not children understand them, children's books are stuffed with references to mental states; this is so even for books aimed at 3- to 4-year-olds, and more so for slightly older children (Dyer, Shatz & Wellman, 2000).

Children's understanding of mental states

Among the most basic mental states you need to understand to explain or predict behaviour are beliefs and desires. If I *want* a cookie, and I *believe* reaching inside the cookie jar will get me a cookie, then I will reach inside the cookie jar—all things being equal. (This last proviso is important because the causes of behaviour are complex. If I have a fear of being caught with my hand in the jar, I may prefer to go hungry. Similarly, I may be on a diet.) Surprisingly, the question of when children can predict people's behaviour based on beliefs and desires was not addressed until the 1980s. Until then, developmental psychology was still very much under the influence of Jean Piaget, the great Swiss psychologist. According to Piaget's theory, young children are profoundly egocentric: They are only able to consider things from their own point of view until they are about 7 years or older. What is now known as theory of mind was considered to emerge as part of a general escape from the confines of egocentrism in middle childhood. This diverted attention away from the surprisingly rapid development of the ability to understand others' beliefs around the age of 4 years. Researchers driven by a powerful theory can sometimes miss the blindingly obvious.

The change was brought about by an influential paper by two primatologists, David Premack and Guy Woodruff (1978): "Does the Chimpanzee Have a Theory of Mind?" This question of chimpanzee theory of mind remains hotly contested, but in a commentary on the paper, the philosopher Daniel Dennett suggested a way of determining the answer. He briefly sketched what has become known as the false belief task, taking as one example a Punch and Judy show. Children squeal with glee as Mr Punch prepares to throw a box over a cliff. Although they have seen Judy escape from the box while Punch's back was turned, it is "obvious—obvious enough for four-year-old children—that Punch believes (falsely) that Judy is in the box" (Dennett, 1978, p. 569). Dennett's reference to 4-year-olds is a notable piece of foresight. The method was put into developmental practice by Heinz Wimmer and Josef Perner soon after. They found that 4- to 5-year-old children can indeed predict the actions of someone with a false belief.

Younger children do not appear to understand belief. They predict that people will behave in a way that makes sense according to how things really are. If Daddy wants a cookie, and if the child has put the cookies in the toaster, Daddy will go to the toaster. If Daddy instead goes to the cookie jar, children find this difficult to explain. Younger children do seem to have a good grasp of desire, however. As a result, understanding of desire has received less attention. There is good reason to suspect that young children understand desire in quite a different way to adults, but their way of understanding is adequate for most situations they encounter.

Development of the research field

During the 1980s, psychologists explored different aspects of the child's theory of mind. By the start of the 1990s, some of them began to contest the claim that children only understood beliefs from the age of about 4 years. Literally hundreds of experiments addressed this issue; a surprising number of developmental psychologists object to claims of development—this is particularly so for cognitive development. There were dramatic demonstrations of early ability, as well as failures to replicate these findings or revelations that they were due to experimental artefacts. The sheer number of studies with conflicting findings was an obstacle to forming any sensible overall opinion. Fortunately, Wellman, Cross and Watson (2001) entered a large number of such studies into what is known as a meta-analysis. This showed that although certain methodological changes may alter the difficulty of the task, none of them causes 3-year-olds to perform better than chance.

This cleared away residual doubts about the validity of the central finding of the field, that preschoolers undergo a major change in their understanding of the mind at roughly 4 years. Researchers then became free to ask more interesting questions. This was one reason why I decided to write this book: The field has finally acquired a degree of stability, coherence and depth. Recently, however, Onishi and Baillargeon (2005) have shown that 15-month-old infants may be sensitive to false belief (see Chapter 2). A long-standing tension in the field is between those who believe theory of mind abilities are innately specified, and those who believe they are constructed through interaction with the physical and social world. Although Wellman et al. (2001) convincingly demonstrate that 3-year-olds cannot make explicit judgements of behaviour based on false beliefs, Onishi and Baillargeon's findings suggest that the seed of this ability may be present very early. The next few years promise to be very enlightening about the nature and origins of theory of mind.

One reason for the vibrancy and success of the field is that it lies at the intersection of several academic disciplines. Research into theory of mind was begun by two primatologists; the false belief task was suggested by a philosopher, and put into practice by two developmental psychologists. Since then, theory of mind has continued to be of central interest to primatologists, philosophers and developmental psychologists. They have been joined to varying degrees by abnormal psychologists, linguists, neuroscientists, palaeontologists, anthropologists and cross-cultural psychologists. This should not be surprising: Our ability to understand our own minds and those of others is central to what it means to be human.

Plan of the book

As Dennett argued, we can only be sure someone has a theory of mind when they understand beliefs. The book is organized around this critical insight. Chapter 2 concerns children's understanding of belief, particularly *false* belief. False belief has been so widely used because it creates a distinction between reality and someone's mental representation of reality. Research over the last 25 years is reviewed, covering children's ability to predict or explain the behaviour of people who have false beliefs, and children's attempts to induce false beliefs by lies or deception. The conclusion of this research is that these abilities are not in place until children are roughly 4 years old. However, some sensitivity to beliefs may exist much earlier.

Chapter 3 covers the three main theories of children's ability to ascribe beliefs to others: The Theory Theory asserts that our theory of mind really is like a theory; according to Simulation Theory, we use our own minds as a kind of "working model" of other people's minds, to predict what we would do if we were in their shoes; Modularity Theory assumes that we have evolved a specialized piece of neural hardware that does the job for us. These theories are all still in the running, and it is possible that our theory of mind is to some extent a hybrid of the three. My own opinion is that the data strongly support Theory Theory for the everyday ascription of beliefs and desires; Simulation Theory may well play a role in more complex theory of mind tasks, particularly those involving emotions; there is presently little specific evidence for involvement of specialized neural systems in development.

If the development at 4 years solely concerned understanding of false belief, it would be of only limited interest. Chapter 4 concerns developments in understanding of other mental states. At the same age children start to pass false belief tasks, they become able to ascribe knowledge and ignorance, distinguish between appearance and reality, and demonstrate a sophisticated understanding of desire. These abilities form the basis of sophisticated abilities to ascribe beliefs and knowledge, and to infer complex emotions. Chapter 5 extends the area of study to nonmental representational media. There is impressive evidence that children's ability to reflect on mental states is mirrored by comparable abilities to reflect on words and pictures.

Understanding of mental representation does not arise out of nowhere, and several precursors have been suggested. Chapter 6 deals with pretence. Children begin to pretend from 18 months, and pretending that something is the case appears similar to thinking that something is the case. However, most researchers think that children's initial understanding of pretence is in much simpler terms. Nevertheless, experience with pretend play probably gives useful practice at component theory of mind skills, and enhances children's social abilities. Chapter 7 looks at understanding of others' attention, particularly their gaze. Children become very good at following gaze in infancy. It has been argued that understanding what is before someone's eyes is a simple form of understanding what is currently in their mind. However, gaze *following* does not equate to gaze *understanding*. In fact, explicit understanding of visual attention does not develop until children are 3 years old. Understanding of eye direction therefore may not be a precursor to understanding of belief, but a concurrent related development.

Other cognitive abilities are developing around the age of 4 years. Chapter 8 looks at children's executive functioning: abilities involved in controlling one's own thought and attention processes. These abilities are related to theory of mind development in potentially complex ways. Insight into one's own mental states might allow better self-regulation and control; better self-control might be necessary to properly focus on mental states. The evidence suggests that both ideas have some merit, and development is likely to involve a complex interplay between theory of mind and executive functioning. As well as having rapidly developing executive skills, children's language is developing rapidly during the period they start to understand mental states. Chapter 9 considers the relationship between language and theory of mind. Children's use of mental state words gives an insight into their level of understanding—which generally confirms findings using experimental tasks. There are claims that specific aspects of language development, particularly syntax, are necessary for theory of mind development. The evidence reviewed suggests this is not so. However, conversational experience, particularly with parents, seems closely linked to theory of mind development. This chapter also covers social and cultural influences on theory of mind, many of which seem to be mediated by language.

The final chapter concerns autism. It was quickly realized that the symptoms of autism might result from a lack of theory of mind (Baron-Cohen, Leslie & Frith, 1985). The possibility of explaining this puzzling tragic disorder gave theory of mind research much impetus. Chapter 10 gives an account of autism, and reviews research on the theory of mind hypothesis of autism. The predictions of the hypothesis are largely confirmed. However, whether a lack of theory of mind is the cause of autism, one of several causes or an effect of some other cause, remains controversial in what is a fast-moving research field.

Chapter 2

Understanding belief

Introduction

THE PHRASE "THEORY OF MIND" hit the literature in 1978 when Premack and Woodruff posed the question, "Does the chimpanzee have a theory of mind?" Chimpanzee theory of mind remains controversial (see Chapter 7), and the answer to Premack and Woodruff's question is, "probably not". However, posing the question in such explicit terms caused others to wonder when young children could be said to have a theory of mind. Premack and Woodruff give a short broad basic definition of theory of mind: "the individual imputes mental states to himself and others" (p. 515). Since then the phrase has been used in such a variety of ways that it is impossible to give it any more precise definition. It is best treated as an umbrella term for children's understanding of mental states.

Arguably the most fundamental of mental states are belief and desire. What you think is the case and what you want will determine how you act. This chapter concerns belief, which has been the main focus of research in theory of mind. There are three main reasons why you might want to understand beliefs:

(1)   In order to predict behaviour. Behaviour is reasonably

predictable if you know what someone desires and what they believe. Other things being equal, they will behave in a way that would satisfy their desires if their beliefs were true.

(2)   In order to explain behaviour. If you see someone do something, especially something strange, their actions can be explained by inferring particular beliefs and desires. Knowing the person's beliefs in these circumstances can also help predict their subsequent behaviour. Their beliefs may also be informative, perhaps causing you to update your own beliefs about the situation.

(3)   In order to manipulate behaviour. In particular, if you can cause someone to believe something false (and your behaviour-prediction ability is sound), then they may behave to your advantage.

If beliefs were always true, it would be impossible to make someone believe something false, and prediction and explanation of behaviour would be relatively easy. This is because, if beliefs are true, there is no reason to consider them at all. Instead, behaviour prediction and explanation can be done on the basis of what is really the case. This is much less complicated than inferring and representing an invisible mental state and basing behaviour predictions on that. Furthermore, beliefs normally *are* true; they are supposed to be. Adults probably base much of their prediction of other people's behaviour on what is really the case, since this is simpler and generally quite reliable.

This poses a diagnostic problem. For example, imagine a particular child could predict or explain the behaviour of someone whose beliefs are true. This would not allow us to conclude that the child understood anything about beliefs: She or he might simply be basing her or his judgements on what she or he knows to be the real situation. What is required is a test that distinguishes between reasoning on the basis of the state of the world, and reasoning on the basis of someone's beliefs about the state of the world. Fortunately, this is possible, because people's beliefs are sometimes *false*. This causes them to behave in ways that cannot be predicted or explained by reference to the real situation.

In a commentary on Premack and Woodruff's original research, the philosopher Dennett proposed a critical test of the ability to impute mental states to others, one involving the understanding of *false belief*. Most subsequent research on the development of theory of mind has concerned false beliefs, and their role in the prediction or explanation of behaviour, and in attempts to manipulate behaviour. The rest of this chapter covers these three main areas of false belief understanding, beginning with prediction.

False belief prediction

The unexpected transfer false belief task

The most common test for theory of mind in children is the "false belief task". Two versions of the false belief task are widely used. The most straightforward version follows Dennett's (1978) minimal criteria for ascribing a theory of mind. It was first put into developmental practice by Wimmer and Perner (1983). The classic false belief task is a story acted out with dolls and props. Other versions are pure stories, or involve real people, or involve pictures or videos of real people. The format does not affect the basic finding. Here is the original version (translated from German):

> Maxi is helping his mother to unpack the shopping bag. He puts the chocolate into the GREEN cupboard. Maxi remembers exactly where he put the chocolate so that he can come back later and get some. Then he leaves for the playground. In his absence his mother needs some chocolate. She takes the chocolate out of the GREEN cupboard and uses some of it for her cake. Then she puts it back not into the GREEN but into the BLUE cupboard. She leaves to get some eggs and Maxi returns from the playground, hungry.

> Test question: Where will Maxi look for the chocolate?

The findings were that children began to pass the task at around 4 or 5 years old.

Notice that the story creates a sharp distinction between what Maxi thinks and what the child thinks. This means that the child cannot answer simply on the basis of what he or she knows to be true. The children who fail the task appear to do this: Failure is not random. Instead, younger children systematically respond with the current location of the chocolate. Predicting behaviour on the basis of current reality is a reasonably successful strategy: If someone wants to get something, predict that they will go to where it is. This will work most of the time because beliefs are usually true, because they are supposed to be true. The false belief task is deliberately designed to disrupt the normal relationship between beliefs and reality.

The original task is quite long. It can be shortened and simplified. For example, Figure 2.1 shows the story I normally use (played out with two dolls, a box, a jar and a marble):

> (1) Here's Sally, and here's Tony . . . and here's a jar and here's a box. (2) Now, Sally has a marble, and she puts her marble into this box, like that, and then she goes out to play. (3) But, while she's away, *what's happening here*? (4) Tony *goes* to the box, and he *takes* Sally's marble . . . (5) and he puts it into this jar, like that. And then he goes out to play too [Tony leaves in the opposite direction to Sally]. (6) A bit later, Sally comes back.

Belief question: Where will she look first for her marble?
Reality question: Where is the marble really?
Memory question: Where did Sally put the marble in the beginning?

This version was adapted from Baron-Cohen et al. (1985). (Their version had two female dolls, Sally and Ann. I found children had difficulty remembering which doll was which. Changing one doll to a boy eliminated this memory difficulty.) The reality question and memory question check that children followed the main events of the story and know where the marble is really. A small minority of children fail the memory question, usually the younger ones. Children rarely fail the reality question.

Children pass this and other simple versions of the task at around 4 years old. The precise age of success is not important. What is important is that the transition from success to failure is fairly rapid. Typically, almost all young 3-year-olds give the wrong answer, older 3-year-olds have a mixed performance and most young 4-year-olds give the right answer (e.g., Perner, Leekam & Wimmer, 1987). A number of tasks measuring related abilities are passed at roughly the same time.

FIGURE 2.1 A typical false belief procedure. (1) and (2) Sally places her marble in the box. (3), (4) and (5) In her absence it is moved to the jar. (6) Children are asked where she will look for it first on her return.

Methodological variations to the task can make it slightly harder or easier, and giving the task to children who differ in mental age, social background and nationality will produce slightly different ages of transition, discussed below. The basic finding remains the same: Younger children do not pass the task; slightly older children do.

The unexpected contents false belief task

This task was devised to demonstrate to children that their own beliefs can be false (Hogrefe, Wimmer & Perner, 1986; Perner et al., 1987). It was thought that after personal experience of having a false belief, children might be more willing to attribute a false belief to someone else. In the task, children are shown a familiar container, often a tube of Smarties (an ever-popular British sweet, similar to M&Ms) and asked what is inside. Typically children answer "Smarties". Then they are shown that they are mistaken: The container contains only a pencil. Children are now asked what someone else, often the child's friend, will think is inside when first shown it.

Despite recent personal experience of having the relevant false belief, children perform just as poorly on this task as on the unexpected transfer task. More surprising still, when asked to recall what they themselves thought was inside when they first saw it, they are equally unable to remember. They say they thought there was a pencil (Gopnik & Astington, 1988). (These two questions are the own-belief and other-belief questions.)

This finding has radical implications. We tend to think that we know what we think, believe, intend and feel. It may be difficult to work out what goes on in others' minds, but not our own: We can find out by simple introspection. However, if this were the case, it should be easy to remember one's own false beliefs—especially ones that were held until a moment ago. The fact that young children cannot recall recently held false beliefs raises the possibility that we may not have very good access to our own mind. Instead, perhaps we attribute beliefs to ourselves in the same way we attribute them to others.

One practical problem with the unexpected contents task is that children do not always say that the box contains Smarties (or whatever the normal contents would be). The worst possible answer children might give is "pencil". This usually indicates the presence of another developmental psychologist in the area. More commonly, children say "I don't know". Usually with a little encouragement they can be induced to guess "Smarties". The details of this are rarely reported. Obviously, these children may not have had a false belief about the contents. After all, they frequently encounter and are responsible for empty Smarties tubes. Thus when asked to consider their own previous belief, "Smarties" is not the correct answer. "Pencil" is not either, of course, but it has the advantage of having been objectively true. There is a strong pragmatic pressure to come up with a specific answer. Some children may answer "pencil" to the own-belief question simply because they did not previously have any particular belief about the contents of the box. Similarly for the other-belief test question: If the child did not have a false belief about the contents of the box, why should she or he attribute one to her or his friend?

Criticism of the false belief tasks

Perner (1991) identified a popular activity amongst developmental researchers: "Piaget Bashing". Jean Piaget was probably the greatest developmental psychologist of the 20th century, building up a massive and general theory of cognitive development in Switzerland, while psychology in the United States was largely under the sway of behaviourism (which tried to avoid considering mental states altogether). Piaget's work continues to provoke criticism, frequently involving claims that he underestimated children. Despite the validity of many of the criticisms, Piaget discovered some powerful and highly replicable effects in which children appear to show cognitive deficits.

The rules of Piaget Bashing are as follows: (1) Take any one of Piaget's claims about what 6- to 8-year-old children cannot do; (2) devise a more child-friendly research method; (3) show children have the ability (or some significant components of it) much earlier.

Wimmer and Perner's (1983) false belief study is a prime example of Piaget Bashing. Piaget claimed that children are profoundly egocentric until the age of around 7 years, unable even to consider what a scene might look like from another viewpoint. Understanding that a situation could be thought of differently by different people should be at least as difficult, and therefore completely beyond, children younger than about 7 years, according to Piaget. In fact, this seems to be in the grasp of the average 4-year-old.

The popularity of Piaget Bashing led naturally to variants of the sport: The first rule is simply amended to replace Piaget with one of his "bashers". This second-order Piaget Bashing has been directed with some vigour at Wimmer and Perner and like-minded researchers concerning the supposed 4-year-old shift in false belief understanding.

Any cognitive test measures two factors: the conceptual competence that is being tested, and performance factors required to take the test. These rely on other cognitive abilities the child is assumed to already possess. The false belief task measures understanding that behaviour is based on an agent's mental representation of the world. To perform the task children must also be able to follow a simple narrative and remember the key events. They must understand the questions—in the same way that adults would understand them. They may also need to have the ability to suppress their own representation of reality, or a default tendency to assume that beliefs are true, or overcome any of a number of hypothetical difficulties that have been suggested.

Theorists differ on which of these two factors causes failure on the false belief task. The major theories of false belief understanding are presented in detail in Chapter 3 and Chapter 8. Very briefly they are as follows. According to "Theory Theory" and "Simulation Theory", the false belief task validly measures belief-reasoning ability. The Theory Theory holds that children develop knowledge of the representational nature of mental states at around the age of 4 years. This is accompanied by a theory of how mental states relate to each other; how states such as belief are formed; and how belief, desire, and so forth are related to behaviour. Simulation Theory holds that this kind of abstract theoretical structure is unnecessary. Instead, children use their own mind as a model of others, with appropriate adjustments. Adjustments are needed to take account of differences in experience, point of view, existing beliefs, and so on. Having done so, children essentially ask themselves what they would do if they were in the position of the other person. The ability to make the adjustments necessary for belief tasks develops around 4 years.

Opposing these theories is a variety of accounts that hold that theory of mind develops in infancy[1], or is innate. Children cannot pass the false belief task because of additional non-theory-of-mind-specific performance factors. Some theorists believe that children can reason about beliefs much earlier but this ability is not captured by cognitive tasks. Others believe that children have a genuine difficulty with belief reasoning, but this is not due to a lack of mental state concepts.

During the 1990s there was a concerted effort to show that the false belief task drastically underestimated children's understanding of belief. The size of the literature produced by this effort is a major obstacle to determining whether it was successful or not. There are literally hundreds of studies examining variations of the false belief task. I could pick a few examples and conclude that children cannot reason about beliefs until 4 years old. I could pick another few examples and conclude the opposite. What was required was a meta-analysis.

Wellman, Cross and Watson's (2001) meta-analysis

A meta-analysis integrates findings from a number of studies, and can give an overall picture of the development of success on the false belief task. The unit of analysis is not individual children (as is usually the case) but conditions within studies; specifically, the proportion of false belief questions answered correctly. This can demonstrate which variables reliably affect success.[2]

Wellman et al. (2001) chose 591 conditions from 178 studies described in 77 reports or papers; more than 4000 children were represented. Conditions where too many children failed control conditions, dropped out or were excluded for any reason were not used. The cut-off date for inclusion was January 1998, 15 years after the first false belief study was published. Thus the analysis included most of the false belief data publicly available at the time.

13

The study allowed an estimate of the probability of passing the false belief task at various ages: At 2½ years, children were less than 20% likely to pass; at 3 years 8 months, children were 50% correct; and at 4 years 8 months children were about 75% correct. Thus, children 3 years 5 months or younger were performing *below* chance, and children older than about 4 years were performing above chance. If you want to pick a specific age for false belief success, a reasonable estimate is somewhere just before 4 years 0 months, the age at which children start to perform above chance.

The main aim of the study was to determine which factors affected performance on false belief tasks, and by how much. The analysis found that several factors did *not* affect performance: Given the size of the study, absences of effects are also informative. First, Wellman et al. (2001) found that the findings of false belief studies had been consistent over the period analysed: More recent studies appeared not to find better performance than earlier ones. Second, the type of test question did not seem to matter. Studies have probed false belief understanding by asking children about what a target character will do, think, know or say. These variations make little difference. Nor did it seem to matter whether the unexpected transfer or unexpected contents task was used, or whether the question was about another's false belief or the child's own previous false belief. Finally, it made no difference whether the character in the false belief story was a real person, a puppet, a pictured person or a videotaped character.

In sum, performance was unaffected by who held the belief, how children had to demonstrate they had inferred the belief, or which version of the false belief task was used. This makes it unlikely that performance depended on any surface feature of the task. It is consistent with success depending on the development of abstract concepts, or on some critical skill required to demonstrate these concepts.

Six variables were found to affect the age of success. The key issue is whether any of these variables preferentially improved performance in younger children. If this were so, it would suggest that younger children understand something about false beliefs, but this understanding is masked by performance factors. An improvement across all age groups, on the other hand, would simply suggest that the task can be made easier. So long as there remained a clear developmental improvement, a performance increase following some manipulation would still be most consistent with the idea that the false belief task measures an underlying conceptual change.

Variable 1: Temporal marking

Only one of the six variables that improved performance interacted with age, but in the opposite direction to that predicted by early competence accounts: The inclusion of "temporal marking" in the test question improved performance of older children only. A common concern has been that children do not interpret the false belief question in the way that the adult expects. One potential ambiguity with the test question is *which point in time* is being asked about. For example, in the Smarties task, "What did you think was in here?" is intended to refer to when the Smarties tube was first shown to the child. Children might conceivably fail to realize this, and give an answer based on the period after the most salient event, the revelation of the pencil.

Several research groups modified the question to explicitly indicate that it was about "before" the box was opened. Gopnik and Astington (1988) and Moses and Flavell (1990) found that emphasizing this in the test question made no difference. Lewis and Osborne (1990) criticized these studies primarily for using "before", which they claimed may be harder to understand than "when", and also for embedding the temporal marker within the sentence. Lewis and Osborne constructed sentences of the form: "What did you think was in the box when the top was still on it?" and "What did you think was in the box before I took the top off?" However, contrary to their hypothesis, this time the "before" question improved performance, whereas the "when" question did not. Furthermore, this result does not appear reliable; Lewis, Freeman, Kyriakidou, Maridaki-Kassotaki and Berridge (1996) again compared the different question types as part of a larger study and found no difference.

Siegal and Beattie (1991) argued that children understand false beliefs but misinterpret the question to mean something like "Where will Maxi have to look in order to find his chocolate?" Why children should go beyond the literal meaning of the sentence is not clear. However, Siegal and Beattie found that preschool children performed much better when answering questions about a false belief story when the question was altered to "Where will [character] look *first*?" This result is also hard to replicate. Clements and Perner (1994) compared the two question forms in a more standard false belief scenario, and found no difference in performance. Peterson and Siegal (1999) also found no difference for normal and deaf preschoolers, and children with autism.

Despite a lack of consistent effects with temporal marking test questions, both Lewis and Osborne's "before" question and Siegal and Beattie's "look first" question seem clearer, better questions and both have been frequently adopted by subsequent researchers. This shift in practice is vindicated by Wellman et al.'s (2001) meta-analysis. Making the test question more temporally explicit seems to improve performance; however, it does so only for older children, not younger ones. If children's performance was being masked by misunderstanding the test question, the opposite should be the case: Younger children should be selectively assisted by temporal marking. Instead, temporal marking probably produces a sharper improvement of false belief task performance at around 4 years.

The remaining variables identified by Wellman et al. were as follows.

Variable 2: The motive

Sometimes false belief tasks are presented to children with no explanation of why the object is moved (in the unexpected transfer task) or why there is a pencil in a Smarties tube (in the unexpected contents task). Other versions of the task present an incidental reason (Mother needed to use some chocolate in cooking, for example, or we needed somewhere to keep the pencil). However, when the task was explicitly presented to the child as a deliberate attempt to trick the protagonist, performance on the task improved significantly across all ages.

Many researchers have had the intuition that theory of mind understanding might first be seen in deceptive contexts: fooling people, hiding things and telling fibs. There seems to be some truth in this. Later in the chapter, I examine more dramatic claims of early competence in lying or active deception.

Variable 3: The salience of the false belief

When the false belief is explicitly stated or depicted in some way, children's performance can improve. Similarly, children do better if the protagonist's absence at key moments is emphasized. One example of this comes from Mitchell and Lacohée (1991), who used a procedure in which children were shown a Smarties tube and invited to post a picture of what they thought was inside the tube into a miniature postbox. Having posted a picture of Smarties, children found out the real contents—a pencil. They now found it easier to report their prior belief. Mitchell (1996) argued that children's mental state understanding is masked by the salience of current reality. Having a physical tokening of their past false belief, even an unavailable one, makes it easier somehow for them to judge on the basis of belief rather than reality. [However, see Mitchell (1996) for a discussion of mixed success in attempts to replicate this finding.]

This theory assumes that, by 4 years, children can resist the pull of reality. However, the meta-analysis shows that increasing salience improves the performance of older children as well as younger ones. The salience of current reality might make false belief tasks harder, but it cannot explain why false belief competence develops.

Variable 4: Participation

In some tasks, children are simply passive onlookers. Children perform better if they participate in the task, helping to set up the props or to make the essential transformation.

Variable 5: Children performed better if a real target object was absent

Sometimes the object in the unexpected transfer ceases to exist (the chocolate is eaten, for example) or the unexpected contents of the Smarties tube turns out to be nothing at all. In these cases, children typically performed better. Younger children did not perform above chance, and it is possible that the absence of a target object improves performance because it removes the obvious wrong answers. In the typical unexpected transfer task, for example, younger children systematically answer with the real location of the object. If the object ceases to exist, they may simply indicate one of the two locations at random: An "improvement" from 0% to 50%.

Variable 6: Country

Children in different countries performed differently, ranging from especially good performance in Australia to poor performance in Japan: At 44 months, American children were 50% correct, Australian were 69% correct and Japanese were 40% correct. Nevertheless, within each country the age profile had a similar shape, with poor performance in younger children and better performance in older children, just shifted up or down the age range.

Summary

These six variables show that it is possible to modify performance on false belief tasks. To summarize Wellman et al.'s (2001) meta-analysis: During the first 15 years of false belief research there was a concerted effort to show that the false belief task underestimated the belief understanding of younger children. The literature was large, and the variations in type of task and findings were sizeable. The meta-analysis provides some order to a body of literature that was becoming intractable and hard to interpret. The findings are that, out of numerous variables suggested to alter performance, six reliably improved performance; none of these improved performance of 3-year-olds beyond chance, and the one that raised performance to chance may have done so by inducing 3-year-olds to guess. This is problematic for claims of early competence. Nevertheless, even a modest improvement in performance might be taken as evidence of early competence if the manipulation selectively improved performance in younger children. No variable did this. The only one to interact with age involved modifying the question to make clear which point in time the question referred to. This selectively improved performance in older children.

This strongly suggests that existing accounts of early false belief understanding are wrong. Wellman et al. (2001) favour the idea that passing the false belief task marks a conceptual change. Modifying the task can alter the age at which children can demonstrate this change by a few months. The nature of the conceptual change remains a subject for debate: Wellman et al. favour Theory Theory; Simulation Theory is also consistent with the empirical findings. There is a debate over the implication of this conclusion for other theories. For immediate reactions, see the commentaries on Wellman et al.'s article by Moses (2001), and Scholl and Leslie (2001).

False belief explanation

There are lots of reasons why we need to explain behaviour. In particular, being able to say why a person behaved as they did can help us learn to predict or influence behaviour more effectively. Behaviour is caused by a person's beliefs and desires, and unlike mental states, behaviour is visible. Children's first attempts to reason about beliefs may be after someone does something odd, like searching in an empty location. For adults, interpreting behaviour in terms of the underlying mental states may alert us to individual differences, such as someone's personality traits (he stayed at the office all evening—perhaps he's a workaholic; she donated the money— she must be a generous person) or more temporary dispositions such as mood.

A plausible idea is that explaining behaviour may be easier than prediction of beliefs. Predicting beliefs requires a number of things that may be difficult: Children must remember what Maxi saw and did not see, and infer from his experience what he knows or does not know. Thus children have to understand *belief formation*. They must typically also be aware of what Maxi wants. They may also have to temporarily suppress their own, correct understanding of the situation. Then, from their understanding of Maxi's belief and desire, children must work out what he will do. Explanation, on the other hand, presents children with the finished state of affairs, and they simply have to explain why he did something odd. Anyone with at least a rudimentary concept of belief should be able to provide an explanation of the form "He thought it was in there", even if they cannot explain why he might think it was in there. Maxi's previous perceptual access is relevant but not necessary, since however it came about, a plausible belief can be hypothesized simply on the basis of his odd behaviour.

The first study to examine explanation suggested it was considerably easier than prediction. Bartsch and Wellman (1989) told children stories like the following. Bill (a puppet) had a cut, and wanted a Band-Aid. He went to a Band-Aid box, which children had previously seen was empty. Children were asked "Why do you think he's looking in there?" and prompted with "What does Bill think?" Three-year-olds gave belief-based explanations 66% of the time, mostly following the prompt (e.g., "What does Bill think?", "That there are Band-Aids in there"). In the prediction task children were asked where Bill would look for a Band-Aid: in a Band-Aid box that was empty or in a plain box containing a Band-Aid. Children were correct only 31% of the time.

However, as Wimmer and Mayringer (1998) point out, there is no obvious alternative to the explanation question, whereas there is a highly salient wrong answer for the prediction question. One might therefore expect children to do better on the explanation task regardless of whether they understood belief. This is especially likely if they use phrases like "thinks it's in there" before they develop a proper understanding of belief (see discussion of Perner's "prelief" hypothesis in Chapter 6). Even though the task may be prone to false positives, the improved performance has not proved easy to replicate. Moses and Flavell (1990) conducted a study similar to that of Bartsch and Wellman and found very few justifications in terms of belief. Children generally explained behaviour in terms of the character's desire (somewhat anomalously, since the desire was not satisfied by going to the wrong location). One contributory reason for this may be that Moses and Flavell did not ask the prompt question, "What does Bill think?" (in response to which children could be credited as having correctly explained Bill's belief simply by mentioning Band-Aids).

Wimmer and Mayringer (1998, following Wimmer & Weichbold, 1994) used a rigorous questioning technique to probe beyond desire-based explanations and lack of response. For example, if children said the character went to the empty location "because she wants to look at the book", the experimenter would say "Yes, Ann wants to look at the book, but why then does she go to the *cloakroom* to get the book?" If children produced no response, the experimenter told them exactly where Ann goes, and where she thinks the book is, and asked children "Why does Ann think the book is in this cupboard?" They found that explanation was no easier than prediction (Experiment 1) or was harder (Experiment 2).

Explanation might be difficult because it requires verbal skill, and a willingness to talk. Liz Robinson and Peter Mitchell (1995) had an ingenious way to remove the need for verbal explanation, and thus get round the problem of shy or inarticulate preschoolers, and of children using mental state terms they do not yet properly understand. Their false belief task involved identical twins. The twins placed an object in a box. Then one twin left the room, and the object was moved while the other twin watched. Later, both twins went to find the object: one twin to the real location, and one to the wrong location. The question was why one twin went to the wrong place: Was it because he had been outside or stayed inside? This explanation condition produced considerably higher success than a condition in which children had to predict where the absent twin would look on his return: for example, 37% correct prediction compared to 85% explanation (Experiment 1). However, as Perner (1995) points out, the chance baselines are different on the two tasks. In Robinson and Mitchell's explanation task, children have a 50–50 chance of picking the correct explanation. In the standard false belief task, children do not guess: They consistently give the *wrong* answer. It is usually assumed that passing the prediction question indicates an understanding of belief, rather than a lucky guess. For Robinson and Mitchell's children, then, the roughly 40% who pass the

19

prediction question probably understand belief, and should also pass the explanation question. The remaining 60% should guess in the explanation task, half guessing correctly. This would yield about 70% success, not far from the 85% of children who actually pass the explanation task. Analysing other experiments from the same study in this way gives an explanation advantage of about 10%. Wimmer and Mayringer (1998) cite a personal communication from Robinson that, in subsequent use of the procedure, 3-year-olds did not differ from the guessing baseline in this task. Perner, Lang and Kloo (2002a) repeated the twin task and confirmed that there was little evidence for explanation being better than prediction, and the two abilities were strongly related, even after partialling out control measures and verbal ability.

Thus, although there are good reasons to think that simple belief explanation might be easier than simple belief prediction, the evidence for this is not strong. The best conclusion from the available evidence is that explanation may be slightly easier than prediction—but only maybe, and only slightly.

Manipulating behaviour

Concealing information

One of the most useful properties of a theory of mind is that it allows you to manipulate the behaviour of others. A very direct way of doing this is through *deception*. Deliberate deception may therefore be one of the earliest signs of a theory of mind. Note, the aim of deception can be to manipulate beliefs or to manipulate behaviour. If children only aim to manipulate behaviour, then we would not want to conclude that the deceiver had an understanding of belief. A cute illustration of this is provided by Joan Peskin (1992):

> Jeremy (aged 3): Mommy, go out of the kitchen.
> Mother: Why Jeremy?
> Jeremy: Because I want to take a cookie.

Jeremy clearly knows that his mother's presence will make it difficult to get a cookie. His aim is to get his mother to leave, but he appears oblivious to the role of her mental states in the situation.

This is an example of inability to withhold information. Peskin and Ardino (2003) looked systematically at preschoolers' ability to keep a simple secret. Two experimenters took a child into the preschool kitchen. First they looked in the fridge, and the experimenter pointed out some food. Then the second experimenter said it was her own birthday, and left the room to fetch a present she wanted to show the child. While she was away, the other experimenter showed the child a birthday cake for the other experimenter, saying "It's a secret. Don't tell Vicky the secret". The cake was wrapped up and put on a table. When Vicky returned she told the child that she was very hungry. Two thirds of 3-year-olds told her about or pointed to the cake; two thirds of 4-year-olds and almost all 5-year-olds kept the secret, usually telling Vicky to look in the fridge. The tendency to keep a secret was very strongly related to performance on a battery of standard false belief tasks ($r_{54} = .62$, $p < .001$). Thus, until they pass the false belief task, children seem to be poor at withholding information, in this case despite the obvious possibility of directing Vicky to the food in the fridge.

Peskin and Ardino also looked at children's ability to play hide and seek. This also requires the withholding of information: Children must hide while the seeker's back is turned, must conceal themselves fully, and must remain quiet and not, for example, announce loudly where they have hidden. When playing the seeker, children must withhold information from themselves: They must turn around and cover their eyes while the other hides, not peek and not tell the other person where to hide. Peskin and Ardino played a game of hide and seek with children in the kitchen, which had been set up so there were four places to hide: under the table (covered with a table cloth), behind a curtain under the sink or inside one of two cupboards. Children had turns both as the hider and the seeker. The 4- and 5-year-olds were even better at the hide-and-seek game than they were at keeping a secret; 3-year-olds were even worse, with only 3 out of 18 children passing the task. The 3-year-olds were quite good at explaining the rules of the game, but they did not seem to understand the point. A few told the experimenter to hide and then also hid themselves. Most other children did not hide properly: Either they hid before the seeker turned her back to count, told the seeker where they were going to hide, did not hide from view, or did not remain hidden or quiet. When seeking, children either told the hider where to hide or did not turn around and cover their eyes while starting to count. Most of the 3-year-olds were poor at both hiding and seeking.

Performance on the hide-and-seek task was strongly related to performance on the keep-a-secret task ($r_{\phi} = .60$, $p < .001$) and to the battery of false belief tasks ($r_{54} = .62$, $p < .001$). (Interestingly, although these two tasks were related to false belief performance, they were not related to an executive function measure after age was partialled out.) Anyone who has played hide and seek with a toddler will not be surprised at these findings. Although young children find hide and seek hugely enjoyable, they just do not grasp that the seeker is not supposed to know where the hider is. They like the peek-a-boo aspect; the ritualistic search in the wrong places before finally finding the hider with an exaggerated flourish is also great fun. However, the aspect of the game concerned with manipulating the mental states of others seems to completely elude younger children.

Lying

Failing to withhold information does not usually have serious consequences (although, in our distant past, successful hiding may have been very important to survival). Early competence might be more easily revealed in lying or deception, which children might have had reason to learn to do. The simplest form of this is simple denial, especially useful after children have done something wrong or forbidden. Lewis, Stanger and Sullivan (1989) attempted to elicit this kind of behaviour from children who were just about to turn 3 years old. Their procedure was reasonably natural. Children sat down, and the experimenter set up a toy zoo behind them. Children were told not to peek while the experimenter went out of the room for a few minutes (and monitored children with a video camera and a one-way window). Naturally, 29 of the 33 children peeked. When the experimenter returned, she asked the child whether he or she had peeked. About a quarter of the peekers did not respond to the question, and the remaining children were split equally into those who admitted they peeked and those who said "no". (Curiously, most boys admitted to having peeked, but only 13% of girls did so.)

Lewis et al. (1989) concluded that the children who said "no" intended to deceive the experimenter. This would indicate that the children understood that belief could be manipulated. However, there is a simpler alternative explanation. Young children may say things that are not true without intending to make other people believe what they say. This idea has a long history; William and Clara Stern (1909/1999) referred to it as pseudo-lying. This seems to start quite early, often as a means of defence. For example, the children who said "no" in Lewis et al.'s study may simply have wanted to ward off embarrassment or punishment. The "no" functions as a rejection of the question or the topic, rather than an assertion of the opposite.

Denial is the easiest form of pseudo-lying. With simple, flat denials it is difficult to judge whether or not there is an intention to manipulate the beliefs of others. Even more complex denials, such as "I didn't do it", may simply be well-worn strategies to avoid punishment. Other stock phrases sometimes provide persuasive evidence of a lack of insight into the effects on others' beliefs. For example, the Sterns' child Günter would often say "No, 'spensive!" (i.e., "No, that's too expensive!") to indicate something did not suit or interest him (Stern & Stern, 1909/1999). He had learned the phrase from his parents, who used it to refuse to buy things for him. However, Günter used the phrase as a defence, when he did not want to be taken to bed or was disturbed while playing.

Here it is perfectly clear that he did not intend to deceive anyone, since the phrase is practically meaningless in these contexts. Perner (1991) cites an example in which the pseudo-lie can only be detected on some occasions. Perner's 3½-year-old son would use "I am soo tired" as a ploy to get his own way. Sometimes this was appropriate and effective, such as when he wanted to be carried during a mountain hike. At other times it was clearly counterproductive, such as when he wanted to avoid being put to bed.

In general the inflexible nature of early lying suggests that it is probably aimed at manipulating the behaviour of others, and should not be considered as deliberate deceit. However, it can be difficult to judge without detailed information about the context of individual cases. One way to look for early ability to lie would be to ask people who know the children well. Stouthamer-Loeber (1991) asked the parents and teachers of 4-year-olds at what age children were capable of deliberate lies. There were 80 mothers and 21 teachers from middle-class daycares. Figure 2.2 shows percentages of each group judging when children can tell a deliberate lie.

A few mothers and teachers thought that even very young children can lie, and some judged that even 5-year-olds were not capable of deliberate deception. However, most of the mothers and teachers thought that 3-year-olds could not lie, and 4-year-olds could. The agreement between parents and teachers was very close. Clearly, this result supports false belief studies: At least in the opinion of their mothers, children start to lie at about the time they can pass false belief tasks.

Of course it is possible that parents and teachers tend to underestimate children's devious abilities. Although they know the children better than anyone, everyday life may not provide many optimum opportunities to show early ability. Peskin (1992) tried to provide the best possible conditions in a game with two puppets. Three stickers were put in front of children: one they liked most, one they liked somewhat and one they liked least. They were told they could choose one, but only after one of two puppets had chosen. Before the puppets chose, each asked the child

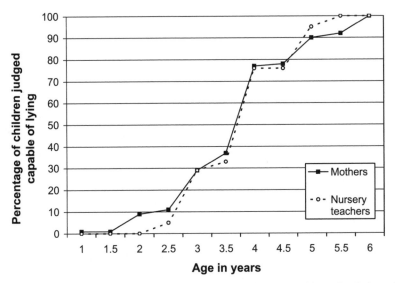

FIGURE 2.2 The age at which parents and teachers of 4-year-olds judged that children become able to tell deliberate lies. (Drawn from tabulated data in Stouthamer-Loeber, 1991.)

which sticker he or she liked best. The nasty puppet would choose the one the child indicated. The nice puppet would choose a different one. Children were therefore motivated to point to the sticker they liked best when playing with the nice puppet, but to point to another sticker when playing with the nasty puppet. The results were very clear. Almost all 3- to 5-year-old children indicated their preferred sticker when playing with the nice puppet. More than half the 4-year-olds and nearly all the 5-year-olds were able to conceal their preference when playing with the nasty puppet. However, fewer than 20% of 3-year-olds could conceal their preference, even after five trials. Most 3-year-olds did spontaneously try physically to stop the puppet taking the sticker however, showing that they knew what he was up to, and that they wanted to keep that sticker. They just did not have the conceptual ability to do so by deceptive means.

Misleading others

Young children are not very good at lying or withholding information. Both skills involve a large verbal component; it remains possible that children can mislead others by nonverbal means. Chandler, Fritz and Hala (1989) used a procedure that appeared to show that they could. In their hiding game, a doll walked across a whiteboard to hide a "treasure" in one of several bins at the far end. As she walked she left a trail of inky footprints. When they were cast as the seeker, children of all ages successfully used the footprints to find the treasure. The question of interest was whether they could generate deceptive strategies when they were the hider. The footprints could be wiped up with a cloth, and the doll could be walked to one or more of the empty bins to leave a misleading trail. Chandler et al. found that, after a considerable amount of prompting, even about half of the 2½-year-olds were capable of wiping up trails with the sponge, and leaving false trails. Half the time 4-year-olds also managed this; 3-year-olds did less well, with only a quarter of them ever managing this.

Thus, it appeared that some toddlers were capable of manipulating evidence so that another person would remain ignorant of the true location, and were even able to plant a false belief. There are several possible interpretations of the finding. Children may have understood the effect of the false trails on the other person's beliefs. Alternatively, they may have understood the effect of false trails on the other person's behaviour. This does not require consideration of the other's mental states: People follow trails; if you want them to go somewhere, lay a trail to there. There is also a less theoretically interesting possibility: If you give a 2-year-old a way of making marks on a whiteboard, and a way of wiping them off again, then they are likely to make a bunch of trails and wipe them off again, until the adult stops hinting that they should do something further. Sodian, Taylor, Harris and Perner (1991) replicated the procedure to find out which of these strategies accounted for performance.

They replicated Chandler et al.'s (1989) findings regarding laying of false trails: At least half of children in each of the 2-, 3- and 4-year-old groups laid a false trail at least once. However, although most children laid a trail at least once during the experiment, they did not do so often: only 5 of the 42 children laid trails on all three trials, and 18 children never did. Children were also able to remove the genuine trails, but this required fairly explicit hinting. Sodian et al. (1991) used a graded series of hints. Most 2- and 3-year-olds only wiped up all traces of the trail after the second hint "Look at the tracks. Will that help [experimenter 2] to find the driver?" Many of the 2-year-olds also required the third hint: "What about the tracks. Can you do something to the tracks so that [experimenter 2] can't find the driver?" So younger children needed explicit reference to the tracks, and even the suggestion that something could be done about them, before they would remove them. Given that not much else could be done to the tracks other than remove them, this is not good evidence of deliberate deception.

After the second experimenter's initial (deliberately) incorrect search, the first experimenter whispered to the children to tell the second experimenter where to look next, suggesting they try to trick the second experimenter again. Virtually no 2-year-olds pointed or told the second experimenter to go to an empty cup; 3-year-olds did some of the time; 4-year-olds did so frequently.

Perhaps the most telling evidence came from questioning children before the second experimenter returned about where he would search, and where he thought the object was. If children were deliberately manipulating the other person's beliefs or behaviour, they should predict he will go to the wrong location. Two- and three-year-olds very rarely did this, even on the third trial (despite the fact that the second experimenter had deliberately gone to the wrong location on the two previous trials). Four-year-olds did so over half the time on the first trial, and more frequently on the second and third trials. Children's judgements of where the second experimenter thought the object was followed the same pattern. Finally, after the second experimenter looked in the wrong place, younger children were typically at a loss to explain his behaviour. This strongly suggests that children were not attempting to manipulate the other person's beliefs or behaviour. Instead, they were just wiping stuff up and making trails, because they had been given the tools to do both. This impression was strengthened by a second experiment in which a group of 3-year-olds were offered the opportunity to help a nice character find some treasure (e.g., by strengthening the trail) or to prevent a robber from doing so (by the usual means). Children typically wiped up the true trail and laid false ones as before, and followed the experimenter's suggestions to reinforce existing trails. However, they did so indiscriminately, so were as likely to deceive the nice character and help the robber as to do the reverse.

In conclusion, it appears that young children are no better at deceiving people with deceptive cues than they are at lying or withholding information. Chandler et al.'s (1989) procedure was imaginative and cute, but it lacked a necessary control condition. It seems to be that including an element of deception in false belief tasks improves performance somewhat, as Wellman et al. (2001) found. Children do use lying, concealment and deception to manipulate others' behaviour, but this begins quite suddenly at around the same time that they can pass the less morally dubious false belief task.

Implicit understanding of belief

The balance of evidence is that children do not *show* understanding of belief until they are about 4 years old. None of the alterations to the false belief task reviewed by Wellman et al. (2001) produced above-chance performance in 3-year-olds. The natural conclusion is that younger children do not understand belief. However, it can also be claimed that children do understand belief but this understanding is *implicit*.

To make this claim requires a clear definition of what is meant by "implicit". This term is used in a variety of ways by different authors, and frequently is left undefined (its meaning might be said to be implicit). It is often identified with processes that are unconscious or cannot be verbalized (and, if nothing more is implied, it would be clearer simply to speak of unconscious or unverbalizable processes). For present purposes, for understanding of belief to be implicit there are two criteria:

(1) The child cannot show understanding of belief in circumstances that require a judgement based on another's belief. Judgements are considered to indicate explicit understanding.
(2) The child's behaviour nevertheless varies according to whether someone else's belief is false or true. Methodologically, it must be shown that behaviour varies as a function of the difference in beliefs, rather than because of some incidental difference in the stimuli or task.

Wendy Clements and Josef Perner (1994) satisfied these two criteria with a modified false belief task. The task followed the standard format, with a story about two mice, one of whom has a piece of cheese. There were two mouse holes, both leading to the mice's bedroom, and a box outside each hole. Sam mouse puts his cheese into the box outside his hole and goes off to bed. While Sam is asleep, the other mouse, Katie, moves the cheese to the box outside the other mouse hole. Children were then told: "Later on, Sam woke up and gave a big stretch. 'I feel very hungry now', he said. 'I'll go and get the cheese' ", and the experimenter added "I wonder where he's going to look?"

Anticipating the mouse's return, children naturally looked towards the hole they thought Sam would come out of. If children were sensitive to the mouse's false belief, they should look to the hole he originally exited. If not, they should look to the hole with the cheese outside (since the mouse's stated intention was to retrieve his cheese). Children's anticipatory looking may therefore measure an *implicit* sensitivity to understanding of belief.

Children were then asked the usual *explicit* false belief question: "Which box will he open?" or "Which box will he open first?" (The difference in wording was to test out Siegal and Beattie's (1991) claim that adding "first" to the test question massively improves performance. In this study it made virtually no difference, with 36% of children passing the "look first" version, and 32% passing the standard version of the explicit task.) Children were also given a true belief task, in which Sam sees Katie move the cheese to the other box.

The results were remarkably clear. Until the age of 2 years 11 months, there was no evidence of looking towards the false belief location, and no success on the explicit questions. Around the age of 3 years, however, children suddenly began to look to the false belief location in the false belief task, and the true belief location in the true belief task: 77% of children showed this pattern. However, only 23% passed the explicit false belief questions. The older children continued to show the correct looking pattern, but it was not until they were about 4 years old that a majority passed the explicit questions. Children were able to look towards the correct location a year earlier than they could pass the explicit false belief question.

Clearly there is some knowledge of false belief before children pass the explicit task. The question is what form the knowledge takes. One possibility is that children are developing an awareness of false belief, but they lack confidence in this novel idea. They look correctly, but when asked verbally they fall back on their former strategy of predicting behaviour according to reality. This idea was tested by Ted Ruffman (Ruffman, 2000; Ruffman, Garnham, Import & Connolly, 2001; Wendy Garnham is the married version of Wendy Clements). The basic experimental design was similar, with the mildly exciting addition that the mouse came down a red or a green slide to one of two locations. In addition, children were asked to make a "bet" on where the mouse would appear. They were given 10 counters and could divide them between the two locations however they liked (they received 10 new counters for each trial, and had to use them all). Betting is a measure of explicit knowledge, because it involves a public commitment to one of the two possibilities.

First of all, we have to be sure that children can "bet" appropriately under conditions of certainty and uncertainty. Ruffman et al. (2001) showed children a bag of 10 green balls that, because of their shape, could appear down the green slide but not the red slide. Children were asked to bet with their counters where one of these balls would appear from. Almost all children very confidently put all their counters by the green slide. They were also shown a bag with nine red cubes (which could only go down the red slide) and one green ball, and again asked to bet. Even this minor uncertainty caused children to dramatically hedge their bets: Children of all ages put on average between five and six counters by the red slide. This procedure seems to be quite sensitive to children's uncertainty.

Next children were asked to bet on where the mouse would appear in true and false belief tasks, again with their eye movements monitored. For the true belief tasks, children of all ages confidently bet nine or more counters on the true belief location. For the false belief task, however, there was an interesting effect of uncertainty. Most children passed the looking measure, as before, and about half passed the verbal question. The younger children who looked to the correct location but failed the verbal question were extremely confident about their *wrong* answer: Almost all of them bet all 10 counters on the wrong slide. The older children who failed the verbal question were slightly less confident, but still bet an average of about eight counters on the wrong location. The most interesting group was the younger children who passed the verbal question. They had probably only recently developed the understanding required by the false belief task. They tended to hedge almost as much as in the nine red and one green object game, only betting on average six of their counters on the correct location. The older children who passed the verbal question had increased in confidence, betting about eight counters on the correct location.

Thus, the children who fail the standard verbal task are very confident in their wrong answer—even most of the older children, who are presumably closer to success than the younger ones. On the other hand, the young passers were not at all confident in their correct answers, although they rapidly became more sure of themselves.

This suggests that children who failed the false belief task did not have correct knowledge of beliefs that they were too uncertain to use. Children were very confident about their incorrect behaviour predictions. The children who were uncertain were the younger children who *passed* the explicit task. This suggests that they had recently acquired an understanding of false belief, and still lacked confidence in it.

Younger children's correct looking therefore seems to be based on a different form of knowledge than the older children's correct answers to the false belief question. This knowledge is implicit. We still do not know what this means, however. The working definition of implicit—knowledge that is not verbalizable—certainly seems appropriate, but so far it is difficult to conclude more about the nature of the knowledge. Clements and Perner (1994) speculate that the difference between the two kinds of knowledge may depend on: (1) representing a fact, and (2) being able to make a judgement of that fact. Younger children may be able to represent the other person's false belief, for example, by conjuring up a mental model with the content of the false belief. Because they do this, they tend to look in the direction consistent with the model. However, they are as yet unable to base judgements on this model, possibly because they do not yet understand its relationship to the real world.

Infants' understanding of false belief?

Clements and Perner (1994) showed quite clear implicit understanding of false belief around the age of 3 years. They also showed, however, that children younger than about 3 years did not even look to the correct location, and therefore did not seem to have this implicit understanding. This seemed to resolve the issue of early understanding: If children do not even look to the right location in anticipation before the age of 3 years, it seems unlikely that they have any understanding of false belief, implicit or otherwise.

However, recent findings by Onishi and Baillargeon (2005) call this strongly into question. They used the "violation-of-expectation" paradigm with 15-month-old infants. This is a method commonly used with preverbal infants. The idea is to find out whether children have a particular concept by showing them something that should be surprising if they had that concept. For example, Baillargeon (1987) showed infants a screen that rotated through 180°. The drawbridge-like screen started out flat, laying on the table in front of the infant. After rising to 90° it was upright and broadside to infants, such that they could no longer see behind it. It then continued rotating to 180° until it was again flat. After infants had become habituated to this (and were thus starting to show less interest), a solid object was placed behind the screen. The object was visible initially, until the screen had rotated sufficiently to occlude it. In one condition, the screen continued to rotate until it hit the (now invisible) object, at which point it stopped—the expected outcome. In another condition, the screen continued to rotate, passing through the space where the object should have been (an experimenter surreptitiously moved the object out of the way each time the screen rotated "through" it)—the "impossible" event. Children from the age of about 4 months looked much longer at the "impossible" event, suggesting that by that age they know that objects are solid, and other objects do not usually simply squash them flat. (However, there is a lively debate about this and other similar demonstrations, concerning both whether they can be replicated and what they mean. For example, see Rivera, Wakeley & Langer, 1999, and Houston-Price & Nakai, 2004).

Onishi and Baillargeon (2005) used the violation-of-expectation paradigm to probe for infants' concept of belief. The setup involved a woman sitting behind a table top facing a yellow box and a green box. The woman wore a visor so her eyes were not visible. (Infants are sensitive to eye direction, and cues from eye gaze would have introduced potentially complicating factors.) Initially there were three familiarization trials, one in which the woman placed a toy watermelon slice inside the green box, then two more in which she simply reached into the green box and paused.

The experimental trials involved the object moving so that the woman should either have a true or a false belief. Each 15-month-old infant only saw one condition. In the true belief condition, the woman remained visible behind the boxes. As infants watched, the melon moved from the green box to the yellow box (apparently of its own accord, which is slightly odd). The woman then reached into the green box or the yellow box. The infants looked longer when the woman reached into the empty green box. This is not surprising—children probably expect that if someone reaches, they reach to an object. This is a simple regularity of behaviour. The condition of interest was the false belief condition. During the belief induction trial, the woman was not visible (a screen was put between her and the boxes) and therefore disconnected from subsequent events. The melon moved as before, so in this case it is reasonable to infer that the woman falsely believes that the melon is still in the green box. This time, the infants looked longer when the woman reached into the yellow box, where the melon was. Infants apparently expected the woman to reach to the wrong location, where she last saw the melon, and were surprised when she reached to the correct location.

Interpretation

The natural conclusion is that 15-month-old infants have some understanding of false belief. This finding has prompted a furious debate. Onishi and Baillargeon (2005) have carefully ruled out most plausible alternative explanations. At minimum they consider that children must expect people to look for things where they last left them. What is at stake here, of course, is the idea that there is an innate theory of mind. Leslie (2005), for example, takes these findings to vindicate his idea of "a specialized neuro-cognitive mechanism that matures during the second year of life" (p. 459). Onishi and Baillargeon also favour the conclusion that their results show a representational theory of mind, albeit a rudimentary implicit one. The results make this plausible, although further research will be required to make any stronger conclusion.

Perner and Ruffman (2005; Ruffman & Perner, 2005) suggest other possibilities. One is that infants may have rules for predicting others' behaviour. In this case, people look for objects where they left them, a possibility that Onishi and Baillargeon acknowledge. Children have very sophisticated statistical learning abilities (e.g., Gómez & Gerken, 2000) which might allow them to draw up such rules based on associations between situations and behaviours. (I discuss young children's sensitivity to *engagement*—another's general involvement in an object or activity—in Chapter 7.) Because older children fail explicit false belief tasks, these rules would have to be implicit, unavailable for making judgements.

Another possibility is that infants' looking behaviour may be based on low-level processing. In order to process actions on objects, children may typically create three-way associations between an actor, an object and a location. When they see the woman put the melon into the green box, they create a woman–melon–green box association. If they are presented with the same association later, they will need less time to process it because it will still be active in memory. Thus, old three-way associations will be looked at for less time. However, if infants are presented with a new association, this will take longer to process. In the false belief condition, the melon has moved in the absence of the woman, so the three-way association when she reappears is new. This would explain the difference in looking times. It also produces an easily testable prediction: If the woman did something different at one or other box, the same pattern of looking times would occur. For example, if the woman simply wiped the top of one box (on all trials, including test and familiarization), then children would still take longer to process new three-way associations in the false belief trials.

This has yet to be tested, but a recent experiment with young 2-year-olds is not easily explained in terms of low-level processing. Onishi and Baillargeon's (2005) findings are puzzling because they seem inconsistent with Clements and Perner's (1994) implicit false belief findings. Clements and Perner showed quite clearly that most 2-year-olds looked in the wrong place when anticipating the behaviour of a character who had a false belief. If infants understand false belief, why do not 2-year-olds? Victoria Southgate and colleagues (Southgate, Senju & Csibra, 2007) suggest that the difference might lie in the verbal element of Clements and Perner's task. They removed the verbal element from the design, combining it with elements of Onishi and Baillargeon's task.

Twenty-five-month-old children watched a video in which a woman (again with a visor) could reach through one of two flaps, as shown in Figure 2.3. In front of each flap was a box. In the two familiarization phases, a puppet placed a ball in one of the boxes; there was a tone and the flaps lit up, then the woman reached to the box with the object. During the false belief phase, after seeing the ball placed in a box, she turned around (apparently distracted by a phone noise) and did not see the puppet remove the object from the scene. When the woman turned back, the flaps lit up to signal she was about to reach. Most of the 2-year-olds first looked at the flap next to the box where she had seen the object, and looked at it longer. Apparently they expected her to reach through that flap.

This finding is reasonably convincing: Children anticipate behaviour based on a false belief a year earlier than previously shown. There are two major differences between this study and Clements and Perner's: the absence of a verbal prompt and the fact that the object was entirely removed from the scene. Southgate et al. (2007) suggest that when children heard the verbal prompt, "I wonder where he's going to look?", they prematurely interpreted the "where" as referring to the location of the object rather than the behaviour of the protagonist. Another possibility is that the difference results from the disappearance of the object. In Clements and Perner's study, younger children looked towards the real location of the object. The attraction of the object may have masked sensitivity to the mouse's false belief.

The discovery of implicit false belief understanding in young 2-year-olds and perhaps infants is an important development. Clearly, something precedes children's success on explicit false belief tasks, and precedes it by a considerable period.

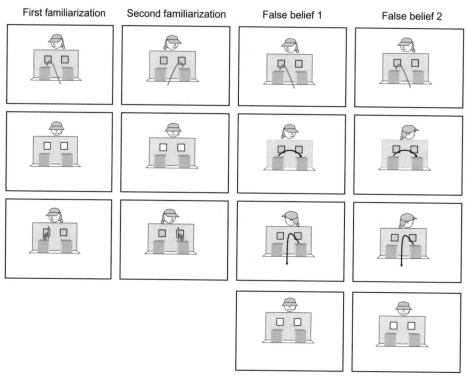

FIGURE 2.3 Schematic illustration of Southgate, Senju and Csibra's (2007) implicit false belief procedure. In the familiarization trials, a puppet places a ball in a box, the windows light up, and the actor reaches through a window to the box containing the ball. Children then experience one of the false belief trials, in which the ball is removed while the actor is not watching. The actor turns back and the windows are illuminated. If children are sensitive to the actor's false belief, they will look in anticipation towards the box where she last saw the ball. (Based on Figure 1, Southgate et al., 2007.)

At present, it is only possible to speculate about the nature of 2-year-olds' under-standing. The extremes of the debate are clear. Children may have a represen-tational theory of mind from infancy. This would strongly imply that it is innate. This theory requires an explanation of why much of this early theory of mind is unavailable for use, and can only be detected by very subtle methods. A plausible suggestion has been that it relies on other abilities that develop more slowly, par-ticularly executive functions. These are processes relating to self-control, including control of actions, of thoughts and of attention. Some minimum executive ability may be necessary to direct attention away from current reality. In Southgate et al.'s (2007) task, for example, the absence of a distracting object, and of verbal refer-ences to it, may make it much easier to direct attention to the other person's mental states. However, extensive research on the relationship between executive function and theory of mind makes this simple masking theory untenable. The relationship between the two abilities is much more complex, as discussed in Chapter 8.

The other extreme is to attribute apparent early understanding of mental states to low-level processes and sensitivity to behavioural regularities, such as an expectation that people will look for things where they last saw them. This is a reasonable assumption until the data prove otherwise. However, the few studies now existing begin to look like they are telling a consistent story, from early surprise at another's action (after the fact), to 2-year-olds showing anticipation of false belief based action (initially only in the absence of a distracting object and verbal prompts), culminating in 3- to 4-year-olds' success on an explicit task.

Thus it begins to look likely that the truth lies somewhere between these extremes. Two-year-olds already show an impressive ability to think about nonreal situations in their pretend play (see Chapter 6). It may be that they start to think about nonreal situations when observing others' behaviour. At present, it is too early to make any definite conclusion. What will certainly be needed is some explanation of what "implicit" involves in this context.

Summary: The truth about false belief

More than two decades of research has shown that children's ability to reason about beliefs develops with remarkable consistency. Researchers have examined children's ability to predict behaviour based on false beliefs, to explain behaviour that plausibly results from false beliefs, and to manipulate behaviour by creating a false belief or maintaining another's ignorance. Children start to do all these things at around the age of 4 years. Some procedural alterations can improve performance, but never by very much. Three-year-olds continue to perform at or below chance. Nevertheless, something precedes this competence. Two-year-olds will look in anticipation to the correct location in false belief tasks, then give the incorrect answer to the explicit question. Even infants look longer when a character who should have a false belief searches in the correct location. This does not undermine work on explicit false belief understanding, but promises to give valuable insights into how it develops. This is going to be one of the big research issues of the next decade.

Chapter 3

Theories of theory of mind

Theoretical perspectives

WHAT EXACTLY IS A theory of mind? Premack and Woodruff (1978) introduced the term "theory of mind" to mean the ability to impute mental states to the self and others: "A system of inferences of this kind is properly viewed as a theory, first because such states are not directly observable, and second, because the system can be used to make predictions, specifically, about the behaviour of other organisms" (p. 515). The term "theory of mind" was quickly adopted by developmental psychologists, initially with little commitment to the issue of whether it is really a theory. Over the years, at least three different theoretical positions have emerged, not all of which take the idea of it being a theory seriously.

In everyday conversation, we talk about other people's mental states in two distinct ways. One way is apparently theoretical: Mental state concepts like "want", "think" and "see" are causally linked; "because he saw it, she thought he knew, and she did what she did because she doubted that he wanted it", and so on. We have ideas about how experience, perception, beliefs and desires interact with each other and with behaviour. This allows us to predict and explain what people do. The idea that our theory of mind is theoretical in this way is called the "Theory Theory". However, there is another way of thinking about behaviour: We ask ourselves, "If it were me, what would I do in that situation?" This may involve imagining ourselves in the other's position, and within this pretend scenario, deciding what we would do. Plausibly, we do this by running through the same decision process we would use if we really were in that situation. This may require little or no theory about how mental states interact: We simply use our own mind with appropriate adjustments, relying on the fact that people typically react and think in similar ways. The idea that we understand mental states in this imaginative way is known as the "Simulation Theory" of theory of mind. Both Simulation Theory and Theory Theory describe quite plausible ways that we might think about others' mental states and behaviour. In fact, we probably use both.

The third main theory of what develops involves postulating a mental module: a piece of neural architecture that is dedicated to theory of mind processing. The other two theories are neutral as to how they are instantiated in the brain. Modularity Theory, on the other hand, makes very specific claims.

What mental states are

Before dealing with specific theories, it is helpful to clarify what the theories are about. Most people, including the majority of philosophers, agree that behaviour can be accurately explained in terms of beliefs and desires. A mundane example: I *want* a cup of coffee; I go to a café because I *believe* that I can get one there. This is basic and unmysterious.

In all three theories discussed below, it is claimed that people think about beliefs and desires in terms of *propositional attitudes*. Propositions are states of affairs or situations. They may or may not be true. For example, "this is a cup", "this chicken is delicious", "I left the baby on the bus", and so on. Importantly, propositions can be judged as true or false.

The statement "I believe that I can get a cup of coffee in this café" is a propositional attitude. It can be divided into four parts:

(1)   The agent: The person who holds the belief or desire.
(2)   The proposition: The content of the belief or desire.
(3)   The attitude: The kind of mental state we are talking about. Adults recognize many kinds of attitude: think, believe, know, doubt, desire, hope, fear, and so on.
(4)   The anchor: The bit of the real world the proposition is about (technically speaking, according to which the proposition is to be evaluated).

In the café example, I am the agent, the proposition is "I can get a cup of coffee in this café", the attitude is *believe*, and the anchor is the café. Note that this propositional attitude statement can be true even if the café has stopped serving or has run out of coffee. What makes it true or false is whether it accurately describes my belief. Whether my belief is true or not is irrelevant.

Desires can also be described in terms of propositional attitudes—although the way we talk about them obscures this. In the example, "I want a cup of coffee", "a cup of coffee" is not a proposition: "a cup of coffee" is clearly neither true nor false. However, the abstract "a cup of coffee" is not going to satisfy my desire. More explicitly, I want that *I have a cup of coffee*. I am the agent, the attitude is desire, the anchor is me here and now, and the proposition is "I have a cup of coffee". Since this results in rather an unwieldy sentence, we say "I want a cup of coffee" for short.

Theory Theory

This position takes the term "theory" of mind seriously. The term "Theory Theory" was coined by the philosopher Adam Morton (1980) to refer to the view that commonsense psychology is theory-like in nature. Our commonsense theory posits a range of mental states, causally linked to each other and to behaviour and perception by fairly lawful relationships. Morton did not think that this theory is necessarily much like a scientific theory. Most theory of mind researchers subscribe to the notion of a "theory" of mind in this rather loose sense. This is not universal: Others have provocatively claimed that children's theories are very much like scientific theories, and develop in much the same way as theory change in science (Gopnik & Wellman, 1992, 1994). However, in this chapter, I will concentrate on the best articulated Theory Theory account. Perner (1991, 1995) argues that by 4 years old children acquire a *representational understanding of mind* (a RUM thing).[1] Children conceive of mental states in terms of propositional attitudes, represented and evaluated in the minds of themselves and others. Prior to 4 years old, children should not be credited with a theory of mind, but perhaps with a theory of behaviour.

Getting the hang of reality: Birth to 18 months

During most of infancy, children are credited with a *single updating model* of the world. Their primary goal is to faithfully represent objects (including people and animals) in their environment. This is not trivial: Children have persistent problems with object permanence; when objects pass out of sight, young infants behave as though they have ceased to exist. From roughly 4 to 8 months, infants begin to anticipate the reappearance of objects and will search for partially occluded objects. However, children make bizarre errors. For example, the infant reaches for and grasps a visible object. If an experimenter then covers the child's hand and the object with a cloth, infants will stop retrieving the object. Instead, although they continue to hold it, they behave as though it were no longer there (Gratch, 1972).

From 8 months onwards, children will search for completely occluded objects, but make the "A-not-B error". An attractive object is hidden several times in location A (typically, under a cloth) and retrieved by the child. Then it is placed under a second cloth, B, while the child watches. The child nevertheless searches again at A. This bizarre error has received a lot of attention [see Smith & Thelen (2003) for a recent review and theoretical perspective].

The A-not-B error is largely overcome by 12 months. At this point, children seem to be good at representing their immediate environment and the positions of objects within it—even objects that are not currently visible. However, this is the limit of their ability. Children continue to have difficulties with *invisible displacements*. For example, a ball is hidden under an up-turned cup. The cup is then slid under a cloth and slid out again. The cup is lifted to reveal no ball! Children will search inside the cup, but nowhere else. They do not seem to be able to imagine any other possible hiding places based on the object's past movement. This problem is overcome from about 18 months onwards (Flavell, Miller & Miller, 1993).

Multiple models: 18 months onwards

Once present reality can be faithfully represented, children start to be able to represent nonpresent situations. As well as their single veridical updating model of the world, children are now able to entertain other models. These models may represent past situations, possible future situations, desired situations and purely hypothetical situations. They are also referred to as secondary representations.

Understanding invisible displacement is one of the earliest signs children can do this. After the object has vanished, children have a model like this:

Model 1
[present: "Cup empty. Ball . . .?"]
This is the single veridical updating model. It contains no suggestions about where the child should search for the missing ball. In order to pass the task, children must have a model like this:

Model 2
[past: "Ball in cup under the cloth"]
Comparison of the models allows the child to alter the first model to:

Model 1
[present: "Cup empty. Ball might be under cloth."]

At this stage, children seem to become aware of the existence of the models to some extent. Previously, the single updating model is effectively transparent to children: They are aware of the world it represents, but not of the model itself. However, Gopnik and Meltzoff (1984) report, for example, that once children start to get good at invisible displacement tasks, they also begin to comment on disappearances with statements like "All gone!" This implies awareness of the relationship between the immediate past (when the ball's location was known) and the present (when it has apparently vanished). This suggests that they now explicitly represent that present reality *is* present reality, whereas previously this fact was only implicit, in their use of the model as their basis for action.

The use of multiple models is also evident in children's ability to indulge in pretend play. Here, according to Perner (1991), children are able to conjure up a model that is in many respects quite different to the real situation (see Chapter 6 for further discussion of this). The ability to entertain more than one model is also necessary for language, at least to understand talk about more than the here and now. It is also necessary for recall—to conjure up memories of past situations. It is necessary for effective planning, and even to be properly credited with a desire, since the child must have a representation of the desired situation (e.g., me holding an ice cream) in order to know whether the desire is satisfied or not, and to help bring about the desired situation. This aspect is a little difficult to accept; Jarrold, Carruthers, Smith and Boucher (1994, p. 453) certainly consider it to be incorrect, at least on intuitive grounds.

One crucial point is that at this stage, although children have some awareness of the status of models, they do not conceive of these models *as models*. They conceive of these models in terms of reality: current reality, past reality, potential reality and the bizarre other-reality of pretend. Children are not aware that these are mental representations. That awareness requires metarepresentation.

Metarepresentation: 3 to 4 years onwards

The term "metarepresentation" was first used by the philosopher Zenon W. Pylyshyn (1978) to mean "representing the representational relation itself". Perner argues that to understand belief, children need to be capable of representing that representations are representations. That is a lot of "representations", and is confusing. It is worth going slowly and carefully here.

At the multiple model stage of development, children are capable of having mental models of reality, past situations and hypothetical situations. Now, from the point of view of psychologists, these mental models are *representations*. The veridical model represents current reality, models of past situations represent past situations, models of pretence represent hypothetical situations. That is from our point of view, as psychologists. The young child does not have to conceive of these things as representations. For the 2-year-old child, the veridical model *is* reality, models of past situations *are* the past, models of pretence *are* nontrue situations. The child is *not* aware that these things are mental models. What they are aware of is the content of the models, along with an evaluation of the status of the content, including importantly, whether it is true or false.

The question is, what is the value of going beyond this simple conception? This conception is quite adequate for pretending, even with other people (as argued more fully in Chapter 6). This is because, in pretence, typically everyone evaluates the truth of the proposition in the same way, as false. However, this conception is *not* adequate to predict the behaviour of someone who *misrepresents* reality, for example through having a false belief. In the case of false belief a person evaluates a particular proposition as true, whereas we (the child and the experimenter, say) evaluate it as false. The person wants to act effectively. However, because they have a false belief, they will behave according to a false proposition. Maxi looks in the wrong place for his chocolate, even though he genuinely wants to find it: the "puzzle of false belief" (Perner, 1988, p. 157).

In order to explain or predict this, the child needs to understand that pro-positions can be evaluated. Evaluation of a proposition means to judge whether it is currently true. To understand that people evaluate propositions, the child must make a clear distinction between: (1) the proposition and (2) the state of the world according to which the proposition is to be evaluated. The child must also know that (1) is about (2). Otherwise, Maxi would not behave according to a false proposition when he wants to behave according to the true state affairs. Figure 3.1 illustrates why it is necessary to understand that people evaluate propositions (see pp. 42–43).

The distinction between a proposition and what it is about is a key property of representation: Representations always represent things in a particular way, what Perner (2000) now refers to as "perspective".[2] For example, a photograph of you does not simply represent you, but you from a certain physical point of view—profile, portrait, from behind, and so on. Similarly, Maxi's representation of the location of his chocolate represents it in a particular way, a way that differs from how it truly is. In the case of misrepresentation it is absolutely essential to distinguish between the proposition and the relevant state of the world because Maxi's behaviour is not caused by reality, but by his representa-tion of reality.

Summary

Children begin life with a shaky ability to represent their immediate environ-ment. Their single veridical updating model improves over their first year: *primary representation*. At this point children are explicitly aware of the content of their model. They are *not* aware that it is a model, or that it is of reality, or that it is true.

Sometime during their second year, children become able to construct additional models: *secondary representations*. These models represent nonreal situations, and can represent the past, desired or hypothetical situations. Children are now explicitly aware of the truth value of models; that pretend models are not true, and that their primary representation is true. They remain unaware however that there are such things as models, seeing them rather as reality, or the past, or pretend situations.

At around 4 years, children become able to distinguish between models and what models represent. At this point they realize that the truth of propositions can be evaluated, and independently evaluated by themselves and others. Now they are aware of the models, conceiving of them as representations of other things. This awareness is *metarepresentation*. Children are also aware that models can misrepresent. This is what allows them to pass the false belief task.

Evaluation

The endpoint of Perner's account is widely accepted as a description of how older children and adults conceive of mental states. This is as it should be, since Perner has cast philosophical ideas about the Representational Theory of Mind into a developmental story that also pretty well describes how we adults think we understand beliefs.[3]

Objections to the theory have chiefly concerned the developmental timescale, particularly the idea that the ability to pass false belief tasks arises because of conceptual change. Instead, several theories claim that children possess the relevant conceptual understanding, but it is masked by other considerations, usually poor executive functioning. These theories are considered in Chapter 8. However, Wellman et al. (2001) found that no manipulation has reliably raised 3-year-olds' false belief performance to above chance; there is no evidence that younger 3-year-olds possess the relevant conceptual understanding.

Perner's account predicts that 4-year-olds should understand not only mental representation, but any form of representation. The evidence concerning this is dealt with in Chapter 5. Perner's (1991) account of earlier behaviour has received less attention. One positive aspect of it is that it explains a lot of developmental phenomena in a systematic way. For example, infants do not recognize themselves in the mirror until they are about 18 months old. (Monkeys never do, although most great apes—certainly chimpanzees, bonobos and orangutans—are capable of this.) The standard test of mirror self-recognition is the "rouge test", in which a coloured mark is placed on an infant's face without him or her noticing (under the guise of wiping some dirt away, for example). The infant is then left in front of a mirror. Children younger than 18 months tend to try to touch the rouge on the image of themselves in the mirror. Older children wipe their own faces and look at their hand, just as an adult might.

FIGURE 3.1 How to represent mental states: A worked example.

The cartoon describes an unusual mental state of a 6-year-old. The question is: How do we represent Calvin's mental state? Clearly we need to represent: Calvin; the situation his mental state is about; and the fact that the two are related. A first attempt might look like this:

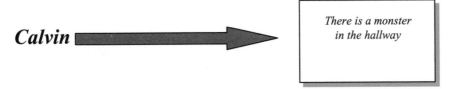

It is also important to keep Calvin's mental state separate from our own, to avoid confusion. In the present case, we might become confused about whether there really is a monster in the hallway. The content of Calvin's mental state must be quarantined and marked as false, like this:

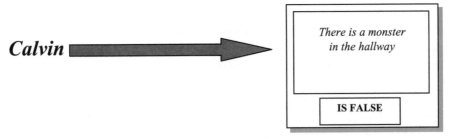

This seems quite promising. If Calvin is pretending that there is a monster in the hallway, this scheme seems to capture what we need to know: Calvin's behaviour relates to a particular proposition, which is false. But it is not clear that Calvin *is* pretending. The present scheme cannot capture the difference between pretending there is a monster in the hallway and falsely believing it. We can make this distinction if we incorporate a way of marking how Calvin evaluates the situation, shown below:

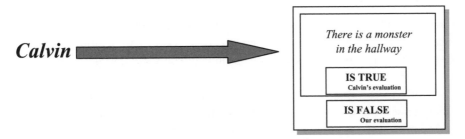

This scheme now allows us to distinguish between Calvin's belief, that there is a monster in the hallway, and our belief, that there is not. A proper understanding of belief involves the recognition that people evaluate propositions independently of their objective truth. However, children can take part in pretend play without making this distinction, since in pretence typically everyone evaluates the false proposition the same way, as false.

On Perner's account, mirror self-recognition requires two models to capture the idea that the person in the mirror is the same person on the other side of the mirror, i.e., me. Mirror self-recognition occurs at around 18 months because it requires children to know that the image is themselves "in another situation", in this case in the mirror. Roughly the same understanding is required to understand that people or things in photographs are the same as the corresponding people or things in the real world. Children can start to understand something about photographs when, for example, they can conjure up a model containing Daddy on a mountain wearing skis to go alongside their veridical model of the here-and-now Daddy, who is in an armchair wearing slippers (see Chapter 5).

Simulation Theory

According to Simulation Theory, we do not need a *theory* of mind. Instead we have a good working model of other people's minds: our own. If we assume that all minds work in basically the same way, we can predict what others will do by predicting what we ourselves would do under the same circumstances. Building a theory, when you already have a working model, seems quite unnecessary.

Simulation Theory entered the theory of mind debate in 1986, independently proposed by the philosophers Robert Gordon and Jane Heal. Subsequently it has produced a lot of interest in philosophy of mind, and there are a number of versions of the theory. Here I will concentrate on the version proposed by Paul Harris (1992), which is grounded in developmental psychology and tailored to explain the development of theory of mind skills.

Harris's developmental version of Simulation Theory

Harris's (1992) version of Simulation Theory rests on children's capacity for pretence. By the age of 2 years, children are very good at pretending, attributing pretend properties to objects and imagining nonexistent objects. By the age of 3 years, Harris hypothesizes, children can also imagine having mental states— beliefs or desires—that they do not truly hold. For example, a child who is not thirsty can pretend to want a glass of milk. Children can reason on the basis of these pretend mental states to infer other mental states or actions.

Harris proposes that there are *default settings* that correspond to the child's own current mental states. These are of two types: One type specifies the current state of reality (i.e., what the child believes or perceives to be the case); the other type specifies the child's own mental states associated with that reality (Intentional states of the self—the child's representation of her or his own mental states). For example, one set of default settings specify amongst other things what is on the table (a milk carton, cookies, broccoli), and the other set specifies that the child *thinks* the milk carton is empty, *wants* the cookies, does not *like* the broccoli. The theory assumes the child is able to introspect accurately, and therefore knows her or his own current beliefs, desires, and so on.

Reasoning about other people's mental states requires temporarily altering your default settings to match what another person's mental states should be. Harris (1992) assumes that tasks are more difficult if more default settings need to be altered. The appeal of the theory is that this plausible assumption accounts for much of the developmental findings concerning difficulty of different tasks. Children's first experience of altering default settings is in the context of pretence. This requires altering default settings associated with current reality. Children also seem adept at altering Intentional states of the self towards current reality by about 3 years of age. They understand that others can see, want, like, and perhaps know different things to themselves. All these tasks involve altering just one set of default settings.

False belief tasks, on the other hand, require altering two sets of default settings. For example, in the Maxi task, children must: (1) imagine a nonreal state of affairs and (2) imagine having a different mental stance towards that state of affairs. Children become able to alter two sets of default settings around the age of 4 years. Harris (1992) also argues that a similar process occurs for the child's own past beliefs. Children are assumed to be able to know their own current beliefs by introspection, but previously held beliefs must be reconstructed. This is done by altering the appropriate default settings. In the case of false belief, this involves the same processes as attributing someone else a current false belief: imagining a reality that differs from the true past state of affairs, and imagining a different stance towards it.

Evaluation

The theory explains most of the data very well. Harris, like Perner (above) and Leslie (below), believes our theory of mind is based on ascribing propositional attitudes to others. However, we do not do this by theorising (Harris, 1992, p. 121). As discussed, Harris's version of Simulation Theory requires children to be able to accurately introspect on their own mental states. This in turn requires children to already have concepts of belief, desire, and so on. Harris does not speculate about whether these concepts develop or are innate.

However, it is unlikely that the "theory" can entirely be removed from theory of mind. Certainly, an appropriately set up simulation can replicate the mental states of another person. For example, in the false belief transfer task, Maxi sees the chocolate put in location 1, and we set our hypothetical belief state to match that. Then we imagine Maxi's experience as he goes out to play and does not observe the chocolate moved to location 2. Having run through this process, we can introspect on our (hypothetical) belief state, and attribute to Maxi the belief "the chocolate is in location 1". Critically, we did not have to consider differences between our and

Maxi's belief states at the beginning of the simulation, because the false belief was acquired during the events simulated.

However, this is often not the case. In the unexpected contents task, for example, before simulation can begin, the child must realize that the other person is ignorant of the true contents of the Smarties tube. This ignorance cannot be inferred by simulating their experience, because there was no event or experience that caused them to be ignorant: They were always ignorant. This fact needs to be specified before running the simulation To do this, children presumably infer that because the person has not seen inside the tube yet, they do not know what is inside. This bit of reasoning is theory-like, inferring a mental state (ignorance) using a rule (does not see = does not know). And the Smarties task involves very basic mental state reasoning: More complicated theory of mind reasoning can require considerable initial adjustment of default settings, for example to match the person's knowledge, education, traits and emotional states (how would an embittered coal miner with a reputation for meanness and a history of violence react at the bar during his daughter's graduation ball?). Some theoretical knowledge seems indispensable to get simulations started.

There are also cases where simulation just will not work. Perner (1991, p. 269) considers visual perspective taking. No amount of simulation will tell you how, for example, three mountains look from the perspective of a person on the other side. You simply have to work it out. Another example is the case of judgements of knowledge versus ignorance. If I observe someone looking inside a box, can I judge their knowledge state through simulation? Yes, if I happen to know what is in the box. I can then imagine myself looking inside the box, and let my knowledge-formation mechanism act on the imaginary input (e.g., the coin in the box). Introspecting, I realize that, in this hypothetical case, I know what is inside: a coin. However, if I do *not* know what is inside, the simulation does not work so well: I imagine myself looking inside but, introspecting, I find I am still ignorant of the contents. If I attribute this ignorance to the other person, I will misjudge their state of knowledge. (In fact, children's ability to judge the knowledge of others' in this task is not affected by whether they know the contents or not; Wimmer, Hogrefe & Perner, 1988.)

The argument from error

Setting these concerns aside, it is empirically difficult to decide between the Theory Theory and Simulation Theory. One way researchers have tried to distinguish between them is by focusing on errors in mindreading (Saxe, 2005). Social psychology is full of examples where actual behaviour is very different to what people would predict. A striking example is Milgram's (1963) study of obedience. The study was published a year after Adolf Eichman was hanged in Israel for his part in the Holocaust. Eichman's defence had been that he was only following orders. Milgram wondered whether this might actually have been the truth (although naturally this would not have absolved Eichman of guilt or responsibility). In Milgram's experiment, participants were paired with a stooge in a supposed "learning experiment". The stooge went to a separate room, where he could be heard but not seen. Participants were asked to administer electric shocks of increasing voltage to the stooge when he gave incorrect answers to test questions. In reality, no shocks were administered, but the stooge soon began to bang on the wall, demand the experiment stop, and at about 135 volts, stopped responding altogether. Nevertheless, most participants, when prompted by the experimenter, continued to increase the voltage of shocks until it reached the maximum 450 volts. Milgram's fellow psychologists had unanimously predicted that only a tiny minority of participants would do this.

How can the findings be surprising if we use simulation? The Milgram experiment is an extreme and emotive case, but there are many more prosaic examples from social psychology in which people behave in markedly different ways to how they predict they would behave. Stich and Nichols (1992) describe a lottery experiment in which participants bought a US$1 ticket for the office lottery. Some participants were allowed to choose from several tickets, whereas others were just given one. On the morning of the draw, the experimenter offered to buy back the lottery ticket. Participants who had been given no choice of ticket were prepared to sell for just under US$2 on average; participants who had chosen a ticket, even though it was clear the winner would be randomly determined, on average were only prepared to sell for nearly US$9 (Nisbett & Ross, 1980, p. 136).

This is intuitively surprising—would you have predicted such a big discrepancy? The inability to predict behaviour in these sorts of situation suggests that we are not using simulation. If we use a theory, it may or may not correctly describe human behaviour. In unusual situations, it is quite plausible that a theory would produce the wrong prediction (just as Newtonian physics does not work at very small scales, which require quantum theory, or at very high speeds, which require special relativity theory). However, if we use our own decision-making apparatus to predict what others will decide to do, we should be able to predict reasonably accurately, especially in situations where we would presumably behave the same way. This "argument from error" (e.g., Saxe, 2005) is one of the most powerful arguments against Simulation Theory.

Supporters of the theory, however, can argue that simulation fails occasionally because people do not simulate accurately. Harris (1992), for example, points out that the lottery example would require you to simulate the vacillation and decision of the participants who got to choose, and also set aside the reminder implicit in the description of the study that winning was entirely random. The finding may be surprising simply because you did not do this. Accurate simulation depends on having the right pretend inputs.

It is very difficult to determine what inputs people use, so this counterargument is difficult to refute. However, Ted Ruffman (1996) devised a developmental task that does this quite elegantly. He adapted an inference task used by Sodian and Wimmer (1987). In one condition, children were shown a round dish full of red sweets, and a square dish of green sweets. A sweet is transferred from the round dish to a bag. A doll does not see this, but is told that the sweet came from the round dish. Children up until about the age of 7 years judge that the doll does not know what colour the sweet is, failing to understand that the doll can make a simple inference (round dish = red sweet). Moreover, they judge that the doll thinks the sweet is green. This seems to imply two theoretical rules: a "seeing leads to knowing" rule is used to infer that the doll, who has not seen, does not know; a "not knowing leads to wrong answers" rule is used to infer that the "ignorant" doll has a false belief.

Simulation Theory cannot readily explain the finding: The doll ought to have the same belief as the child—that the sweet in the bag is red. This would lead to the correct answer without the need to adjust default settings. The only option is to argue that a simulation is run that for some reason uses incorrect inputs. The key inputs are: (1) the message given to the doll (that the sweet came from the round dish); and (2) the doll's knowledge of the colour of the sweets in the round dish (red). If either of these was omitted or incorrectly entered, children would incorrectly simulate the doll's knowledge and belief. To see whether this was plausible, Ruffman added a false belief condition, in which the doll was given the same message, that the sweet had been transferred from the round dish (with the red sweets), but this time it was untrue; in fact it was from the square dish (with the green sweets). In this case, children have to use (1) and (2) to infer the doll's false belief. Even 4-year-olds could do this. Clearly children were working with the correct inputs in the false belief version of the task. The fact that they nevertheless could not correctly infer the doll's true belief in the standard inference task strongly suggests that they are not using simulation in this kind of task. Instead they seem to be overapplying theoretical rules.

Synthesis

After a lively debate about whether Theory Theory or Simulation Theory best describes mindreading, a consensus seems to be developing that it involves both (e.g., Nichols & Stich, 2003). What is uncertain is to what extent, and which processes involve simulation, and which theory. The sort of theory of mind tasks usually used in developmental research probably are best described by Theory Theory. However, there are clear cases where we must use simulation. For example, imagine you have to predict how someone else will answer the question: "What is 2 plus 2?" The natural way to do this is to answer the question yourself, and then attribute the answer to the other person: a clear case of simulation. It would be absurd to suppose that you have a theory of how other people do mathematics. Many of our predictions of everyday behaviour are probably of this sort, particularly those that involve predicting others' inferences. This simple simulation has to be initiated with a piece of theoretical knowledge, such as "He will answer it in the same way as I do", but thereafter our own reasoning process can be used.

Perner (1991) suggests that Simulation Theory is also very plausible when considering emotions. For example, suppose that while walking home at night you imagine being followed by a suspicious-looking character. The imagination evokes real feelings of fear and anger. This shows that our emotional mechanism can respond to situations that are simply imagined. Thus we can simulate the emotions of others if we can effectively imagine ourselves in their situation. Nevertheless, emotions also require appropriate adjustments based on theoretical knowledge. Perner considers predicting how a colleague will feel if his mother-in-law dies. Simply imagining how you would feel if your mother-in-law died is not adequate. The colleague may feel quite differently from you about his mother-in-law, and this fact must be taken into account for accurate simulation.

Much of the speculation about Simulation Theory has died down recently, with the acceptance that theory of mind reasoning probably involves both. Former opponents of Simulation Theory, Nichols and Stich (2003) now propose a hybrid theory that mixes simulation-like and theory-like elements. Perner and Kühberger (2006) are developing an empirical approach to determining whether any given prediction is based on theory or simulation. A general theory of which types of processes are supported by theory and which by simulation is now possible, in principle. For the time being, it is reasonable to conclude that simulation may be used in some theory of mind tasks, but it also requires theoretical knowledge to start the process.

Modular theories of mind

Mental module accounts hold that our theory of mind is handled by a specialized piece of mental hardware: Some part of the brain is dedicated to theory of mind processing. Modular theory is essentially a hardware version of Theory Theory. Children have concepts of belief, pretence, desire, and so on, and are able to reason with them to predict and explain behaviour. However, this is not an abstract theory, but is instantiated in a particular set of neural circuits. The theory is innately specified, along with core concepts like belief and desire.

Modules are often considered to have been put there by evolution: Being able to predict behaviour is so important that there would be pressure not to leave it up to chance or a slow process of theory building in childhood. Instead some or all of our theory of mind is hardwired and begins to operate after appropriate neural maturation and/or the right environmental triggers. There may, in fact, be several modules, perhaps in a layer, representing evolutionarily more primitive theories of mind. This could explain the developmental pattern of preschool theories of mind, as more evolutionarily recent modules mature and take over from their forebears (Segal, 1996).

One attractive feature of this idea is that it explains why, with a few minor possible exceptions, theory of mind development is culturally uniform. If children were left to build a theory using more general mechanisms, considerable variation might be expected (even within cultures). It also suggests a simple (although perhaps simplistic) explanation for the developmental disorder of autism. Two striking features of autism are a deficient theory of mind, and a lack of pretend play and other imaginative activities. This could be because a theory of mind module is damaged, abnormal or absent in autism. (Note, to also explain the lack of pretend play in this way requires a commitment to the idea that pretending requires understanding pretence in terms of propositional attitudes. Most theorists consider that the younger pretender conceives of pretence in much simpler terms. See Chapters 6 and 10.)

Fodorian modules

Discussion of modules in psychology derives from Fodor's (1983) influential book, *The Modularity of Mind*. The essence of modularity is "informational encapsulation". A module is basically a black box: It takes a specific kind of input (information about behaviour), and produces a particular output (descriptions of mental states). The black box cannot draw on other parts of the system to help processing, and the rest of the system has no access to what is going on inside the box.

In addition to being encapsulated, modules have a number of hypothetical properties, as follows:

(1) They act only on specific kinds of information, so a theory of mind module would act only on information concerning (certain types of) behaviour and mental states. It is a specialized system.

(2) Their operation is mandatory. In other words, we cannot help interpreting behaviour in terms of mental states. This is very plausible. Heider and Simmel (1944) showed adults a film involving three geometric shapes: a valiant little triangle, his circular girlfriend and a large bullying triangle. The film involved a fight between the couple and the large triangle, who tried to abduct the circle—but the valiant little triangle put up a good fight and the couple managed to escape, much to the rage and frustration of the large triangle. The film is impossible to watch without forming something like this kind of interpretation, but in fact is simply an unnarrated sequence of moving shapes. Our tendency to interpret interactions as social, and behaviour in terms of psychological traits or states, is clearly very powerful.

(3) Modules are fast. This could be a consequence of encapsulation, which limits the information the module can or needs to consult, along with mandatory

operation that removes the delay involved in considering whether or not to process incoming information.

(4)   Their outputs are restricted to low-level concepts. This feature does not seem appropriate to a theory of mind module.

(5)   They exhibit characteristic and specific breakdown patterns. This might be the case in autism.

(6)   Their development has a characteristic pace and sequencing.

Leslie's Theory of Mind Mechanism theory

At present, the most comprehensive modular account has been presented by Alan Leslie. This was also one of the earliest theories of theory of mind (beginning with Leslie, 1987). Leslie argues that theory of mind reasoning is handled by a module in the Fodorian sense. Specifically, Leslie proposes a processor called the Theory of Mind Mechanism (ToMM)—an innate modular piece of brain hardware. As input, it takes information about the behaviour of other people and uses this to compute their probable mental states. It outputs descriptions of mental states in the form of propositional attitudes.

The theory was first developed in the context of pretence. For example, if the child's mother holds a banana to her ear and starts to speak into it, the watching child's ToMM might output the following propositional attitude statement: Mother pretends of the banana that "it is a telephone". The ToMM also produces descriptions of beliefs, true or false. So, if a child observes a false belief task, his or her ToMM will output a description of the agent's final false belief: i.e., Sally believes of her marble that "it is in Box 1".

A key assumption of the theory has arguably led to theoretical problems ever since: When children start to pretend, they understand what they are doing in adult-like terms, representing pretence in terms of propositional attitudes. Children begin to pretend with others at 18 months. The ToMM is therefore assumed to be fully functional from this age. This claim results in an immediate empirical problem. If the ToMM is fully functional at 18 months, why are children unable to pass false belief tasks until they are around 4 years old?

This problem of how to integrate children's skill at pretence with their incomprehension of mental states is shared with other theories of theory of mind. Theory Theorists and Simulation Theorists have argued that one can pretend, even with others, without an adult-like conception of pretence (see Chapter 6). Predicting or explaining behaviour, however, requires a proper concept of belief. Leslie, however, remains committed to the idea that early pretence is understood in terms of propositional attitudes in exactly the same way that belief is. Thus the gap between being able to pretend and being able to pass false belief tasks must be explained in some other way.

His initial suggestion was that children do not understand how beliefs are

51

formed (Leslie, 1988). Pretend scenarios are just invented, more or less at whim. Beliefs have an orderly but complex relationship to the world. Perhaps children take time to learn the causes and effects of belief. A modular account of this sort may be possible, perhaps assuming that the module has parameters that need to be set by specific environmental inputs. Parameters concerning belief formation might require specific input or additional maturation. However, Leslie (1991) abandoned this idea. Instead, Leslie and Thaiss (1992) suggested that the ToMM's difficulty with belief was assumed to be because it could not compute the proposition. The ToMM was able to compute propositions if they can be "read off" behaviour, which is assumed to be possible in pretence. However, belief tasks require the reconstruction of the proposition based on the agent's exposure history. This was too hard for the ToMM. Instead a device called the Selection Processor (SP) computed the missing proposition (Leslie, 1994; Leslie & Roth, 1993; Leslie & Thaiss, 1992). It then passed the proposition to the ToMM, which computed the remainder of the propositional attitude statement, e.g., Maxi believes (of) his chocolate that "____".

This suggestion seemed unsatisfactory. If the ToMM is a specialized device for computing mental state descriptions, it would be odd if it was typically unable to compute mental state descriptions. Perhaps for this reason, the theory has been modified further. In the current version, the ToMM once again has the power to compute propositions, and may pass on more than one proposition at the same time. For belief, the ToMM always attributes a true belief to the agent. Any plausible false beliefs are also attributed. These are passed on to the SP. This is an executive mechanism that may not be restricted to operating in theory of mind tasks. The SP's function is to select a single belief description. When more than one is received, it selects the true belief proposition by default. This is why younger children fail the false belief task. The inhibitory ability of the SP is initially poor, and it cannot suppress its own default tendency. Its inhibitory ability improves with age, until at around the age of 4 years the SP can override its default in order to accept the false belief description and pass the task.

Evaluation

The theory makes definite claims, which is attractive, and provides a fairly simple explanation of autism. It also has the potential to be turned into a processing account of false belief performance. This is already being done for a more complex version of the false belief task. Cassidy (1995, 1998) modified the standard false belief task, in which Maxi wants to find his chocolate, to one in which the protagonist wants to avoid the object. She found that whereas her 4-year-olds all passed the standard task, most failed the novel avoidance–desire task. Leslie and colleagues (Leslie, Friedman & German, 2004; Leslie, German & Polizzi, 2005) have developed two complex models of the inhibitory processes that may be involved in this task. Recent evidence for infant sensitivity to false belief (Onishi & Baillargeon, 2005: see Chapter 2) can also be taken as supporting an innate modular ToMM (Leslie, 2005).

There is an unresolved problem at the core of the theory, however (see Doherty, 1999). At first glance it seems like there is a fairly straightforward division of labour between the two processors. The ToMM handles theory of mind process-ing, and a functioning theory of mind is in place from 18 months onwards. The SP performs the executive inhibition that is necessary to pass the appropriate outputs of the ToMM to the rest of the system. The SP is not intended to perform theory of mind calculations in its own right. However, examining the role of the SP in false belief tasks more closely shows that this cannot be so. The SP receives two different belief descriptions, for example, "Maxi believes it is in box 1" and "Maxi believes it is in box 2". The ToMM supplies *no* further relevant information. The SP must select one of the descriptions, but is given no basis to choose.

How it makes its choice is simply not addressed: "What triggers the inhibition is an interesting question but not one we will address here. Presumably, the recogni-tion that Sally does not see/know that the bait is in the new location plays a role" (Leslie et al., 2005, p. 53). The only other mention of this issue is that the "SP accesses a learned database of circumstances relevant to selecting between candidate-beliefs" (Leslie et al., 2004, p. 532).

In other words, the SP knows about belief formation: It has to recognize which of the beliefs it has been given is consistent with the facts. Knowing how circumstances lead to particular beliefs requires quite a sophisticated understanding of mental states. Furthermore, in order to select which of the two candidate beliefs Sally should have, the SP will have to work out, from its knowledge of what Sally has seen, what Sally ought to believe. It could then compare this belief description to the outputs of the ToMM. However, if the SP could do this, it would not need to consult the ToMM. It would be much more straightforward to do the job on its own. One or other of these two mechanisms seems redundant.

These theoretical problems all stem from the attempt to explain pretence and belief by the same mechanism without allowing for any development in the mech-anism. Developmental effects are attributed solely to maturation of the SP. A differ-ent modular theory has been proposed by Baron-Cohen (1995), in which several modules cooperate and feed into each other. He has as his final module a ToMM that operates from around 4 years. He does not attempt an explanation of pretence. This theory is covered in more detail in Chapter 7. Segal (1996) suggests another alternative. He suggests that there are a series of "switches" inside the theory of mind module, allowing theories of mind with slightly different parameters. How and when parameters get set depend on environmental input, and possibly some-thing like an internal clock. So children might start with a particular parameter set to "prelief", an undifferentiated concept of belief and pretence (see Chapter 6). At some point it will get set to "belief". Prelief might be a hangover from an evolutionarily earlier theory of mind module. This is reasonably compatible with the problematic division of labour discussed above. The SP may act as a second theory of mind mechanism. The ToMM may come with a concept of prelief, useful for alerting children to the possibility of alternative mental states. This might allow them to think about nonreal situations and reflect on their relationship to behaviour. It would also be sufficient for pretence. It could pass its outputs on to a maturing SP (modular or otherwise) that would eventually take over the job of theory of mind reasoning. This seems a potentially fruitful way of modifying the ToMM-SP theory. Functionally, it would be very similar to Perner's (1995) version of Theory Theory, but make definite claims about hardware.

Modular theories of mind have a persistent appeal. The apparently universal development of theory of mind, resulting in very similar "theories" across many cultures, and following the same or at least a similar timetable suggests that there is something biologically predetermined about theory of mind. It is plausible that evolution would have fitted us out with some innate basis for theory of mind, although there is as yet no evidence concerning this; our nearest relatives, chimpanzees, do not appear to have theory of mind skills (although this is still controversial: see Chapter 7). Modularity Theory is compatible with Theory Theory in general: The module's theory of mind could be theory-like; it would not develop in a way that is remotely analogous to the development of scientific theories, but most theory theorists do not claim this. It also seems plausible that part of the simulation process could involve a specialized module, perhaps serving the purpose of setting up starting conditions for simulations; as yet there have been no proposals along these lines.

Summary

All three theories have continuing potential. It has often been assumed that one or other type of theory must be correct, and the others therefore incorrect. In fact, all three types of theory might have elements of truth. If so, the question would become one of demarcation: Which bits of theory of mind are best described by each individual theory? The idea that we understand emotion through a form of simulation, and belief through a more theoretical process is perfectly reasonable. Our theory might be implemented within a specialized brain area that may have the characteristics proposed by Modularity Theorists. Alternatively, we may come equipped with an innate primitive theory of mind module that causes us to attend to mental states (and allows some primitive theory of mind reasoning), which causes us to develop a Theory Theory of mind by the time we reach about 4 years. It seems likely that our theory of mind is some kind of hybrid of at least two of these theories, possibly all three. As stated at the end of innumerable undergraduate essays, more research is needed.

Chapter 4

Associated developments 1: Beyond belief

Introduction

NATURALLY THERE IS MORE to having a theory of mind than passing the false belief task. The false belief task has dominated theory of mind research, for both bad and good reasons. Much of the 1990s was spent in attempting to prove that the false belief task underestimated children. Gopnik, Slaughter and Meltzoff (1994) coined the phrase, "neurotic task fixation" for this behaviour, which was largely a failure. It is not possible to make explicit false belief tasks much easier, but the attempt taught us a lot about the factors that moderate the difficulty of the task (Wellman et al., 2001). Despite the massive research time spent on this one task, there are reasons to remain interested in it. First, it is a diagnostic test of the understanding that behaviour is based on internally represented mental states. The neurotic attention it has received means that we can be confident in the reliability of the task.

The second reason is that false belief understanding does not arise in isolation. At around the age of 4 years there is a general change in the way children understand a range of mental phenomena. This change is fundamental, important and has far-reaching consequences. This chapter looks at these wider changes in children's understanding of the mind, and what follows from them. However, first it is necessary to consider desire.

Desire

We predict behaviour by attributing a combination of beliefs and desires. If Maxi wants his chocolate, and he thinks it is in the drawer, then (all other things being equal) he will go to the drawer. Most research in theory of mind has concerned beliefs and related phenomena, and desire has been relatively neglected. This may seem odd, because attributing desires is potentially much more useful. Beliefs are usually true, so they can usually be ignored. Instead, others' behaviour can be predicted on the basis of objective reality. Children only need to consider belief in cases where the usually reliable belief–reality link has broken down. Desires, on the other hand, are idiosyncratic and constantly changing. Maxi may want his chocolate, but I want a beer, and shortly after I may want a curry. This means that some understanding of desire is essential for even very basic behaviour prediction.

Children from late infancy onwards show signs of this understanding. The major unresolved issue is whether children understand desire in the same way that adults do. Adults probably work with two different conceptions of desire. The simplest form is an *objective* concept of desire. This can be a relationship between a person and an object or a situation. If I want a cheeseburger, I can view this as a relationship between me and a cheeseburger. It is a particular kind of relationship, such that I will behave in predictable ways (approaching the cheeseburger, attempting to grab it, and so on). This is probably sufficient to predict my behaviour towards a given cheeseburger in my immediate vicinity. If no cheeseburger is in evidence, a slightly more sophisticated way of viewing my desire is needed, as a relationship between me and a potential future state of the world: the situation in which I have a cheeseburger. This concept of desire is still objective because the situation is a state of the world, albeit a potential future one.

The second, more sophisticated concept of desire is as a *subjective* internal state. The reason why my desire for a cheeseburger drives my behaviour is because I have a mental representation of the potential future state, and a particular attitude towards it: in other words, a propositional attitude (see Chapter 3). To what extent adults use such a complex subjective view of desire, rather than rely on the simpler objective view, is not known. The way we talk about desires in English fits the simple view of desire much more smoothly. The propositional attitude view can only be expressed awkwardly: "I want *that* (I have a cheeseburger)". We are much more likely to say "I want a cheeseburger". (Simply "Cheeseburger!" is often sufficient.) Nevertheless, adults can adopt the complex view of desire when necessary. It is less clear whether young children can. This is difficult to determine because the objective conception of desire is quite adequate for most situations.

One consequence of having an objective concept of desire is that objects may be seen as inherently desirable or undesirable (Perner, 1991). In other words, "spinach is nasty" rather than "I don't like spinach (but others do)". Repacholi and Gopnik (1997) looked at whether infants view desires in this way by looking at understanding of *discrepant* desires. An objective concept of desire cannot accommodate conflicting desires towards the same thing (although, as will be seen, what counts as a single "thing" can be flexible). Repacholi and Gopnik used a clever food-sharing procedure. Infants aged 14 and 18 months were presented with two bowls, one containing crackers and one containing raw broccoli. Children naturally preferred the crackers. The experimenter then ostentatiously tasted each type of food. She expressed disgust at the crackers, and pleasure at tasting the broccoli. She then pushed the bowls back towards the child, held out her hand and said, "Can you give me some?" Of the children who complied with the request, 14-month-old children almost always gave the experimenter crackers. The 18-month-old children gave this peculiar adult broccoli most of the time, suggesting that they understood that her desired food differed from theirs. This ability seems to be developing rapidly around 18 months: When the performance of the younger and older children in the 18-month-old group was analysed, only the older children were consistently handing over the broccoli. The results cannot be explained by selfishness: In a control condition where the experimenter expressed preference for crackers, most children of all ages handed them over.

This finding suggests that by the age of around 18 months children understand that objects are not inherently desirable or undesirable. Repacholi and Gopnik argue that infants understand desire as a subjective internal state that can differ from person to person: There is no accounting for tastes. This would support a proposal by Wellman (1990, 1993) that young children are initially desire theorists. Wellman argues that children develop a psychological theory of desire well before they develop the belief–desire theory necessary to pass the false belief task.

This is not the only way of interpreting the findings, however. Children could still pass Repacholi and Gopnik's task with a slightly more sophisticated but still objective understanding of desire. Rather than simply classifying the foods as "crackers good, broccoli bad", children can consider the desirability of two separate situations: The situation of "broccoli in the experimenter's mouth" is good (because she said so, the child will take her word for it); the situation of "broccoli in the child's mouth" however is self-evidently bad (Perner, Zauner & Sprung, 2005; Rakoczy, Warneken & Tomasello, 2007). This way of viewing desire is subjective in the sense that it allows children to understand that people may have different tastes. However, desires are still conceived as objective features of situations. The distinction is between a simple objective concept of desire, in which desirability is seen as a property of objects (or actions), and a more complex objective concept of desire, where desirability is seen as a property of situations. One or other of these objective concepts of desire would do perfectly well in most circumstances.

One way of determining when children use a truly subjective concept of desire is to ensure that discrepant desires apply to one and the same situation. This is not always as easy as it might appear—the world can be carved up into situations in different ways. For example, Hannes Rakoczy and colleagues (Rakoczy et al., 2007) adapted a discrepant desire task originally used by Lisa Lichtermann (1991). In the task, two characters are on a boating lake in the same boat. They have a brief argument in which Susi says that the boat should go to the tree, and Tom says it should go to the house. Thus they have incompatible desires concerning the outcome of a single situation. At this point the wind blows the boat to the tree. Children were asked where Tom and where Susi had wanted the boat to go. They were generally very good at remembering the two characters' incompatible desires—but these desires had just been stated twice, so this may simply reflect memory for what was said. The more interesting question concerned whether children could judge that Susi will be happy, and Tom will be sad at the outcome.

Lichtermann found that 3- to 4-year-old children were bad at this, and performance correlated with a standard false belief task. Rakoczy et al. found that young 3-year-olds were good at this, despite almost all of them failing false belief tasks. The difference between the studies is striking, and is difficult to know which set of results is correct. One possible conclusion is that 3-year-olds can report discrepant desires, and moreover can reason on them to work out how the two characters felt about the outcome. Thus 3-year-olds conceive of desires as subjective. However, there is a way of solving the task with an objective concept of desire. This involves considering the events in terms of two separate situations, each involving one of the characters: The situation in which Susi goes to the tree is good; the situation in which Tom goes to the tree is bad (pretty much like "broccoli in your mouth, good" and "broccoli in my mouth, bad"). Clearly, these situations are not independent, but as children are only asked to think about them one at a time, they may not consider this.

Rakoczy et al. do not consider this possible counterexplanation, but nevertheless their second experiment is not easily explained in terms of an objective concept of desire. Their new task was a simplified version of a task used by Moore, Jarrold, Russell, Lumb, Sapp and MacCallum (1995). The child and a puppet play a competitive game. A marble drops down a chute and appears in one of two trays. The puppet wants it to appear in one tray and the child wants it to appear in the other. Here it is difficult to consider the two possible outcomes independently: One tray is good for the child and bad for the puppet, and vice versa, since the two are in direct competition (and, incidentally, the game is rigged). Moore et al. found that this task was as hard as the false belief task. Rakoczy et al. found that reporting the players' incompatible desires was significantly easier than the false belief task, but ascribing appropriate emotions to the winner and loser was not. However, when children who performed poorly on the false belief control questions were excluded, there was no difference between the desire and belief tasks.

Taken together, Moore et al.'s (1995) and Rakoczy et al.'s (2007) studies suggest that the incompatible desires task is at best only slightly easier than the false belief task. Yuill, Perner, Pearson, Peerbhoy and van den Ende (1996) provide further evidence that a subjective understanding of desire is developing around the age of 4 years. They told children illustrated stories of characters with *wicked* desires. For example:

> This boy was playing ball. He did not like the boy in the green jumper. He wanted to throw the ball at him to hit him on the head. He threw the ball. It hit the boy in green on the head and made him cry.

> Test question: Is the boy who threw the ball happy or sad, or in between?

Three-year-olds tended to judge that the wicked boy would be sad, apparently unable to understand that he could want something that was objectively bad. Older children recognized that the boy would be happy at the bad outcome, because his desire (however reprehensible) had been satisfied. (Of passing interest: In a similar procedure with an open-ended interview, children of about 10 years began to report the character having mixed feelings: guilt, regret or shame in addition to satisfaction.) Thus, although even infants may understand that someone can want something yucky like broccoli, children under 4 years do not understand that someone may want something objectively bad to happen.

The issue is likely to remain controversial for the time being. What is clear is that at present there is no strong evidence that understanding incompatible desires is any easier than understanding false belief. Repacholi and Gopnik's (1997) findings can be explained by infants' use of a sophisticated objective understanding of desire. This is also the case for Lichtermann's (1991) and Rakoczy et al.'s (2007) boat task. Moore et al. (1995) and Rakoczy et al.'s competitive game task is clever: it requires a subjective understanding of desire. It has proved either as hard as the false belief task, or not much easier. Similarly, Yuill et al. (1996) found that 3-year-olds cannot understand that someone may desire something objectively bad, but 4-year-olds can, and their task does not seem to be at all complex. The balance of present evidence suggests that understanding discrepant desires is about as hard as understanding discrepant beliefs.

Appearance and reality

Sometimes appearance and reality diverge. The shadow behind your wardrobe looks like a monster. The bearded man dressed in a red coat looks like Father Christmas. It appears that there are tiny people inside the television. The magician appears to have just sawn his assistant in half. It is obviously useful to realize that things may not be as they appear. Creating a distinction between how things are and how they appear is the basis of many forms of deception, both malicious and benign. Appreciation of the appearance–reality distinction allows us to go beyond outward appearances.

The distinction was introduced into developmental psychology by Flavell, Flavell and Green (1983). Their work was not initially part of early theory of mind research, instead arising out of research on children's perspective-taking abilities (discussed in Chapter 7). Their basic task is as follows: Children are shown a deceptive object, such as a sponge that looks like a rock. They are then allowed to feel it, and readily agree that it is in fact a sponge. Then they are asked two questions: "What is this *really, really*? Is it *really, really* a rock or *really, really* a piece of sponge?" and "When you *look* at this with your *eyes* right now, does it *look* like a rock or does it *look* like a piece of sponge?" (Flavell et al., 1983, p. 102).

Typically, before the age of about 4 years, children give the same answer to the two questions. In the case of the sponge-rock they tend to say it is a sponge and it looks like a sponge. This is referred to as a realist error. Children of 4 years onwards tend to say it is a sponge but it looks like a rock, just as adults would. There are also versions of the task where a property of an object, rather than the identity of the object, appears different. For example, a piece of white paper looks blue when placed behind a blue filter. Young children in this case tend to say the paper looks blue and really is blue. This is referred to as a *phenomenist* error (although an "appearance error" might be a more user-friendly piece of terminology). This version of the procedure is not used often, perhaps because it is somehow less clear that the paper really is white. Children may think that the filter temporarily changes the paper's colour, and in some sense it does.

Theories

The appearance–reality distinction is clearly related in some way to false belief, which involves what might be called the belief–reality distinction. *Exactly* how it is related proves hard to specify. Most researchers now regard the appearance–reality task as more-or-less another version of the false belief task. Children start to pass the two tasks at around the same time, and they are related (e.g., Gopnik & Astington, 1988). The unexpected contents false belief task is very like the appearance–reality task: the Smarties tube looks like a full tube of Smarties. Furthermore, the appearance–reality task can be quite easily modified so that it *is* a false belief task. Here the distinction is between what we know about the object (its real nature), and what someone else will *think* when they first see the object. Children pass the false belief version of the appearance–reality task at about the age they pass the unexpected contents task: Gopnik and Astington (1988) found the standard and false belief versions of the appearance–reality task to be about as difficult; Rice,

Koinis, Sullivan, Tager-Flusberg and Winner (1997) found the false belief version to be easier.

Flavell et al. (1983) argue that the children's problem concerns dual representation; they find it difficult to simultaneously represent an object's appearance and its reality. It is not clear whether this would be a processing difficulty, caused by an inability to represent one object in two ways, or a conceptual difficulty, caused by an inability to distinguish between identity and appearance. Perner (1991) opted for a conceptual explanation. Our vision represents the world. Occasionally vision can misrepresent it: A sponge is misrepresented as a rock; a white piece of paper is misrepresented as blue. Since 3-year-old children do not understand misrepresentation, they have no way of reconciling the difference between how something is and how it looks. When asked questions about it, they answer on the basis of what they know to be the case. (Interestingly, once you know that the object is a sponge and not a rock, it does not look as much like a rock as it did before. In fact, it begins to look distinctly spongy.)

Perner's explanation may be correct, but it seems to conflict with the way adults typically think about appearances. In Perner's terms, 4-year-olds think of appearance as a property of their visual representations. Adults are probably inclined to think of appearance as a property of an object. It is more natural to say that the sponge-rock has a rock-like appearance, rather than our vision represents it as a rock. The fact that we think certain appearances are misleading may be because of their potential effects on beliefs. Our understanding of appearance–reality could therefore be mediated by our understanding of belief.

This is a conclusion reached by Hansen and Markman (2005), who argue that appearance–reality tasks underestimate children. Naturally, research on the appearance–reality distinction has received the same kinds of criticism as research on false belief. Hansen and Markman's argument is that the test questions are ambiguous. "Looks like" can refer to probable reality as well as to misleading appearance. This may be the default meaning for adults, unless the relevant part of reality is already known by those in the conversation. If I say "That looks like Josef over there", I probably mean that I think that the person over there really is Josef. If, however, I am with a group of people including Josef, and say "that looks like Josef over there", I am probably making a comment about similar appearance. Here, you can work out what "looks like" means on the basis of what I know: If I know Josef is here next to me, I must be making a comment on appearance. If I have no idea where Josef might be, I am probably talking about reality, that that really is Josef over there. Adults may usually interpret "looks like" as "probably is", unless there is reason to think otherwise.

The appearance–reality task therefore might be difficult for children because they do not know what knowledge is shared. "What does this look like?" is ambiguous until the child finds out whether the speaker knows the identity of the object (in which case the question is about appearance) or not (in which case the question is about probable reality). "Overall, 3-year-olds' performance on the traditional tasks may be hindered if the fact that the identity is commonly known is obscured by . . . competing pragmatic factors" (Hansen & Markman, 2005, p. 238). For this to be true, 3-year-olds must think the experimenter probably does not know the real identity of the object. This strikes me as slightly implausible, since the object belongs to the experimenter, was brought by him, he is probably currently holding it, and just a moment ago agreed with the child that it really was a sponge.

Nevertheless, the appearance–reality task *is* a bit odd. Hansen and Markman's account is one of a number of competing accounts about how children's poor understanding of conversational pragmatics would lead them to give wrong answers to appearance–reality questions. For example, others have suggested that the test questions in tasks like this are difficult because the questions violate normal rules of conversation, and so confuse children. Normally, an honest question implies the speaker does not know the answer, but thinks that the listener might. In developmental psychology experiments, however, the opposite is usually the case. If children find the question odd, they may become confused about what the experimenter wants them to say, and give the "wrong" answer as a result. Children are also often posed a number of similar questions about the same thing. Repeated questioning may cause children to assume that different answers are required (e.g., Donaldson, 1978; Siegal & Peterson, 1994). Alternatively, when faced with the same response options, children may persistently give the same response, possibly failing to notice the questions are different (e.g., Deák, Ray & Brenneman, 2003).

Accounts attributing children's difficulties to repeated questioning could explain why children give the same answer to both questions in the appearance–reality task. However, they cannot explain why children answer the appearance question wrong when it is asked first, which 3-year-olds typically do. Hansen and Markman's account can explain this, but only for one version of the appearance–reality task. In the sponge-rock task, for example, the real and apparent identities of the object differ. Children answer the appearance question on the basis of reality (it looks like a sponge), consistent with the claim that they misinterpret the question to be about reality. However, in other versions of the task, the real and apparent properties of an object differ. For example, a white card appears blue behind a filter. In these tasks children tend to answer the appearance question on the basis of appearance, correctly saying it appears blue (but incorrectly saying it is really blue). This is counter to Hansen and Markman's claim. They acknowledge this, simply stating that "Any conclusions about children's appearance–reality abilities in general must be tempered accordingly" (2005, p. 258). Their account is specifically limited. Thus, although there are several competing claims that children's poor understanding of conversational pragmatics would lead them to give wrong answers to appearance–reality questions, none of them seems fully consistent with the evidence.[1]

A further weakness of pragmatic accounts is that they offer no ready explanation for development. Why do children suddenly start to succeed on theory of mind or appearance–reality tasks? Siegal and Peterson (1994) cite evidence that mothers begin to talk more in terms of mental states at around the age children turn 3 years. This simply begs the question of why mothers do this (e.g., because their children are beginning to show signs of understanding mental states. This issue is considered in detail in Chapter 9). Siegal and Peterson also suggest that school and preschool fosters appropriate pragmatic knowledge. There is no doubt that school affects the way children think (it is supposed to, after all). However, children start school at highly variable ages (especially when comparing different countries). There is no evidence that attendance at preschools induces a sudden metacognitive development, or that, for example, keeping children longer at home delays their theory of mind. Hansen and Markman argue instead that pragmatic understanding develops as a result of theory of mind development. This would imply understanding of appearance–reality and false belief are related after all, but by a slightly more circuitous route.

Evidence

Theoretical arguments aside, there is evidence that the appearance–reality task can be made much easier. For example, Hansen and Markman (Experiment 2) compared different versions of the test question: "What does this look like?" and "What does this sponge look like?" The new question version makes it clear that the experimenter knows what the object is really. Three-year-olds' performance rose from 47% correct with the first question to 91% correct with the modified version. In two further experiments, they used tasks in which the appearance and reality were explicitly contrasted, either by mixing up the test objects with other deceptive objects of the same type (e.g., three types of deceptive candle) or by asking children questions like "Can you tell Ernie what this looks like and what this really is?" Success on the modified versions was around 80% or 90%, compared to 40% or 50% on the standard versions. Rice et al. (1997) found that couching the task in terms of deception made it easier. They also found that the task was easier if the deceptive object (e.g., a sponge-rock) was presented in the context of an object with the same appearance (e.g., a real rock) and an object with the same identity (e.g., a normal-looking sponge). The new task was passed by 74% of children compared to 47% passing the standard version.

What is not clear is whether these manipulations selectively improve the performance of younger children. As discussed in Chapter 2, Wellman et al. (2001) have shown that similar manipulations make the false belief task easier, but for all age groups. They do not alter the shape of development, and therefore do not support claims that younger children have conceptual competence that is masked by performance factors. In the appearance–reality experiments discussed, nearly half of the children typically passed the standard version. These samples therefore appear to be in the "zone of proximal development" of the appearance–reality distinction. As a result, appropriate manipulations may dramatically improve performance. It is not yet possible to say that younger children have the conceptual competence to understand the appearance–reality distinction.

Knowledge

Also around the age of 4 years, children start to understand how knowledge relates to experience. For something to be knowledge, it must be: a belief, true and justified by experience. Lucky guesses do not count. Successful false belief task performance suggests children understand something quite complex about this. The false belief is: a belief, not true and justified by experience. A more basic understanding of knowledge may be present in slightly younger children, who may understand that to have a belief at all requires some experience.

Wimmer et al. (1988) looked at children's ability to judge knowledge versus ignorance. They brought two children into a room and showed them a box. One of the children was shown what was inside the box (or was simply told—the results were the same). Children had to judge whether they or the other child knew what was inside. Three-year-olds were not good at this. When the other child had seen inside the box, children denied that the other knew what was inside. Nearly half the 3-year-olds also judged that they themselves knew what was inside the box when they had not seen inside. Four-year-olds and older children were good at this ignorance task.

Subsequent studies by Pratt and Bryant (1990) and Pillow (1989) found better performance in 3-year-olds. The ability to judge ignorance may arise earlier than understanding of belief (although it is worth noting that if children do not understand knowledge, they may guess in this task. In the false belief task, by contrast, they have a strong bias to give the wrong answer). Nevertheless, children's understanding of how experience leads to knowledge is clearly shaky at this age. Gopnik and Graf (1988) let children find out what was in a box in one of three ways: they saw it, they were told by the experimenter or they guessed it from a simple clue. They were then asked how they knew what was inside: did they see, were they told or did they get a clue? Three-year-olds were very poor at this; four-year-olds were much better. Younger children clearly can effectively use experience to update their beliefs, but do not encode the source of their knowledge. They simply do not remember how they found out.

It seems that 3-year-olds may understand that some kind of experience is necessary to have knowledge about something. Four-year-olds additionally can distinguish between finding out through direct experience and finding out through being told. However, even at 4 years, children are poor at distinguishing between different forms of direct experience. For example, Daniela O'Neill and colleagues presented children with a small tunnel that allowed two ways of finding out what was inside: Children could put their hands in to feel the contents, or they could open a window to see the contents (O'Neill, Astington & Flavell, 1992). Children were then shown pairs of objects that differed on one dimension: For example, two piggie banks that looked the same, one of which was full of pennies and therefore heavier than the other empty one; or two toy footballs that felt the same but were different colours. One object was hidden in the tunnel, and children had to work out how to find out which one it was. For the footballs, they had to look inside, whereas for the piggie banks the only way was to feel. Three- and four-year-olds were at chance at this "aspectuality" task, whereas five-year-olds were quite good.

O'Neill and Chong (2001) extended the aspectuality task to all five senses. They instructed children how to find out something about an object. For example, the experimenter sniffed a bottle of bubble bath and told the child to do likewise. Once the child had found out it was strawberry scented, the experimenter asked him or her how he or she knew. Liberal criteria were applied: If the child just repeated the action, for example sniffing again when asked the question, this was counted as a correct answer. Even with these criteria, less than half of 3-year-olds could demonstrate how they knew the scent, and they were equally poor with their other four senses. A different method involved a Mr Potato Head with a full range of attachable sensory organs. Children had to indicate which he would need to use to find something out: a nose for a smell, ears for a sound, and so on. When they played the Mr Potato Head game just after the procedure described above, children did quite well, with even 3-year-olds choosing the correct sense organ 59% of the time. In a subsequent experiment intended to simplify the procedure, however, even 4-year-olds did not pass more than 50% of trials. Children's understanding of the limitations on information conveyed by the different senses seems genuinely poor. Given the age of success, it seems to be harder than the false belief task, by a margin of about a year.

O'Neill and Chong (2001) speculate that children may have the equivalent of severe "source amnesia" suffered by people with frontal lobe brain damage. Source amnesia is the inability to recall how one learned something, and O'Neill and Chong suggest that young children's problem is due to the inability to process the source of information at the time of learning. This may need to be refined slightly; Gopnik and Graf (1988) found that 4-year-olds could distinguish between perceptual access and other ways of finding things out. It may be that in O'Neill and Chong's study, children simply think that any direct perceptual access to an object is sufficient to know all aspects of the object; that is, it is not that they fail to identify or recall the source, but that they do not realize that it matters. This is suggested by children's performance on another theory of mind related task, the "droodle" task.

In the droodle task (Chandler & Helm, 1984), children see a small unidentifiable portion of a picture (see Figure 4.1). They are then shown the full picture. All

(a)

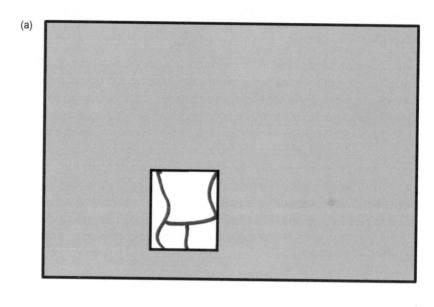

(b)

FIGURE 4.1 The droodle task used by Doherty and Wimmer (2005). Children are first shown an unidentifiable part (a) and then the full picture (b).

but the unidentifiable portion of the picture is covered again, and children are asked whether someone looking at it would know that the picture was of, say, an elephant. Despite their own recent personal experience of not knowing, children up until the age of about 5 years confidently predict that another person will know what the picture is of (Taylor, 1988).[2] This is reminiscent of O'Neill et al.'s

(1992) aspectuality task, in the sense that children overestimate what can be known through direct perceptual access to an object. A similar finding comes from Ruffman, Olson and Astington (1991). Children were shown two toy animals, an elephant and a rabbit, made from the same grey furry material. One of the animals was put behind a screen with a hole in, such that only a small patch of fur was visible. Would someone who only saw the small patch of fur know that the animal was the elephant? Children up until the age of 4 or 5 years tended to judge that they would.

One further example of older children's continuing difficulty with the sources of knowledge concerns knowledge gained through inference. For example, if a ball is taken from a box containing only green balls and put into a bag, even someone who could not see the colour of the transferred ball can infer that the ball in the bag is green. Four- to six-year-old children are quite capable of making this inference themselves. However, they tend to deny that another person who has had the same perceptual experience as them knows what colour the ball in the bag is (Sodian & Wimmer, 1987). Furthermore, if there are also boxes with red or blue balls, children will say that the other person will think the ball in the bag is red or blue (Ruffman, 1996). Ruffman suggests that children overgeneralize two rules: A seeing-leads-to-knowing rule is applied to the situation, and children judge the person does not know because they did not see; a not-knowing-leads-to-wrong-answers rule is used to infer that the person must have a false belief. Ruffman's experiment is discussed in more detail in Chapter 3.

Summary of knowledge understanding

There seems to be a steady progression in children's understanding of knowledge formation around the age that they pass the false belief task. Even 3-year-olds have at least some appreciation that perceptual access or verbal information is needed to know what an object is. This may indicate that children are beginning to consider mental states. At around the age children begin to pass the false belief task, they are able to distinguish between learning something through perception and simply being told about it. It is not until about 1 year later, however, that they can distinguish between perceptual access per se, and different forms or degrees of access: They do not appreciate that the five senses deliver five very different types of information, and they do not understand that seeing just a small portion of something may not be sufficient to know what it is. It is probably not until slightly later still that children realize that things can be learned without direct perceptual access and without being informed about them. Inference is *knowledge* gained through *thought*, and is therefore what is referred to as a second-order mental state. Predicting it involves the coordination of two mental state concepts, and it is not surprising it is somewhat harder to grasp than single mental state concepts. There are several types of higher order task, which I now turn to.

Higher order theory of mind tasks

Theory of mind development does not stop at the ages of 5 or 6 years. We probably continue to gain insights into the minds of others throughout life, or at least until old age diminishes our perceptiveness. Some adults clearly understand what goes on in people's minds better than others. A mark of a good novelist or actor is the ability to communicate insights about the minds of others. However, much of the conceptual basics may be in place around the time children start to go to school. What develops subsequently is probably the ability to apply mental state concepts in a more flexible way and in more complex situations.

An early investigation into more complex belief reasoning was carried out by Perner and Wimmer (1985). They were interested in second-order false belief understanding: what children can understand about one character's false belief about another character's belief. This might involve a novel conceptual insight, that beliefs can take as their object other beliefs. Another possibility is that it simply requires the abilities to keep track of more than one belief and of their rather complex relations to each other and to the world. The story told to children gives some idea of the complexity:

> John and Mary are in the park and decide to buy an ice cream from the ice cream van. Mary hasn't got any money, however. The ice cream man tells her that he will be there all afternoon, so she can buy an ice cream later once she has fetched some money from home. She goes off home. The ice cream man then tells John that because there are no people in the park, he is going to drive to the church and off he goes. As he drives past Mary's house, she sees him and he tells her he is going to the church. Later Mary gets some money and goes off to buy an ice cream. John turns up at Mary's house and Mary's mom tells him she has gone to buy an ice cream. Where does John think Mary has gone?

The answer is the park, of course. John is unaware that Mary has seen the ice cream van move, and therefore should falsely believe that she thinks it is still in the park. Children do not tend to pass this task until the age of about 7 years, and some children continue to give the wrong answer until the age of about 10 years. If we asked about where Mary's mom thinks John thinks Mary is, even older children would experience problems. It seems most plausible, however, that what is developing is the ability to keep track of all the relevant information, and this may indicate more about children's executive function ability than their theory of mind conceptual competence. If this were the case, the precise age at which children pass second-order tasks could vary considerably according to the complexity of the task. This seems to be the case: Sullivan, Zaitchik and Tager-Flusberg (1994), for example, constructed new simplified second-order stories in which false beliefs arose through deception rather than in the more incidental fashion in the original story. Even the youngest group, mean age 4 years 8 months, passed the novel tasks 65% of the time—although they also passed the original second-order task 43% of the time, so they were probably an unusually able sample.

Perner and Howes (1992) devised an even more direct method of probing second-order beliefs. They had a standard false belief task in which John's chocolate is moved to a new location. Mary observes the transfer. Children are asked about John's belief, Mary's belief about John's false belief, and John's belief about John's false belief. This latter question went like this: "What if we ask John: 'John, do you know where the chocolates are?' What will he say?" The correct answer is yes, since John falsely believes he does know where the chocolates are. Note, this is a second-order false belief, concerning John's belief about his own false belief. All the 4- to 6-year-olds in this experiment answered the first-order false belief question correctly. However, only about half of the younger group (children up to 5 years 8 months) correctly predicted John's belief about his own belief: Instead they said that John would say "no", he did not know where the chocolates were. This question did not differ from a question about Mary's judgement of John's false belief: "If we ask Mary: 'Mary, does John know where the chocolates are?', what will she say?" The method is quite ingenious, since it is clear that children have followed the story because they correctly predict John's false belief, and yet they fail to realize that John *thinks* that he knows.

Allowing for differences in method and samples, children seem able to pass second-order false belief tasks from the age of 5 or 6 years. This is about 2 years later than the first-order false belief task, and about 1 year later than the droodle and aspectuality tasks. Even more complex tests of theory of mind have been used, often to probe the mental state understanding of people with autism or acquired brain damage. Francesca Happé (1994) developed a set of short stories to probe complex understanding of thoughts and feelings. For example, in the "Double Bluff" story participants were told about a captured soldier who is questioned about the location of his army: in the mountains or by the sea. They are really in the mountains. The other side know he will certainly lie to them. He tells them his army is in the mountains. Participants are asked to explain why he said that. Happé's normal participants, with a mean age of 8½ years, had little difficulty explaining the soldier's double bluff. They had more difficulty in stories involving sarcasm, such as one in which a girl's mother is cross at her failure to thank her for dinner, and says "Well that's very nice isn't it! That's what I call politeness!" A third of children had difficulties explaining this kind of story. Children with autism, even those who could pass second-order false belief tasks, had difficulty with both kinds of story.

Belief-based emotions

Second-order and higher order theory of mind tasks typically require children to reason about one person's beliefs about another's beliefs. In the case of the sarcasm story above, for example, the girl's mother intends the girl to understand the opposite of what is said, so plausibly children must reason about the mother's intention concerning the girl's belief. A sophisticated understanding of emotions is similar. Children initially judge others' emotions according to the state of the world: If you have what you want, you ought to be happy; if your desires are thwarted, you will probably be unhappy. Children understand the contingency between satisfied or unsatisfied desire and happiness or unhappiness from late infancy (Wellman, 1990). However, sophisticated understanding of emotions requires children to realize that they are *belief* based. Regardless of whether your desires are satisfied or unsatisfied in objective reality, you will be happy if you *think* they are satisfied. Understanding of emotions is therefore second order. Unlike the second-order belief tasks above, which concern one person's mental states about the mental states of another, reasoning about emotion requires children to understand how two mental states within the same person interact.

Harris, Johnson, Hutton, Andrews and Cooke (1989) looked at when children could do this. They told children stories in which, for example, Ellie the elephant only likes Coke, and hates milk. Mickey the monkey has sneakily emptied a Coke can and filled it with milk. Children were asked whether Ellie will be happy or sad when she first sees the can. This is similar to the Smarties task, so most of the 4- to 6-year-old participants presumably were aware of Ellie's initial false belief that the can contains her favourite drink. Nevertheless, the 4-year-olds judged that she would be sad when she first sees it. Children were judging emotion on the basis of what they themselves knew to be true, failing to realize that the emotions of someone else are based on what they believe to be true.

The quintessentially belief-based emotion is surprise. Surprise results from a mismatch between what you believe and the state of the world. To properly understand surprise, therefore, one must understand belief, and be able to base an emotion judgement on it. Children use the word "surprise" from 2 years onwards, but typically use it to refer to something pleasant such as a wish fulfilled, a party or a present. They do not appear to understand the defining unexpected element (Hadwin & Perner, 1991). Hadwin and Perner presented children stories in which, for example, a character discovered unexpected contents (jelly babies) in a Smarties box. Almost all of the 4- to 6-year-old participants correctly predicted Tommy's false belief before he opened the box. However, when asked to judge Tommy's emotion, by pointing to a surprised or a neutral face, 4-year-olds were at chance. About half the 5-year-olds and nearly all 6-year-olds correctly indicated the surprised face. Hadwin and Perner also used Harris et al.'s (1989) procedure, and found equivalent results in judging belief-based happiness.

Ruffman and Keenan (1996) confirmed that understanding of surprise develops around the age of 5 or 6 years. This did not depend on whether children had to use the word "surprise", or children could judge surprise by pointing to a surprised face. Children seem to be delayed on judging belief-based emotion relative to judging belief. An obvious possible explanation is that having to consider the relationship between two mental states is simply harder than having to consider only one, and therefore develops later. Ruffman and Keenan examined this with a control task that matched the information-processing demands of the surprise task. However, this did not cause problems. Instead, the lag seems to result from children having to revise their theory of emotions, from one based on objective reality to one based on beliefs about reality. Curiously, they also found that 5- and 6-year-old children tended to erroneously judge that surprise resulted from ignorance as well as belief: For example, if a character knew that a dish contained green or white pieces of paper, but did not know which, children tended to judge that he would be surprised when he found out. Children's understanding of surprise therefore continues to mature after they realize that emotions are based on beliefs.

The apparently gradual development of understanding of belief-based emotions is supported by a study by Rieffe, Meerum Terwogt and Cowan (2005). They looked at children's explanations of stories in which the character should feel happy, angry or sad, or afraid. Four-year-olds gave explanations in terms of the objective situation most of the time, and rarely mentioned beliefs or desires. Six-year-olds gave belief-based explanations for happiness, but rarely for sadness or anger. Ten-year-olds gave belief-based explanations for all of the stories. Curiously, even 4-year-olds gave at least some belief-based explanations of fear. This may be because, unlike the happy and angry/sad stories, the fear stories focused on an unknown quantity: an unidentified dark figure or a strange bump in the night. The unknown objective reality therefore could not be mentioned. Even so, 4-year-olds referred to beliefs considerably less often than older children.

Summary

Clearly there is much more to a theory of mind than understanding false belief. One thing that makes this area of research interesting is that there seems to be a general change in the way children understand their world at around age 4 years. Arguably the false belief task marks a watershed in children's social cognition. Two- and three-year-olds have a basic grasp of other people's behaviour: They know that people act to satisfy their desires, and that people will be happy when good or desirable things happen, and sad when the opposite happens. However, their understanding is limited. Children younger than 4 years do not understand the subjective nature of mental states. Research on the false belief task makes this clear

71

for beliefs. Desire has been less extensively researched, and the findings discussed above can be interpreted in several ways. However, there are good reasons to think that young children are limited to an objective concept of desire, where behaviour is seen as motivated by desirable and undesirable situations, rather than an internal mental state. There is also reason to think this also changes around 4 years, although conclusive research has yet to be done.

At the same time, children begin to distinguish appearance (a subjective aspect of an object) from reality (an objective one). They also begin to understand knowledge and ignorance. However, at this age children still have difficulties determining how much can be known from limited perceptual access; it is another year or so before they realize that only seeing a small part of a picture is not enough to know what it is of, or that some aspects of objects can only be known through specific senses. This understanding of knowledge and belief causes children to re-evaluate their judgements of emotion. By the age of 5 or 6 years children realize emotions are based on people's beliefs rather than objective reality. All of this can be seen as part of our basic theory of mind, and it is much more than just false belief.

Chapter 5

Associated developments 2: Understanding nonmental representation

Introduction

VIRTUALLY ALL THEORISTS AGREE that theory of mind involves the understanding of mental representation: By the time children pass the false belief task they understand the representational relationship between a belief and the state of the world it represents. Where theories differ is in whether this understanding develops at 4 years. Modularity Theory holds that children's capacity to understand representational mental states is innate, and operates from infancy. What develops at 4 years is the ability to express this understanding in the false belief task; it may be expressed in other contexts earlier or later, depending on complexity. Executive function accounts of theory of mind development make similar claims. According to Simulation Theory (Harris's developmental version), what develops at 4 years is the ability to imagine having a different attitude to a nonreal situation: belief rather than disbelief. Children understand mental representation much earlier, perhaps through direct introspection. Neither theory makes any natural claim about understanding of *nonmental* representations, such as pictures or language.

Theory Theory is different. The shift in children's social understanding at 4 years is taken to be because children begin to understand mental representation. The false belief task requires an understanding of *misrepresentation*, which is a critical test of proper understanding because it creates a mismatch between a belief and the state of the world that it represents. However, a concept of representation need not be limited to mental representation: In principle the same insights can be applied to nonmental representation. In Perner's version of Theory Theory, this is an explicit claim: What develops is an understanding of representation as such. It predicts that equivalent representational puzzles will be solved for belief, for language and for pictorial representation at the same time. This would mean that theory of mind marks a much more general development. In our culture, photographs, paintings and drawings are ubiquitous, as are writing and speech. Children may start to properly understand these at around 4 years too.

The widespread nature of linguistic and pictorial representation causes problems for assessing this claim, however. Children see pictures and hear language all the time. It would be weird if they did not have some working understanding of them. The photo of Grandma on the mantelpiece never moves, but the real Grandma does. Children do not have to be very observant to notice this. Similarly, their parents may point at the photo and say "look, that's Grandma", so children have good reasons to think that the person in the photo and the person who visits at holidays are the same, even if one is rather flat and motionless. Children can understand these things simply by observing what happens; they do not need to understand the representational nature of pictures. It may therefore be difficult to determine exactly when children do have such an understanding. This chapter reviews attempts to do this. The issue is a test of Theory Theory against its rivals. If comparable developments occur in theory of mind and understanding of nonmental representation, Modularity Theories and Simulation Theory have no ready way to explain this. If they do not, Theory Theory (Perner's version at least) is plain wrong.

Children's understanding of pictorial representation

So it seemed like good news for Theory Theory when Debbie Zaitchik (1990) found that a "false" photograph task was about as hard as the false belief task. Zaitchik's study was ingenious. Children were introduced to a Polaroid camera, which takes a photograph instantaneously. The photograph emerges from the camera and takes a minute or two to develop. Once children were familiar with the workings of the camera, they were shown a scenario designed to correspond closely to the typical false belief task. For example, Bert (from Sesame Street) is lying on a mat in the sun. Ernie takes a photograph of him lying on the mat. Then they both go inside. While the photograph is gradually developing, Big Bird comes along and lies down on the mat. At this point, children were asked, "In the picture, who is lying on the mat?"

Only about a quarter of 3-year-olds correctly answered that Bert was on the mat in the picture; most answered that Big Bird was on the mat. By 4 years old, most children passed the task. Children also had a typical false belief task, in which, as usual, someone acquires a belief about the situation that becomes false (comparable to a camera taking a photograph of the situation that becomes "false"). Children found this task slightly easier than the photograph task, but again most 3-year-olds failed and most 4-year-olds passed. Zaitchik concluded that children may have difficulty with mental representations "not because they are *mental* but because they are *representations*" (Zaitchik, 1990, p. 61).

However, in order to be really certain that the Polaroid task and the false belief task tap the same underlying competence, one would have to show that performance on the two tasks was associated. It might simply be that the two tasks just happen to be of similar difficulty. Oddly, Zaitchik did not report the association between the two tasks. Several studies have done so since. Perner, Leekam, Myers, Davis and Odgers (1998) replicated the basic task. They found, like Zaitchik, that the Polaroid task was, if anything, slightly harder than the false belief task. However, the correlation between the tasks was very small ($r_\varphi = .15$), and nonsignificant. They also noticed that children tended to give the photograph only a cursory glance, and were typically looking at either the experimenter or the real scene when they answered the test question. In subsequent pilot work, when children's attention was focused on the back of the developing picture, they did very well. In a second experiment, this was systematically examined. The experimenter pointed to the back of the picture, making sure that the child was looking at it when answering the question. The results were dramatic: 53% of children were successful on the standard version, compared to 94% of children in the new attention-directed condition. In a final experiment, they examined whether this attention-directing procedure would improve performance on the false belief task, by making children look at the doll who held a false belief. This had little effect, improving success from 28% in the standard condition to 33% in the attention-directed condition. The technique worked once again for the Polaroid task, improving performance from 35% to 67%.

Lewis and Freeman (1992) used a technique that had the same effect. Instead of one photograph, there were two. The first was taken of the original scene; a second photograph was taken after the scene had been altered. Children performed much better on the two-photograph version (71% correct) than on the standard one-photograph version (41% correct). The contrast between the two photographs, with the experimenter asking, "in *this* picture", made it clear what the question referred to. A similar method for the false belief task, having a second doll observing the altered location of the object, made no difference.

Neither study is published, so it is reassuring that Virginia Slaughter (1998) replicated Perner et al.'s (1998) findings using the attention-directed version of the Polaroid task. Slaughter also used a "false" drawing task, in which the experimenter draws the scene, turns the drawing over and alters the scene. Both drawing and photograph tasks were significantly easier than false belief and appearance–reality tasks, and the belief and picture tasks were not correlated.

Perner et al. and Slaughter conclude that children perform poorly on the Polaroid task because of "referential confusion" over whether the test question refers to reality or to the situation in the photograph. There are two things that match the question: two mats for example, one in the real world and one in the picture. Children are unsure which one the experimenter is referring to. The real mat on the table in front of them is more salient, so they tend to tell the experimenter about that one. Any procedure that clarifies what the test question refers to improves performance.

The representational function of pictures

So, straightforward clarification of the test question leads to even quite young children passing the Polaroid task; comparable clarification does not affect performance on the false belief task. This might be taken to show that children's difficulties with mental representation tasks are due to the *mental* part after all, and not the *representation* part. However, although the "false" photograph task is superficially comparable to the false belief task, photographs and beliefs are quite different in their representational function. To put it baldly, "false" photographs are not false.

Zaitchik, recognizing this, put the *false* within inverted commas. The "false" photograph certainly does not correspond to the current situation, but it is not supposed to. Photographs are supposed to correspond to the situation that held when the photograph was taken. Beliefs, on the other hand, are typically supposed to correspond to the situation that holds *now*.

Photographs are usually accurate representations of past situations. Therefore, children do not need to make a clear distinction between what a photo represents (the past situation) and how it represents it (as it was). In that sense they are like beliefs about the true state of a past situation (i.e., accurate memories). By contrast, false beliefs require a distinction between the situation and how it is represented (because the protagonist's behaviour towards the situation will not be driven by the situation, but by how the protagonist represents it). For this reason, Theory Theory makes no specific predictions about the "false" photograph procedure. Simulation Theory and Modularity Theory can also comfortably ignore the "false" photograph task. They make no prediction about a relationship between the false belief and photograph tasks, and there does not seem to be one.

Children's understanding of pictures

On reflection, Zaitchik's findings should always have been very surprising, given even young children's extensive experience with pictures. Even a child with no understanding of representation is likely to notice that pictures do not change. Children begin to grasp the nature of pictures from a very early age. Judy DeLoache and colleagues (DeLoache, Pierroutsakos, Uttal, Rosengren & Gottlieb, 1998) showed 9-month-old children realistic pictures of small plastic toys. Most of the children attempted to grasp the objects, and some of them were highly persistent in their attempts. They seemed to think that they might be able to pick up the depicted objects. However, in a second experiment, the pictures were paired with their real counterparts (glued to the page). Children were twice as likely to touch the real object, suggesting that they could at least make some minimal distinction between objects and pictures of objects. The tendency to try to touch objects in pictures rapidly fell off with age in this study: 15- and 19-month-old infants were increasingly less likely to do so, and correspondingly more likely to simply point at the depicted object.

Nevertheless, infants in their second year can still sometimes be seen trying to interact with depicted objects. For example, Perner (1991) reports seeing his 16-month-old son trying to put on a shoe in a picture, and expressing surprise when he could not. Observations of this sort of behaviour are not uncommon. However, from late infancy children seem to have learned that objects "in" pictures are different to other objects: flat, two-dimensional,[1] and not available to manipulation. Plausibly, children gradually learn which characteristics pictures share with real objects and which they do not. For example, Beilin and Pearlman (1991) found that preschool children sometimes attribute nonvisual properties to pictures, predicting that a picture of an ice cream would be cold, or a picture of a flower would smell nice. This sort of confusion reduces between 3 and 5 years (and may simply be a form of referential confusion, similar to that discussed above. After all, these are very strange questions to ask).

An important issue is when children understand that the object in a picture is the *same* object as an object in the real world. Children will frequently see photographs of people or objects that they also come across in the real world. For example, when seeing a photograph of their father on the beach last summer on holiday, their father may also be sitting in the armchair right now. What is a child to make of this? One possible solution is to assume there are numerous fathers, most of them small, motionless and flat. A more satisfactory solution involves understanding that the same person can occur in more than one situation. So the child's father occurs here and now, and also in numerous pictures. This requires two mental models: the child's model of the real here and now, and a model containing their father on the beach last summer. The second model is marked as "in the picture". This means that for young children, interpreting a picture may be cognitively similar to recalling a memory. When remembering daddy on the beach last summer, the child also needs a second model, marked appropriately: in this case as "last summer". As discussed in Chapter 3, this requires children to be able to represent multiple models, which probably begins around the age of 18 months.

The ability to recognize that the person (or object) in a picture is the same entity as a person in the real world is an important precursor to understanding the relationship between a picture and its referent. It is nevertheless just a precursor: Without a proper understanding of representation, children are limited to the rather odd idea that people and other objects occur in multiple contexts. A proper understanding of representation makes it clear that this is not because the person occurs more than once, but because they can be represented multiple times, and in many different ways. However, this precursor to understanding representation can in principle be a very powerful tool, particularly if combined with an understanding of *correspondence*, as a set of experiments by DeLoache and colleagues has shown.

DeLoache and Burns (1994) examined 2-year-old children's ability to use pictures to find hidden objects. This means children have to draw inferences from the object's location in the picture to the real situation, which plausibly requires them to understand that the same object occurs in each situation. The experiment involved a room, furnished as a typical living room with a couch, a coffee table, and so on. While children were outside the room, an object was hidden (e.g., behind the couch). Children were shown an accurate photograph of the room, and the hiding place was pointed out: "This is where Snoopy is hiding in his room: Can you find him?" Thirty-month-old children successfully went into the room directly to the hiding place 72% of the time. Only one of eight 24-month-olds ever managed to do this. This shows that by the time they are 2½ years, children readily understand that an object in a picture can correspond to a real object.

In a series of additional experiments, DeLoache and Burns (1994) made numerous attempts to get 24-month-olds to pass their task: They produced photographs in which the hidden object could be seen (because of the angle from which the photograph was taken); they used an extensive orientation phase; they took Polaroid photographs. None of these improved 24-month-olds' performance much. These younger children may very well have accepted the experimenter's assurance that an object was hidden behind the couch *in the picture*. They simply did not see how this was relevant to the hiding place in the real room. There are several possible reasons why. Children might be unaware that the couch in the picture and the couch in the real room are the same thing. Alternatively, awareness of this may not be sufficient: If children conceive of the couches as the *same* thing in *different* situations, they may not understand how information about the couch in one situation (the one in the picture) is relevant to the couch in the other situation (the real one). After all, the photo of daddy on the beach last summer is considerably different to daddy right now, and inferences about what he is now wearing or what his mood is cannot be validly drawn from pictures of him. Lastly, it is also possible that children understand that the two objects are meaningfully related, but have performance difficulties drawing the appropriate inferences.

By the time they were 2½ years old, children did well at the picture-correspondence task. With scale models, however, the ability develops somewhat later. DeLoache (1987) gave children a similar hiding game, but used a miniature model of the room instead of a photograph. Children were told that Baby Snoopy and Daddy Snoopy (small and large toy dogs) like to do the same thing, so that wherever Daddy Snoopy is in the large room, Baby Snoopy is in the corresponding location in the small room. The children saw one dog hidden behind a piece of furniture in the real or model room, and had to find the other dog behind the corresponding piece of furniture in the other room. Two-and-a-half-year-olds were unable to do this; young 3-year-olds were very good at it.

DeLoache initially interpreted her results in terms of representational understanding: Older children understand that the model represents the room. There are several reasons why this seems unlikely. The instructions explicitly state that the two rooms belong to different individuals, Baby Snoopy and Daddy Snoopy, and therefore the task virtually requires you to see Baby Snoopy's room as a separate room, rather than as a representation of Daddy Snoopy's room. The dogs' locations correspond for the nonrepresentational reason that the dogs like it that way (according to the experimenter, although in fact the correspondence occurs because the experimenter likes it that way, for reasons that a 3-year-old is unlikely to understand). Thus, in the model task children are given good reasons to think that the model room does *not* represent the real room. In the photograph task, on the other hand, the photo is referred to as if it is the real scene.[2]

The difference in wording between the model and photo tasks is therefore probably why the model task takes longer for children to solve. Dow and Pick (1992) showed that when the wording from the model task is used in the photograph task, it too becomes difficult. The large room was described as belonging to Big Teddy, and the room in the photograph belonging to Little Teddy. Under these conditions, 2- and 3-year-olds' performance was as bad as on the model task. When the room in the photograph was described as *being* the large room, however, 2½-year-olds' performance went from chance to 68% correct retrieval. In other words, the difference between the two tasks may not be in the stimuli used, but in the way the task is presented to children.

Another reason to suspect that the model task does not measure understanding of representation is that performance is symmetrical: Children are as likely to succeed if the toy is hidden in the model and found in the room as when the reverse is the case. Representation, on the other hand, is asymmetrical: The model represents the room, but it would be strange to describe the room as representing the model.[3] Instead, the task seems to measure a subcomponent of representational understanding: Representations must correspond in some systematic way to their referents. Newcombe and Huttenlocher (2000) refer to this understanding as element-to-element correspondence. Elements in the model correspond to elements in the real world: The toy couch corresponds to the real couch, the toy wardrobe to the real wardrobe, and so on. This relationship is perfectly symmetrical.

Children understand element-to-element correspondence at least by the age of 3 years. Blades and Cooke (1994) looked at when children understood a slightly more complicated form of correspondence—*geometric* correspondence. This is when the arrangement of objects in one space corresponds to the arrangement in another space. The most familiar form of this is a map, where shapes on a piece of paper are positioned in ways that correspond to the positions of objects in the world. In DeLoache's model task, the furniture was laid out in the same way in the model and in the room. However, each piece of furniture was unique—there was just one sofa, one wardrobe, and so on. Thus using element-to-element correspondence was sufficient to pass the task.

Blades and Cooke adapted the model room task to include identical and unique items of furniture: two identical chairs, as well as one wardrobe, and one bed. All children performed well when the object was hidden under the bed or in the wardrobe, since they could use element-to-element correspondence. When the object was hidden under one of the identical chairs, however, the task was harder. Not only did children need to understand that the object was hidden under a chair in the other room, they had to use the arrangement of the chairs in one room to work out which chair the object was hidden under in the other room. Three-year-olds were at chance finding the object in this condition. Four-year-olds performed reasonably well, and 5-year-olds perfectly. The younger children were not able to use the position of the furniture items as a cue to finding the object. Understanding the geometric correspondence of two spaces is the beginning of the ability to read maps [see Newcombe and Huttenlocher (2000) for more on map reading].

This finding is interesting—children can use the geometric correspondence between two spaces around the same age as they pass the false belief task. It is possible that as children become able to grasp that one space is supposed to represent the other, they become better able to exploit the correspondence between the two spaces, and thus able to solve these more complex correspondence tasks. However, understanding of geometric correspondence is not conclusive evidence that children understand pictorial representation. Understanding that two spaces correspond does not require you to understand that one represents another. Perner (1991) draws an interesting analogy with British houses. Houses built in the same area in the same period often have identical layouts. If you are in a neighbour's house, you will have no trouble finding the bathroom, because it will be in the "same" place as in your house. This does not mean that your house represents their house. The houses just happen to correspond in systematic ways, and if you know this you can use the information. The tasks discussed can be solved by understanding correspondence, and do not require an understanding of representation (although an understanding of representation would help). This straightforward fact means that we do not know when children have a representational understanding of pictures.

Or at least we did not until recently. Recent research on ambiguous figures, which are pictures with rather special properties, may constitute a test of children's representational understanding of pictures. This is discussed at the end of the chapter.

Linguistic representation

The other main form of nonmental representation is language. This section concerns when children understand the representational nature of language. I will argue that it is at the same time that they understand the representational nature of mind.

The ability to reflect on the representational nature of language roughly corresponds to what is known as metalinguistic awareness. There is an extensive literature on this, although the topic is somewhat out of fashion of late, and the age at which metalinguistic awareness begins is controversial. There are roughly two views. One view is that children have a reflective understanding of language from the time they start to speak, before the age of 2 years. This is known as the Inter-action hypothesis (Clark, 1978; Clark & Anderson, 1979; Marshall & Morton, 1978). According to this hypothesis, a reflective understanding of language inter-acts with learning, and may be necessary for language to be learned at all. The opposing view is that children can use and understand language without the ability to reflect on what they are doing: Metalinguistic awareness develops as a separate metacognitive skill between 5 and 7 years (e.g., Gombert, 1990/1992; Hakes, 1980; Tunmer & Herriman, 1984; Van Kleeck, 1982). According to this Autonomy hypothesis, early behaviour that has been interpreted as metalinguistic before the age of 6 or 7 years is merely "epilinguistic", not based on systematically represented knowledge that can be intentionally applied (Gombert, 1990/1992, p. 9).

The controversy is difficult to resolve because there are numerous conflicting definitions in the literature (so it is quite possible that the two hypotheses are referring to different phenomena). These definitions classify metalinguistic aware-ness as requiring some or all of the following criteria:

(1) The ability to reflect on language as an object.
(2) The ability to control, monitor and plan linguistic processing.
(3) Consciousness/awareness/intentionality.

All definitions include the first criterion, but vary as to the other two, and the emphasis put on them. The second criterion, control of processing, roughly corres-ponds to what is now known as executive functioning, applied to language. Consciousness is obviously problematic as a definitional criterion, since we do not properly understand it and cannot know whether someone else is or is not conscious, let alone what they might be conscious of.

If consciousness is discarded as a criterion, the definition of metalinguistic awareness closely parallels theory of mind: Theory of mind involves the ability to reflect on mental states; metalinguistic awareness involves the ability to reflect on language. Both require executive functioning, at least to demonstrate the reflective ability, and possibly to develop it at all (see Chapter 8 for the lively debate about this in the theory of mind literature). The fundamental difference between theory of mind and metalinguistic awareness may be only in the domain of application: language or mind. If so, they may share most of the same conceptual developments.

One of the most critical cognitive developments in theory of mind is the understanding that mental states represent things as being a certain way. Maxi's belief about his chocolate, for example, represents the chocolate as being where he left it. In the false belief task, things are represented as being different to known reality. Thus children must distinguish between what is represented and how it is represented, which requires *metarepresentation*. According to Theory Theory, children are able to pass the false belief task when they begin to understand this aspect of representation. Language also represents states of affairs in a certain way, so metarepresentation must be a critical component of metalinguistic awareness.

Thus Josef Perner and I predicted from theoretical grounds that metalinguistic awareness should arise at roughly 4 years, in contrast to both the Interaction and Autonomy hypotheses (Doherty & Perner, 1998). Demonstrating this would be a critical test of Perner's (1991) theory, since other theories of mind do not predict any association between development of theory of mind and of metalinguistic awareness. Simulation Theory and Modularity Theory are cast in terms of mental states, and they do not naturally extend to metalinguistic awareness. Executive function theorists could argue that the expression of both theory of mind and metalinguistic awareness are constrained by common executive difficulties. However, the domains are very different, so it seems unlikely that tasks in the two domains would make comparable executive demands.

The obvious strategy to test this claim is to adapt the false belief task to a false statement task. However, statements are naturally seen as expressing the content of the speaker's beliefs—or what the speaker wants the hearer to believe. Common developments in the understanding of false statements and false beliefs could therefore result simply because both require understanding of false beliefs [this is a problem with de Villiers and de Villiers' (2000) memory for false complements task, discussed in detail in Chapter 9]. Instead we decided to look at children's understanding of a simple formal aspect of language: synonymy. Synonyms are words that mean the same thing.

Understanding synonymy requires children to understand a straightforward relationship between linguistic form and what the form represents: Two different forms can represent the same thing. Again, children must distinguish between what is represented and how it is represented, which requires *metarepresentation*. Understanding synonymy and understanding false belief therefore require children to make a very similar distinction.

It is important to distinguish between understanding the fact that there can be two words for the same thing and knowing two words for the same thing. It was an open question whether children would know more than one word for the same referent. It is easy to see how children might unwittingly learn synonyms. They are not uncommon, but they are rarely used in the same conversation. Speakers quickly converge on using the same word for a particular referent, a phenomenon known as lexical entrainment (Brennan & Clark, 1996). Thus the chances of hearing two words for the same referent within a conversation are limited, but not between contexts. For example, children may hear the couch at playgroup called "sofa", whereas the couch at home is called "settee" (or "couch", for that matter). They might therefore learn each word without realizing that they have learned two words for the same thing.

On the other hand, children may actively avoid learning synonyms. It has been suggested that children have a bias against learning more than one word for the same referent. Most of the time, people use the same word for a given type of object: A dog will be called a dog most of the time, rather than an animal or a Springer spaniel. Assuming that objects only have one name would therefore be approximately correct, and would reduce the number of meanings children need to consider when trying to work out what a new word refers to: nothing they can already name (the Mutual Exclusivity bias: Golinkoff, Hirsh-Pasek, Bailey & Wenger, 1992; Markman, 1989; Merriman & Bowman, 1989). Although this hypothetical bias might make it easier to learn words in general, it would make it harder to learn overlapping words, including synonyms and words in a hierarchy, like spaniel–dog–animal.

The existence of the Mutual Exclusivity bias is controversial. Furthermore, according to the theory, children relax the bias word by word when there is good evidence that a particular word really does overlap with another—repeatedly hearing the sofa called a settee, for example, would eventually prompt children to accept the name. We therefore did some pilot work to see if 3-year-olds had synonym pairs in their vocabulary. The following pairs were fairly reliably known:

(1) Truck/Lorry.
(2) Lady/Woman.
(3) Cup/Mug.
(4) TV/Television.
(5) Coat/Jacket.
(6) Jumper/Sweater.
(7) Bunny/Rabbit.

We were therefore able to test children's understanding of synonymy. The general idea was for a task that required children to monitor difference of form and sameness of meaning. In one task, children were given one synonym (e.g., "truck") and asked to think of another way of saying "truck". Clearly, children might do poorly at this because of word-finding difficulties or an inability to inhibit the word used by the experimenter. Therefore, in another task, children watched someone else trying to produce synonyms and had to judge whether he had succeeded. The other person was played by Puppet, who sometimes used a synonym (correct), but frequently repeated the word the child used (incorrect) or misnamed the object (incorrect).

Performance on these synonym tasks was compared with false belief performance over four experiments. In each case the synonym and false belief tasks were of equivalent difficulty, and strongly associated even after statistically controlling for verbal mental age (so that the association was not simply because older or more intelligent children did better on both tasks). Overall, the correlation between the two types of task was $r = .70$, and of 118 children involved, only 18 did not either pass both or fail both types of task (Doherty & Perner, 1998).

This is good evidence for the hypothesis: On the surface, understanding synonymy and understanding false belief are quite different abilities. The specific tasks certainly have little in common. The Production task may share some inhibitory demands with the false belief task, but in the Judgement task children simply have to compare the word they said with the one Puppet has just said. In fact, the Judgement task was no easier than the Production task, and if anything was more strongly associated with false belief performance. We concluded that the association was because the metarepresentational demands of the false belief and synonym tasks are very similar.

One possible concern is that the synonyms were not true synonyms. Strictly speaking, there are probably no true synonyms. Any two words differ either in what they refer to, or in how they refer to it, having different connotations or nuances, or one of a number of other possible differences (Clark, 1988). When children become sensitive to this is another question. Nevertheless, our hypothesis could also be tested by using homonyms. Homonyms are words with the same pronunciation or spelling, but that refer to different things. A good example is *bat*: a flying animal or a piece of sports equipment. Clearly, a word is either a true homonym, or not a homonym at all.

The homonym tasks were analogous to the synonym tasks (Doherty, 2000). For example, in the Homonym Judgement task (Experiment 1), children were shown a sheet with four pictures, two of which were homonymous (e.g., letter—an envelope, and letter—the letter A). Puppet's[4] job was to point to "the other letter, not the same one as [the child] pointed to". As in the Synonym Judgement task, Puppet could point to the other letter (correct), the same letter as the child (incorrect), or to one of the distracter pictures (incorrect). Children's ability to correctly judge Puppet's performance over three trials was compared to their performance on a false belief task and the Synonym Judgement task. All three tasks were strongly associated ($r = .55$ or above, $p < .001$), even after statistically controlling for age and verbal mental age ($r = .35$ or above, $p < .01$). Children's performance on a similar Homonym "Production" task, in which they had to do the pointing rather than Puppet, was also strongly associated with false belief performance ($r = .66$ after statistically controlling for age and mental age, $p < .001$).

More recently, Perner, Stummer, Sprung and Doherty (2002b) extended the basic finding to hierarchically related word pairs such as rabbit and animal. This may require the original explanation to be modified slightly, since rabbit and animal clearly differ in meaning. However, the general hypothesis remains the same: Understanding that words can overlap in meaning requires metarepresentation. The findings are the same too: There is a close developmental link between understanding similar aspects of mental and linguistic representation.

Ambiguous figures

Psychologists have always been fascinated by ambiguous figures, such as Jastrow's duck–rabbit or the Necker cube (see Figure 5.1). These figures have two equally

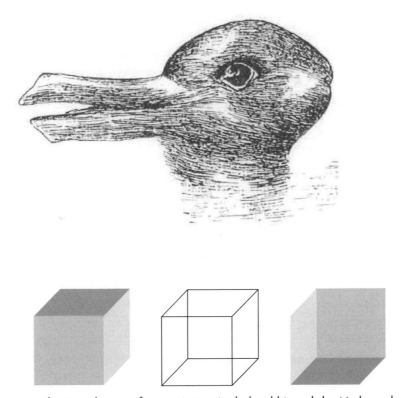

FIGURE 5.1 Classic ambiguous figures: Jastrow's duck–rabbit and the Necker cube with disambiguated cubes on either side.

plausible interpretations. When viewing the duck–rabbit, you first see a duck. Then suddenly it becomes a rabbit, without physically changing. The longer you view it, the more frequently it changes backwards and forwards. Despite more than a century of research on the subject, what exactly is happening when we see an ambiguous figure reverse in this way is not fully understood (see Long & Toppino, 2004, for a review).

The first study of ambiguous figure reversal in young children was carried out surprisingly recently, by Rock, Gopnik and Hall (1994). Irvin Rock had argued that in order to reverse, a viewer had to be aware of the ambiguity, and what the two interpretations were. This had received some support in his previous research: When uninformed, adults tend to reverse infrequently. However, a minority of adults still reversed under these conditions. It is difficult to conclude much from this, because ambiguous figures are common in our society—often found in magazines, on posters, websites, and so on. Participants in experiments therefore may not all be naïve to the ambiguous nature of the stimuli. Moreover, the participants in psychology experiments are usually undergraduate psychologists who are more likely than most to have experience of ambiguous figures. The instruction to stare at a picture and tell the experimenter if anything changes is also a bit of a giveaway. To get a truly naïve group of participants, Rock et al. turned to preschool children. They sat 3- and 4-year-olds down in front of a duck–rabbit (or the vase–faces, or man–mouse figures) and over a minute asked them periodically what they saw.[5] They found that none of the children ever reversed; good support for Rock's hypothesis.

After this they explained the figures to children, showing them disambiguated versions of, for example, the duck and the rabbit. Then they sat the children down again for another whole minute to stare at the figure. This time they found that the older children tended to experience reversals, but not the younger children. Sadly, Rock died in 1995, but Gopnik and Rosati (2001) carried on the developmental work. They found a distinct age effect, with reversal common in 5-year-olds but rare in younger children. They compared performances on the reversal task and the false belief task, but found them unrelated, and children passed the false belief task a year before they were able to experience reversal.

This was something of a surprise. Ambiguous figures are visually analogous to homonyms. A homonym, like *bat*, can be an animal or a piece of cricket equipment, depending on context; the duck–rabbit can be a duck or a rabbit, depending on context. (Homonyms tend not to be presented without context, of course, but if they are we interpret them as one or other of their meanings, probably without noticing the alternative possibility.) The analogy is close, and implies that if children are capable of metarepresentation, they should be able to understand that a figure can have two interpretations (i.e., can represent both a duck and a rabbit). This therefore has implications for the claim that a general understanding of metarepresentation arises at 4 years: On the face of it, this does not seem to extend to pictures.

Marina Wimmer and I decided to investigate this further (Doherty & Wimmer, 2005). If Rock's hypothesis is correct, reversal requires metarepresentation: To be aware of the ambiguity requires children to be able to understand that the figure can have two interpretations or, in other words, can represent two different types of object. However, reversal plausibly also involves extra abilities that children may not have at 4 years—particularly certain executive function abilities. Our aim was to isolate the ability to understand that a figure can have two interpretations. To do this we used a procedure similar to the Synonym task. First we disambiguated a set of ambiguous figures by adding surrounding context, as shown in Figure 5.2. This reliably caused even the youngest children to perceive the alternative interpretation of each figure, so children had the opportunity to learn that figures can have more than one interpretation. We then showed them each figure without context, and said (for example), "This is a rabbit. What else can it be?" After some intervening items, we showed the same picture and said, "This is a duck. What else can it be?" We found that children could not report the two alternatives until they were about 4 years old. However, once they could pass the false belief task, they could report both alternatives, and the two abilities were strongly correlated ($r = .47, p < .001$). Children understood the ambiguity a year before they could experience reversal. We had partially solved the problem. In her PhD thesis, Marina Wimmer (2007) has shown that the reason why reversal takes a further year is that it also requires executive inhibition (see Chapter 8), and visual imagery ability. She has also compared the ambiguous figures production task discussed with the synonyms and homonyms task: All three are strongly intercorrelated.

The general conclusion from this is that children understand that a picture can have two interpretations at around the age of 4 years. This development is associated with comparable developments in theory of mind and in metalinguistic awareness. It suggests that children start to understand the representational relationship between a picture and what it represents at this age.

Summary and conclusions

A possible specific prediction of the Theory Theory of theory of mind is that children will come to understand mental and nonmental representation at the same time: What develops is an understanding of representation per se. If so, this would give children insights into beliefs, and also into the nature of pictures and words. Competing theories of theory of mind make no specific predictions. According to Simulation Theory, the major development is in children's ability to imagine the mental states of others. Nothing clearly follows about pictures or words. Modular theories of theory of mind postulate an innate mechanism specialized to deal with mental states—not specialized to deal with nonmental representation. Again, there are no clear predictions.

FIGURE 5.2 (a) The duck–rabbit; (b) disambiguating duck context; (c) disambiguating rabbit context.

Adapted from Doherty and Wimmer "Children's Understanding of Ambiguous Figures: Which Cognitive Developments are Necessary to Experience Reversal?" *Cognitive Development*, 20, 407–421, Copyright Elsevier (2005), reproduced with permission.

The issue therefore offers a way of testing the three theories: If mental and non-mental representation are understood at the same time, this would support Theory Theory, but could not be readily explained by Simulation or Modularity Theory; if they are not understood at the same time, this would be difficult for Theory Theory to explain, but would not be problematic for Simulation Theory or Modularity Theory.

These predictions were first tested out in innovative research by Zaitchik (1990), who found that a "false" photograph task was of comparable difficulty to the false belief task. However, the scare quotes around the "false" in the photo-graph task were well placed. The photograph is not false, but does what it is supposed to do: faithfully represent the scene as it was when the photograph was taken. This means that an understanding of misrepresentation is not required to pass the "false" photograph task, and subsequent research has demonstrated that substantially younger children can pass this task if the test question is clarified (e.g., Slaughter, 1998).

The other main line of research into pictorial representation has involved using pictures (and models) as sources of information about their referents. DeLoache and colleagues (e.g., DeLoache, 1987; DeLoache & Burns, 1994) have found that children can use pictures to find objects from the age of 2½ years onwards. This seems to be based on the understanding that the same objects can occur in pictures and in reality, and that individual elements in each can correspond. One difficulty with this research is that the correspondence is arbitrary, because, once again, pictures are not usually supposed to represent current reality. On the other hand, maps *are* supposed to represent current reality. Thus it is interesting that children do not develop an understanding of *geometric* correspondence until the age of 4 years. At this age, they understand that the spatial layout of a photograph or model can correspond with the real space. This may be because they begin to under-stand the purpose of maps and diagrams is to represent real-world spaces.

Be that as it may, there was no research into children's understanding of pictorial representation that shows when they start to understand the represen-tational relationship between a picture and its referent. Marina Wimmer and I (Doherty & Wimmer, 2005) carried out what we think is a direct test of this, using ambiguous figures. We found that children become able to report the two interpretations of an ambiguous figure at around 4 years. Younger children, despite having just experienced both interpretations, were unable to recall or report them. This suggests that 4-year-old children become able to represent the relationship between the figure and its two interpretations, which is metarepresentation by definition. Performance on this task was strongly associated with performance on the false belief task. This is therefore good support for Theory Theory: Children's understanding of this aspect of pictorial representation is related to their under-standing of mental misrepresentation, despite superficially very different task formats.

This experiment was inspired by research on children's understanding of syn-onymy and homonymy. As with ambiguous figures, to understand that one word can have two meanings or two words can mean the same thing requires a distinc-tion between the words and their referents, and an understanding that the two are related. Again, this is metarepresentation by definition. Along with Josef Perner, I found (Doherty & Perner, 1998) that children's ability to produce synonyms or to judge a puppet's attempts to do this were strongly related to their understanding of false belief. Experiments with homonyms produced similar findings. Again, this is good specific support for Theory Theory. Simulation Theory or Modularity Theory have no ready explanation for these findings; as far as I know, none has been suggested. The practical implications for children's metalinguistic awareness, or their ability to use and produce pictorial representations, remain an interesting area for future research.

Chapter 6

Precursors 1: Pretence

Introduction

PRETEND PLAY IS GENERALLY viewed as a precursor to theory of mind. Most theories of theory of mind claim that pretence is an early manifestation of some of the skills and concepts that later form part of a theory of mind, possibly in immature form. Some theorists go further, claiming that pretence is an early manifestation of true theory of mind ability. Which of these two views is correct forms the major debate in the area. Most evidence favours the former view. This chapter gives a description of pretend play development, explains the theoretical debate and reviews data designed to distinguish between the two main positions. Finally studies of the developmental relationship between theory of mind, pretence and social understanding are reviewed. The conclusion will be that pretence is a precursor to theory of mind, but is not understood in metarepresentational terms until children begin to understand belief. Experience with pretend play may enhance social understanding and facilitate theory of mind development, and greater understanding of mind almost certainly allows more complex forms of pretence.

Description of pretend play

Play is usually classified as either pretend play or functional play. The main difference is that only pretend play involves situations, objects or properties of objects that are not real. Piling bricks up would be classed as functional play if the intention was to see how high they could be stacked; it would be classed as pretend play if the intention was to build a tower for Rapunzel.

Children begin to pretend around the age of 18 months (very approximately). Pretend play declines after 6 years. This is probably because of social disapproval of pretence in older children, and the availability of other activities such as sports and hobbies. Some people however continue to pretend into adulthood, often in the form of role-playing games. Most adults also indulge in related forms of fantasy activity, such as watching TV dramas and films, reading novels, and playing certain computer games.

Pretend play appears in all cultures. It is almost exclusively human. There is anecdotal evidence of human-raised chimpanzees using pretend objects (Whiten & Byrne, 1991), although this may be limited to symbol-using chimps (Savage-Rumbaugh & McDonald, 1988). When human pretend play begins, it is usually heavily scaffolded by adults, who encourage children to take part in a pretend scenario and suggest to them what they can do. It is also initially heavily dependent on props. As children get older they can invent more of the pretend scenario themselves, and need fewer props. For example, a 2-year-old pretending to be a cowboy might require a toy gun. An older child might be able to manage with a vaguely gun-like object. Older still, children stick their index finger out and thumb up. Finally, by the age of 8 years or so, children can adopt a hand position similar to gripping an imaginary six-gun, moving their trigger finger when they say "bang". Pretence also becomes increasingly social.

There are three main types of nonreal things in pretend play:

(1)   Object substitution: One object is made to stand for another. A classic example of this is a child pretending a banana is a telephone [first used by Leslie (1987), and now mandatory in descriptions of pretence].

(2)   Attribution of pretend properties: A nonreal property is attributed to an object or situation. For example, pretending Teddy's face is dirty, or that today is my birthday.

(3)   Invention of nonpresent objects. For example, pretending to use a nonexistent spoon to eat some nonexistent macaroni cheese.

Is early pretence genuine?

It is hard to be sure whether younger children's play is genuinely pretend, because the nonreal component necessary for it to be pretend is unobservable. Functional play can easily be overinterpreted as pretence. For example, when a kitten plays with a piece of string, is it pretending that the string is a mouse? It is impossible to tell, of course, but the kitten is probably simply reacting to the stimulus properties of the string. Children may be subject to the same overinterpretation. A child pushing a car along may be overlaying a rich fantasy context over the real situation, or she or he may simply enjoy the movement. Even if she or he also makes "brmm, brmm" noises, she or he may simply be imitating what she or he has seen others do. A tea party with toy cups and nonexistent tea may be a pretend situation to adults, but a learned script of arbitrary actions for children.

This is clearly too sceptical when it comes to older children. However, when pretence appears to emerge, it is initially fragile. For example, in one study, when a 2½-year-old knocked over a cup of pretend tea, his mother said "Oh-oh, you spilled your tea. You better wipe it up". The child picked up the sponge, looked puzzled and appeared to be looking for real tea. At least a quarter of the 15- to 30-month-olds showed the same difficulty in maintaining appropriate behaviour within a pretence scenario (DeLoache & Plaetzer, cited in Harris & Kavanaugh, 1993). This difficulty is probably with keeping the pretend state of affairs in mind, even with the mother's help, but it could also be argued it is due to poor script knowledge. In this case, wiping up spilled tea might not be part of the child's script yet.

Harris and Kavanaugh (1993, Experiment 5) addressed this issue by subverting the normal script. For example, during a tea party with a couple of pigs as guests, naughty teddy turns up uninvited. Instead of following the script and pouring tea into a cup, teddy pours tea over one of the pigs. Children are asked to help clear up. Most young 2-year-olds were able to respond by wiping up the appropriate area. Older 1-year-olds, however, did not perform better than chance. Kavanaugh and Harris (1994, Experiment 1) probed this age difference further by simplifying the task. Instead of having to help clear up, children simply had to select which of two pictures showed the outcome of a pretend transformation, such as pretend talcum powder being poured over a cat. One picture was of the cat with talcum powder on, and the other of the cat without talcum powder (i.e., as it was really). Despite simplification of the response, older 1-year-olds still did not perform better than chance. Young 2-year-olds still performed well. (Children with autism also performed well on this task. It is well known that children with autism do not indulge in pretend play, but it has become clear that nevertheless they are capable of it.)

Thus it seems that from the age of 2 years, but not before, children can follow pretend transformations. Harris and Kavanaugh (1993) also included an experiment in which children were asked what had happened. Two-year-olds were surprisingly articulate when asked this, even in response to open-ended questions of the form "what did Teddy do?" They could name the nonexistent substance that had been introduced by the marauding teddy bear, and could also state, for example, that monkey's head was now all "toothpastey". So, not only could children follow make-believe transformations, but they could describe them in a sophisticated way. Importantly, the transformations were performed by someone else. Children were therefore inferring the content of another's pretence. This brings us to another important issue.

What do children understand about pretence?

Joint versus solitary pretence

One of the influential theories of theory of mind development has been Leslie's (1987) ToMM theory, discussed in more detail below (and in Chapter 3). Leslie asserts that the ability to pretend is a manifestation of a general ability to infer the mental states of others. Critical to this theory is the claim that solitary and joint pretence arise at the same time. Clearly the ability to infer what another is pretending is useful for joint pretence. Harris and Kavanaugh's data suggest that the capacity for joint pretence is at least present shortly after the emergence of solitary pretence.

Howes and Matheson (1992) studied the emergence of pretend play longitudinally. In *cooperative social pretend play*, children take part cooperatively in the same pretend scenario. For example, one child will set the table, sit the other child down and "feed" her. The other child makes baby noises and asks for more (Howes, Ungerer & Seidner, 1989, p. 78). This form of pretence emerged from about 2 years 6 months, and most children had taken part in this form of play by the time they turned 3 years. In *complex social pretend play* children also "metacommunicate" about the scenario. Metacommunication is communication about pretence rather than within pretence: Children step out of their play roles briefly to discuss the pretence, assign roles, negotiate the script, and so on. This form of pretence emerged after children turned 3 years, and was not present in half the sample until they were 4 years old. It should be borne in mind that these findings are for relatively advantaged children: Their playgroups were rated "good" on the Early Childhood Environmental Rating Scale (Harms & Clifford, 1980). In a second study, Howes and Matheson (1992) compared children in higher- and lower-than-average childcare. Findings from higher-than-average childcare were roughly comparable with the first experiment, with both pretend forms emerging at the same time or slightly earlier. The lower-than-average childcare findings showed much lower levels of pretence, with cooperative pretend play never seen in more than half the sample, and complex pretend play only seen in 17% of the sample between 4½ and 5 years.

Nevertheless, children's ability to pretend effectively with others begins to emerge between 2 and 3 years of age. At this stage they can also talk about the *content* of the pretence (e.g., that monkey's head now has toothpaste on it). Their ability to reflectively discuss the pretence emerges about a year later. Importantly, older children did not simply talk about the content of pretence, but were talking about the fact that they were pretending, and could negotiate the content (e.g., "let's pretend we don't have any biscuits" or "I'll pretend to be the mommy", and so on). Although children can articulate the *content* of pretend scenarios at 2 years, children do not talk about the *form* of scenarios until about 4 years. This suggests that by the age of 4 years, children have some reflective understanding of what pretence is, but that this understanding may not be present earlier.

Characterizing children's understanding of pretence

One of the most contentious issues in this area concerns whether children conceive of pretence in the same way as adults. The simplest possibility is that children begin with no concept of pretence, and then at some stage acquire the adult concept (either through conceptual development, or through the switching on of an innate module). Alternatively, between these two stages children may first develop a concept of pretence that is quite different from that of adults. This might be hard to detect. Children with such a concept might pass some tests of pretend understanding, perhaps even most, and fail others. Careful consideration is clearly necessary.

Leslie's theory of pretence

Alan Leslie is the principal proponent of the simpler view. His 1987 paper began recent interest in the cognitive underpinnings of pretence. He made the critical point that in order to pretend, children must have some way of *quarantining* their pretend propositions from their representation of reality. Unless you keep absolutely clear what is real and what is pretend, you will become utterly confused. Leslie's proposal was that the brain has a device which copies the child's representation of reality, and passes the copy on to another device, the Manipulator, which can alter it more or less at will. Empty cups can be filled with pretend tea, bananas altered to telephones, and so forth. The Manipulator also adds an "I pretend that" tag to the pretend proposition. It then passes the whole thing back to the rest of the brain.

Tagging "I pretend that" to a proposition produces a mental state expression. This closely resembles the sort of expression adults use when thinking about others' beliefs. "Mother pretends that this cup is full" is very similar to "Mother believes that this cup is full". Only the attitudes *belief* and *pretend* differ [i.e., the agent evaluates the proposition as true in the case of belief, and as not (necessarily) true in the case of pretend]. Thus Leslie asserts that pretence is an early sign of mature theory of mind reasoning.

Embedding the proposition in a mental state expression "quarantines" the proposition: When a proposition is embedded in a mental state expression, the expression can be true or false regardless of the truth of the proposition. For example, the proposition "France is in Asia" is false. But what about the proposition "George thinks that France is in Asia"? This might be true or false, depending on George. The same is true of pretence, perhaps more so since pretend propositions are typically not true, whereas belief propositions frequently are. So, tagging the pretend proposition with "I pretend that" should stop it interfering with the child's other beliefs, i.e., quarantines it.

However, embedding a proposition in a mental state term is an unnecessarily elaborate way of quarantining it. At minimum, the pretend proposition simply has to be marked as false.[1] If children can maintain a clear distinction between true and false propositions, then pretend propositions will not confuse them. The theoretical importance of this fact is that the ability to pretend, or even to understand pretence in others does not require children to conceive of pretence as a mental state.

The philosopher Fodor (1992) disagrees: "Pretending involves acting as though one believes that P is true when, in fact, one believes that P is false. It would thus seem to be impossible for a creature that lacks the concept of a belief *being* false" (p. 290). However, Fodor may be overstating the case. Consider the following revision of the claim: "Pretending involves acting as though P is true when, in fact, P is false. It would thus seem to be impossible for a creature that lacks the concept of a proposition *being* false." This revision seems to me to capture adequately what is required in pretence, without having to posit an understanding of mental states.

The critical point is that you can think of yourself as "acting as though P is true" without thinking of yourself as "acting as though I believe that P is true". This is obvious in normal nonpretend action, when P *is* true. The only difference in pretence is that P is false, and you know that P is false. This means that the ability to pretend does not indicate an understanding of mental states. Children might in principle understand pretence in mental state terms from the time they begin to pretend, but it does not have to be that way.

Pretence as action

Several theorists propose accounts where children see pretence as a special kind of action (e.g., Harris, Lillard & Perner, 1994). The basic idea is simple. Normally people's actions can be understood either by reference to their beliefs or by reference to the state of the world. Because beliefs are usually true, it is possible to ignore them most of the time, and just consider states of the world. This is computationally and conceptually simpler. If you want to know where Sally will look for her marble, you can usually predict successfully that she will look where it is.

A similar account can be made for pretence. Rather than predicting action according to the real world, action must be predicted according to a nontrue situation. For example, in a pretend tea party, actions must be interpreted according to a situation where the empty teapot contains tea, the toy bricks are really cakes, and so on. Then, if a person wants a cup of tea, children can confidently predict they will hold the teapot over a cup, do likewise with the milk jug, and so on.

Children must be able to infer when others are trying to act according to pretend situations, and when according to the real situation. Also they must also be able to infer what the pretend situation is. As discussed above they must also be able to quarantine the pretend situation from their representation of reality. The two situations, pretence and reality, must also be coordinated in a fairly precise fashion: Children must remember what each prop is supposed to be, where nonexistent objects are supposed to be, and so forth. These complexities are shared with Leslie's theory of pretence, of course. The key difference is that children do not need to see the pretend proposition as mentally represented by the pretenders. In general, however, predicting and evaluating action according to either real or pretend propositions would serve the child well as a theory of behaviour.

Evidence for pretence as action

There have been two main tests of the idea that pretence is understood as action according to a false proposition. Both are based on the idea that someone who is ignorant of a proposition cannot be pretending according to it. The first of these tests was carried out by Lillard (1993). She showed children a toy troll, and told the following story:

> This is Moe. He's from the land of the Trolls. Moe's hopping around, kind of like a rabbit hops. Moe doesn't know that rabbits hop like that; he doesn't know anything about rabbits. But he is hopping like a rabbit. Does he know that rabbits hop like that? Is he hopping like a rabbit? Would you say he is pretending to be a rabbit, or he's not pretending to be a rabbit?

Adults and older children view pretence as a representational mental state. So, in order to pretend something you must be able to mentally represent it, and in order to mentally represent something (such as a rabbit), you must know what it is. In other words, Moe cannot pretend to be something that he is ignorant of. However, in Lillard's experiment, most 4- and 5-year-old children claimed that Moe *was* pretending to be a rabbit. This supports the idea that younger children see pretence as a particular kind of action. One can act like a rabbit regardless of whether one knows what rabbits are. So according to this definition of pretence, Moe must be pretending.

Interestingly, most children in this experiment also *passed* a standard false belief task. This suggests that children understand the role of the mind in normal action before they understand it in pretend action. This is perhaps not surprising. Seeing pretence as action works quite well as a practical theory. This is why Lillard had to come up with a rather bizarre situation to tease apart metarepresentational and action understandings of pretence (how often have you had to decide whether someone is pretending something based on their knowledge of the pretend proposition?). However, children may need to understand the role of the mind in nonpretend actions reasonably frequently, in cases of deception and false belief. Therefore, children may apply their understanding of the mind to real action first, since predicting according to the real situation is often inadequate. Gradually, their new conceptual understanding of belief spreads to their understanding of pretence, even though the action theory works well enough.

Prelief

Perner, Baker and Hutton (1994a) have similar findings to Lillard, but a slightly different theoretical explanation. Like Lillard, they argue that children see pretence as false action, but they argue that children's concept of false and true actions develops into a concept of true and false beliefs. They claim that 3-year-olds do not yet differentiate belief and pretence in the same way adults do. Instead, children have a single undifferentiated concept of belief and pretence that Perner calls "prelief" (or "betence"). The difference between prelief and the adult concepts of belief and pretence is that children do not understand that a proposition can be evaluated independently by different people. Thus they cannot distinguish between a person acting according to a false proposition that they evaluate to be false (pretence) or that they judge to be actually true (false belief). This distinction is unnecessary in most situations. Prelief works well for pretence, in which all participants generally know that the proposition is false. It also works well for belief. Beliefs are typically true—or, at least, are supposed to be. When a belief proposition is true, most participants in the relevant situation will deem it true. Children therefore differentiate between two types of prelief: actions according to true propositions (belief), and actions according to false propositions (pretence).

However "prelief" is inadequate as in cases of false belief. Here the proposition is evaluated differently by different people. In the case of Sally and her marble, Sally evaluates the proposition "the marble is where I left it" as true; the child and experimenter evaluate it as false. A child reasoning with prelief will judge that if Sally really wants to get her marble, she will behave according to the true situation. This is the "puzzle of false belief" (Perner, 1988, p. 157): Why should someone who genuinely wants to find an object look in the wrong place? The answer is because the protagonist evaluates the false proposition as true, and will therefore behave according to it.

This evaluation part is why Perner (1995) argues that children must understand mental representation to understand false belief. Evaluating a proposition involves comparing it to the state of the world it is about. This obviously involves understanding that the proposition is *about* something, which is a defining feature of representation (Perner, 1995, p. 248).

Perner et al.'s (1994a) empirical demonstration of prelief involved telling children stories like the following. Jane's rabbit is initially in its hutch. Then her father takes it to the vets. Shortly after, Jane pokes a carrot into the hutch and asks the rabbit if it's hungry. In one version of the story, Jane has seen the rabbit taken off to the vet, and is therefore presumably pretending to feed the rabbit. In the other version, Jane has not seen this, and therefore presumably believes that the rabbit is inside. Children are asked whether Jane was pretending that the rabbit was inside, or whether she really thought that it was inside. Children were given one story like this in the pretend version, and one in the think version.[2] They also received a couple of standard false belief tasks.

They found that appropriately distinguishing between "think" and "pretend" versions of the story was at least as hard as the false belief tasks. Younger children tended to judge that in both cases Jane was pretending. Older 4-year-olds tended to correctly judge that Jane was pretending when she had seen her rabbit taken away, and that she really thought that it was there when she had not seen.

The prelief theory would predict that children are more likely to refer to wrong action as "pretend" than "believe", as was found. Most cases of action according to false propositions will be pretence, in children's experience, and most cases of action according to true proposition will be belief. Children's use of words like "think" and "pretend" would therefore tend to match adults', except in certain exceptional cases (such as behaviour based on ignorance or false belief). This could create problems in diagnosing children's understanding of belief, since in many cases a concept of belief and a concept of prelief will produce the same answer. Note that prelief is not restricted to understanding action. Even someone not acting can be seen as having preliefs (in the same way that they have beliefs).

Divergent pretence

Harris et al. (1994) cite an unpublished study by Freeman, Lewis, Smith and Kelly (1993) examining children's ability to understand that different people can pretend different things of the same real-world situation. Freeman et al. found that this was no easier than standard false belief. Because the study is not published, however, it is difficult to judge. Hickling, Wellman and Gottfried (1997) carried out a study with the same aims. Children and a puppet jointly pretended that an empty glass contained chocolate milk. In the puppet's absence the pretend milk was emptied out. The question was what the puppet currently thinks is in the glass: nothing, or chocolate milk. Hickling et al. found that this pretend task was easier than a false belief task. Most 3-year-olds correctly answered that the puppet thought there was chocolate milk in the empty glass, but failed the false belief task.

This finding has to be interpreted with a degree of caution. As mentioned, Freeman et al. found that the pretend and false belief tasks were of equivalent difficulty. Hickling et al. (1997), in a second experiment, again found the pretend task easier, but this time the difference was very small: Only 6 out of 28 children passed the pretend task and failed the belief task. Furthermore, Berguno and Bowler (2004) failed to replicate Hickling et al.'s findings in one experiment. In a second experiment, they did find that the pretend task was easier, but they found no association between the pretend and belief tasks ($r_\beta = .17$). [See Lillard (2001) for further criticism of Hickling et al.'s study.]

The most likely interpretation of these somewhat conflicting results is that the pretend task *is* easier, but that the effect is small. Three-year-olds, but probably not younger children, may understand that people can hold conflicting pretences. In pretend episodes, it is probably common that different participants have slightly different ideas about what the pretend scenario is. Conflicts can be resolved through metacommunication, which Howes and Matheson (1992) found appears after children turn 3 years, as discussed above. The interesting theoretical question is whether this causes problems for Harris, Lillard or Perner, and whether this supports the claim that early pretence is metarepresentational.

Divergent pretence is clearly a special case. Children may still typically view pretence in terms of action, as Lillard's results suggest. The fact that they may be able to relate different pretenders to different propositions suggests that they are not restricted to conceiving of pretence in terms of action. However, as Hickling et al. (1997) point out, Perner's (Perner et al., 1994a) concept of *prelief* could account for this ability. Prelief fails to distinguish between false propositions evaluated as true and false propositions evaluated as false, but this distinction is not needed in divergent pretence tasks, which simply involve two distinct false propositions. Since everyone involved evaluates both as false, prelief is adequate for the job. Berguno and Bowler's finding of no association between pretence and belief tasks adds weight to the idea that understanding of divergent pretence is not evidence for early understanding of false belief.

Pretence and social understanding

Is pretend play ability related to theory of mind and broader social understanding? There are two possible general relationships. First, extensive experience with pretend play might enhance theory of mind development. All of the theories considered above are compatible with this possibility. For Leslie (1987), pretend play might help children overcome whatever difficulties they have employing their understanding of other mental states. For Harris, children's expertise at altering the default settings of their current representation of reality would enhance performance on the more difficult task of altering the default settings of their *attitude* towards reality. This is especially so for pretence involving adopting another's role. For Perner, expertise at calling up and manipulating mental models might speed up development of metarepresentation. Generally, whether pretence is a precursor to theory of mind, or an aspect of the same ability, anything facilitating the development of pretend ability would be expected to enhance theory of mind ability. Regardless of the theoretical implications, this is also an interesting practical question: Does pretend play enhance social understanding? If so, perhaps pretend play should be encouraged more than it is at present.

The second possibility is that theory of mind development enhances pretence. Howes and Matheson's findings, above, show that complex social pretend play develops around the same age children begin to pass false belief tasks. Metacommunication about play may depend on theory of mind skills arising at about 4 years. Subsequently joint pretence might go much more smoothly, and could be much more complex. These two possibilities are not mutually exclusive. There is good reason to think both may be correct.

In an early study, Burns and Brainerd (1979) looked at the effect of pretend play or construction play (i.e., a kind of functional play) on "perspective taking" (broadly similar to theory of mind ability). Groups of older 4-year-olds had 10 experimenter-led sessions of either pretend play, or construction play. As a result, both groups improved on a range of tests of social understanding relative to a control group who had not interacted with the experimenter. There was a slight advantage of the pretend group over the construction group. Thus play, or at least the adult-guided activity, involved enhanced performance on tests of social understanding. However, because both types of play manipulations were effective, it is difficult to draw more detailed conclusions about the specific effect of pretend play.

Connolly and Doyle (1984) looked at the relationship between pretence and more practical social competence. They rated 3- to 5-year-old children on spontaneous pretence, including the number of identities children assigned to objects, and their flexibility in role play. (Only pretence with others, and not solitary pretence, was considered.) This was compared to their social competence as measured by teacher ratings, popularity with other children, and observations of social behaviour. Children who were "better" at pretence were also the most socially competent. This relationship held even when age and general intelligence were statistically controlled for. There are two obvious explanations for this relationship: Social competence may enhance social pretence, for example by increasing the opportunities to pretend play with friends. Socially competent children could also negotiate more complex scenarios with each other. Conversely, pretend ability may increase social competence. This may be because pretend ability facilitates theory of mind development, or simply because it allows increased social experience with

101

peers. Whether pretence enhances social ability, vice versa, or whether both have beneficial effects on each other is difficult to tell.

This problem is shared with more recent studies in which pretend play has been compared with more specific theory of mind abilities. Astington and Jenkins (1995) compared 3- to 5-year-old children's performance on a battery of false belief tasks with behaviour during a 10-minute play session. They found no relationship between false belief performance and overall amount of pretend play. Pretend play was further analysed for "joint proposals", in which children referred to themselves and another child within the same utterance (e.g., "you have to stay in my arms"), and role assignment, in which children explicitly assigned a pretend role to themselves or others (e.g., "You be mummy"). Both the amount of joint proposals and role assignment correlated strongly with false belief performance (and with each other), even after controlling for age and language ability (false belief and joint proposals, $r = .49$, $p < .01$; false belief and role assignment, $r = .37$, $p < .05$).

Role assignment clearly counts as metacommunication about play. Joint proposals are probably mostly metacommunicative too (i.e., one child proposes something about the pretence to another—although some of the proposals could have been within the play context, with one play character proposing something to another). This suggests theory of mind development may underlie Howes and Matheson's (1992) findings that metacommunication about play develops around the age of 4 years. The issue of causality remains difficult to determine: Does increasingly complex play help development of mental state understanding, or does mental state understanding allow increasingly complex play?

Taylor and Carlson (1997) looked at the relationship between theory of mind ability and the tendency of children to have imaginary friends. The incidence of imaginary playmates was quite high: On strict criteria, 28% of the 3- and 4-year-olds had an imaginary companion, typically an invisible character or a stuffed animal or toy. Examples of these companions included a 91-year-old man called Derek, who, despite being only 2 feet tall, could hit bears, and Joshua, a possum who lived in San Francisco (the study was carried out in Oregon). Other children, especially boys, would impersonate characters instead of treating them as companions. Including impersonation in a combined measure encompassed 25% of 3-year-olds and 47% of 4-year-olds. This combined measure was significantly related to false belief performance for the 4-year-old group, but not the 3-year-old group. Taylor and Carlson also found that false belief understanding was related to the ability to perform self-directed pretend actions (like brushing your teeth), but not with object-directed actions (such as pretending to cut a block in half). Also, interestingly, 4-year-olds who watched less television were more imaginative, and for the whole sample, watching less TV was significantly associated with higher theory of mind scores. Thus there seems to be a relationship between fantasy, pretence and false belief performance. The fact that in this study fantasy and belief understanding were only associated for the older group again suggests a specific relationship between pretence and belief understanding.

All of the studies reviewed in this section found some relationship between pretend ability and theory of mind or social sensitivity. The issue of which causes which is difficult to disentangle because all the designs have been cross-sectional. What would be required would be a longitudinal examination of pretend play, including measures of social sensitivity and theory of mind. The only relevant study was carried out by Youngblade and Dunn (1995), who compared pretend play at 2 years 9 months with belief understanding at 3 years 4 months. However, their older children had not yet developed appreciable theory of mind abilities. Only 14% passed one out of four typical false belief tasks. This measure was therefore abandoned in favour of belief explanation, but even then only 28% passed one out of five—an extremely lenient criterion. Of several measures of pretend play, only the ability to act out a pretend role was associated with belief performance ($r = .30$, $p < .05$). All other measures were completely unrelated. Thus the two abilities actually appear to be only weakly related, but since the false belief understanding was minimal, no strong conclusion is possible from this aspect of their study. Oddly, the study is nevertheless frequently cited as evidence of a pretence–belief developmental relationship.

Do children understand it's just pretend?

The popular idea that children sometimes cannot distinguish between what is pretend and reality is not supported by research. Wellman and Estes (1986) asked children about real and imaginary objects, such as a real cookie or one just thought about. Even most 3-year-olds (72%) correctly judged that only the real cookie could be eaten, touched, seen, and so on. It is widely accepted that from at least the age of 3 years onwards, children do not confuse fantasy and reality.

Children are not always completely certain, however. An interesting demonstration was provided by Harris, Brown, Marriot, Whittall and Harmer (1991). An experimenter took a 4- or 6-year-old child to a room in which there were two large boxes. The child was shown the boxes were empty, and then asked to pretend that either a monster or a bunny rabbit was in one of the boxes. The experimenter asked the child whether the creature was real. Most answered "no".

The experimenter then said she had to leave the room briefly to fetch some sweets. Harris et al. (1991) were interested in whether children would look in the boxes while the experimenter was away. However, four of the younger children would not let her leave because they were frightened. All four were in the group that had been asked to imagine the monster. Half of the remaining children examined one of the boxes, usually the box that they had imagined contained a monster or rabbit (regardless of which). When the experimenter returned after 2 minutes, half the children admitted to wondering whether the pretend animal was really in there. (You might like to imagine whether you would have looked in similar circumstances.)

This probably does not imply difficulties in distinguishing pretence from reality, however. It suggests a certain credulity, caused by imagining the possibility of there being a creature inside the box. This causes some children to test reality. It may not be much different from the adult tendency to be frightened after watching a horror film. We may be absolutely certain that there are no such things as vampires, but may still be extra vigilant before going to bed that night.

Summary

From the age of 2 years, children are able to infer the content of other people's pretend scenarios, track changes in the scenario and verbally comment on it. From the age of 2½, children start to take part in complex social pretend play with their peers. By 4 years, most children are also able to metacommunicate about pretence, suggesting fairly sophisticated ability to reflect on pretend behaviour.

Experiments assessing children's understanding of pretence suggest that, until the age of 4 or 5, children may view pretence in terms of deviant actions rather than in terms of the underlying mental states of the pretender (Lillard, 1993). Children can only differentiate two identical deviant actions (e.g., trying to feed an absent rabbit) according to their underlying mental states (believing or pretending that the rabbit is there) from the age at which they pass the false belief task (Perner et al., 1994a). Experiments directly comparing pretend ability with social understanding or false belief understanding consistently find that more complex forms of pretence arise at the same time as developments in social understanding and theory of mind. The causal relationship between these is difficult to determine on present evidence. However, the rapid emergence of communication about pretence at the same age children pass the false belief task (Astington & Jenkins, 1995; Howes & Matheson, 1992) suggests that insight into the representational nature of mental states allows more complex and rich pretend play. This may also explain why many more 4-year-olds than 3-year-olds have imaginary companions.

There is very little evidence that pretence is understood in mental state terms until the age of 4 years, making Leslie's (1987) metarepresentational theory of pretence difficult to maintain. The evidence that children can understand divergent pretence before they can understand false belief is weak or equivocal, and can in any case be explained by Harris and Perner's nonmetarepresentational theories of pretence. Pretence should properly be seen as a precursor to a later understanding of mental states.

Chapter 7

Precursors 2: Understanding visual attention

Introduction: Theory of mind in chimpanzees

SEVERAL EXPERIMENTS HAVE LOOKED for understanding of beliefs in chimpanzees. Typically chimpanzees fail belief tasks outright, or take hundreds of trials to learn to give the correct answer to the task. A good example is a study by Josep Call and Michael Tomasello (1999), who developed a nonverbal analogue of the unexpected transfer false belief task. In this task, an experimenter hid a food reward in one of two boxes, out of sight of the chimp. Then another experimenter, the Communicator, placed a wooden block on the box with the food. This was to indicate to the chimpanzees where the food was. It took chimpanzees some time to learn this: about 60 trials before they chose this box more often than chance.

Once they were used to this procedure, the false belief task began. The Communicator watched while the experimenter placed food in one of the boxes, with the chimp unable to see which one. The Communicator then left, and the chimp watched as the experimenter swapped the location of the boxes. When the Communicator returned he placed the block on the empty box, i.e., the box he should think contained the food. If the chimpanzees were considering the Communicator's mental states, they should reason that he had a false belief about the location of the food, and that therefore the box with the block on was the empty one. However, the chimpanzees consistently picked the box with the block on: They completely failed to consider the Communicator's false belief. Even after 20 such trials, spread over a number of sessions, the chimpanzees were still picking the wrong box, and thus getting no food. Human 4-year-olds also performed slightly below chance at a version of this task, but 5-year-olds were well above chance at this, and at a verbal version of the same task.

Premack and Woodruff (1978) had coined the term "theory of mind" when they asked "Does the chimpanzee have a theory of mind?" The answer seems to be "no". The ability to represent others' mental states may be a purely human ability. Or at least, this is the conclusion if you accept the false belief task as the definitive test of theory of mind. At present there is a lively debate about whether chimpanzees have capacities that are simpler, but still deserve to be included in a wider definition of theory of mind. These are largely to do with following others' gaze direction.

Gaze direction—an easier form of mental state understanding?

Several theorists have proposed that gaze understanding is a precursor to understanding belief (e.g., Baron-Cohen, 1995; Gopnik et al., 1994). Understanding that someone sees something certainly seems similar to understanding that someone knows something. Compare "Maxi sees that his chocolate is in the cupboard" with "Maxi knows that his chocolate is in the cupboard". The linguistic form of the two statements is obviously similar, and the commonality may go deeper. As Juan Carlos Goméz (1996, p. 334) puts it, "This can also be considered to be an early and simple way to know what is in the other's mind, because the contents of the other's mind—the object looked at—is in front of the beholder's eyes".

This is an attractive idea, although "understand gaze" is a potentially ambiguous term. My strategy in this chapter is to examine on the one hand what monkeys and apes are able to do and, on the other hand, what children of different ages are able to do, attempting to draw the minimal necessary conclusions from the data. This will throw light on: (1) whether gaze understanding is a precursor to full-blown theory of mind, and (2) whether gaze understanding should be considered a simpler form of mental state understanding. As a preliminary, it is useful to note a few things about human and primate eyes.

The unique morphology of the human eye

Eyes differ considerably between species. Most mammals are quadrupeds, and do not move their head and eyes independently (Emery, 2000). To work out what they are looking at, head direction is just as useful as eye direction. Moreover, head direction is easier to detect. It is also typically in the same direction as the body, which is easier still to detect.

Primates are different to most mammals in their very well-developed vision. Kobayashi and Kohshima (2001) analysed the eyes of 88 species of primate, including Japanese, Caucasian and Afro-Caribbean humans. Most primate species have the following:

(1) Colour vision, provided by cone cells. All Old World monkeys and apes are trichromatic—they have three sets of cones. So do New World females, although males are often dichromatic, having only two out of three sets of cones. Most other mammals do not see in colour, possibly because they evolved from a nocturnal common ancestor.

(2) Central foveae: dense concentrations of cones corresponding to the centre of the visual field. This allows very high resolution vision, given sufficient light.

(3) Forward-facing eyes, allowing very good depth perception.

In order to use their foveal vision and superior depth perception effectively, primates have to be able to turn their eyes in the direction they wish to look. For small primates, this can be done by simply turning the head. Their heads are small, and turning them costs little in terms of energy or speed. With increasing head size, it becomes more efficient to turn the eyes independently of the head. Larger primates have wider eyes to allow them to do this. Species that live on the ground, rather than in trees, have the widest eyes (relative to the size of the iris), allowing large gaze shifts in the horizontal plane. Humans move their eyes without a corresponding head turn more than other primates. Kobayashi and Kohshima videoed 18 species eating food by hand, including humans, chimpanzees and a number of smaller primates. They found that humans moved their eyes without a corresponding head turn roughly 60% of the time. The next highest were chimpanzees, with around 25% of eye movements.

This means that it is particularly difficult to tell what humans are looking at by their head direction—two to three times less accurate than for our closest relative, the chimpanzee. However, this difficulty is balanced by a unique feature of the human eye: We are the only primate species for which the "white of the eye"— the sclera—actually is white. All other primates have pigment adaptations that turn the naturally white sclera brown; in almost all cases this is the same colour as the iris, and usually as the face (see Figure 7.1). This appears to be a specific adaptation to make it *harder* to detect where these primates are looking. This gaze camouflage may help individuals disguise direct gaze, which is perceived by others as aggressive. It could also make it difficult for predators to know whether the primate can see them; survival chances are higher if a predator thinks it has been spotted.

Humans are different. Our eyes are wider than those of any other primate

FIGURE 7.1 Clockwise from top left: The eyes of two marmosets, a gorilla, a chimpanzee and two humans. Note that only the humans have visible sclera. (Photos: marmosets, Hannah Buchanan-Smith; gorilla, copyright © Michelle Klailova; chimpanzee, Louise Lock; humans, Martin Doherty.)

species. We move them independently of our head direction. We have extensive visible white sclera. Since we are the only primate species to have this, it seems to be a specific adaptation. This is likely to be so that our gaze direction is easier for other humans to detect, and perhaps to allow us to signal with gaze. If so, we probably have adaptations to detect gaze, and given that our independent eye movement means that judging by head direction is unreliable, and our white sclera makes judging by eye direction easier, gaze detection would be most effective if it was based on eye direction.

The perception of direct gaze

The most basic gaze perception ability is to distinguish direct from averted gaze. Farroni, Csibra, Simion and Johnson (2002) looked at this ability in newborn infants, within the first 120 hours from birth. They showed infants pairs of pictures of faces, one with direct gaze and one with averted gaze. Infants looked significantly longer and more often at the direct-gaze picture, suggesting that even in their first 5 days children can distinguish direct and averted gaze. Other studies have found this skill does not appear until 4 months of age (Samuels, 1985; Vecera & Johnson, 1995). Either way, this ability appears early in infancy. At around this age, infant chimpanzees also prefer human faces with open eyes and direct gaze (Myowa-Yamakoshi, Tomonaga, Tanaka & Matsuzawa, 2003).

Some researchers have argued that this indicates that infants know they are being looked at (e.g., Baron-Cohen, 1995; Vecera & Johnson, 1995). This would mean that children understand that people look at things—in this case, that an adult is looking at the infant herself or himself. While this might be true, it is certainly not warranted by the evidence. Infants may simply be sensitive to the presence of an important stimulus: directly gazing eyes. Many animals are sensitive to being looked at. Being able to detect a predator's gaze, for example, is of obvious adaptive significance. In social animals it is also important to know whether conspecifics are looking at you. Sensitivity to others' gaze may therefore be innate and from our distant evolutionary past. Even if this were not the case, it seems likely human infants would rapidly learn the significance of direct gaze: It is a stimulus they see regularly, and it reliably signals that they will be cooed over, played with or fed. Even newly born infants have seen direct gaze relatively often.

At minimum, infants are sensitive to the surface features of the direct-gaze stimulus, which does not necessarily require them to conceive of the other as "looking at" them. Research suggests that children cannot make *explicit* judgements of direct gaze until they are 3 or 4 years old. Baron-Cohen and Cross (1992) asked 3- and 4-year-olds which of two faces (in photographs) was looking at them. Four-year-olds were nearly perfect at this task (94% of trials correct), but 3-year-olds only judged correctly 75% of the time. This was better than the 50% chance baseline, but consistent with half of the 3-year-olds simply guessing. Doherty and Anderson (1999) found that only one of eighteen 2- to 3-year-old children was able to consistently judge which of two schematic faces was looking at them compared to 60% of a 3- to 4-year-old group. Even 2-year-olds performed well when head and eyes were congruent, indicating that they understood the task, and that their difficulties were specific to judging eye direction. Bruce et al. (2000) and Doherty, Anderson and Howieson (2007) found similar results with photographs, and Thayer (1977) found that even 6-year-olds were poor at judging whether they were being looked at. Thus, although infants show a precocious sensitivity to gaze, there is no evidence that children represent gaze as a relationship between themselves and the viewer until around the age of 3 years or later.

The perception of gaze direction

Nonhuman primates

Few animals other than humans need to follow eye direction. Even other primates largely move their heads and eyes together, and head direction is a much more easily detected stimulus. Chimpanzees move their eyes independently of head and body more than other nonhuman primates, but this tendency is far greater in humans (Kobayashi & Kohshima, 2001).

The ability to use or understand others' gaze cues seems to correspond to roughly how far up the phylogenetic tree a primate is. The most primitive of primates are prosimians, an order including lemurs. Lemurs do not follow head direction; monkeys do. Jim Anderson and Robert Mitchell fed individual black lemurs small pieces of fruit, occasionally breaking off to stare into the distance, making a large head turn. The lemurs rarely looked in the same direction as the experimenter. Adult stump tail macaque monkeys, on the other hand, almost always did (Anderson & Mitchell, 1999). Emery, Lorincz, Perrett, Oram and Baker (1997) showed rhesus monkeys videos of other rhesus monkeys looking at things (with head and eyes directed at the objects). The monkeys tended to attend more to the object or place attended to by the other monkey. Thus, in some circumstances, monkeys follow head and eye cues. However, Anderson and colleagues found that neither rhesus nor capuchin monkeys are able to learn to use head turns in an object choice paradigm. The experimenter turned his head and eyes to look at one of two covered locations, the one that contained a food reward. Despite many trials and the motivation to find the food, the monkeys never learned to use the head and eye cue (Anderson, Montant & Schmitt, 1996; Anderson, Sallaberry & Barbier, 1995). This suggests that although monkeys use others' head cues to direct their own attention, they neither know nor learn the significance of those cues.

Chimpanzees understand more than monkeys, although the extent to which they may understand the significance of others' attentional cues is controversial (chimpanzees, like bonobos, gorillas, orangutans and gibbons, are classified as apes, not monkeys). Povinelli and Eddy (1996a, 1996b) performed a groundbreaking series of studies concerning chimpanzees' ability to follow the gaze of others. Human-reared juvenile chimpanzees can do this very well. For example, the experimenter sat waiting for a chimpanzee to come into the experimental enclosure (behind a Plexiglass barrier—adult chimpanzees are dangerous animals and many primatologists are short of fingers as a result of carelessness around them). As the chimpanzee approached, the experimenter broke off eye contact and turned her head and eyes to look at a spot above and behind the chimp. Chimpanzees turned to follow the experimenter's gaze about half the time. If the experimenter only moved her eyes, they would still turn about a third of the time.

Chimpanzees clearly use human gaze cues to direct their own looking behaviour. Moreover, they can do this in a sophisticated way. In a second experiment, Povinelli and Eddy (1996a) placed an opaque screen along one half of the Plexiglass barrier. As the chimpanzee approached, the experimenter looked at a point on her own side of the screen, invisible to the chimpanzee. If chimpanzees' gaze following was based on a simple orienting response, they might be expected to turn and follow the experimenter's line of sight "through" the screen and on to the back wall of the enclosure. However, they did not do this. Instead they moved to the side in an attempt to see what on the other side of the screen the experimenter might be looking at.

Povinelli and Eddy (1996a) interpret this cautiously, but it suggests the chimpanzees knew that the experimenter was looking at something, that the screen impeded their vision, and that therefore the object must be on the experimenter's side of the screen, invisible to the chimp. This implies that chimpanzees are able to represent a spatial relationship between a person's eyes and an object, and they expect gaze to terminate at an object even if it is invisible to them. This goes far beyond the gaze-following ability of monkeys, and even human children before the age of about 18 months (see below). It is very tempting to draw extensive conclusions: Chimpanzees clearly represent others' looking behaviour. This implies that they understand *seeing* and *attention*. Properly understood, *seeing* and *attention* are representational mental states, very similar to belief and knowledge. In terms of Goméz's (1996) suggestion above, chimpanzees' ability to follow gaze could mean that they have an early and simple way to know what is in others' minds, so long as the contents are in front of the beholder's eyes.

Povinelli and Eddy (1996b) addressed this question in a separate series of experiments using a procedure that might indicate an understanding of the specific mental state "seeing". They took advantage of chimpanzees' species-specific begging behaviour. This is much like ours—holding out the hand in the hope of being given a piece of fruit. If this gesture is not noticed, chimps sometimes reach out further, or slap their palms against the wall or the cage, which tends to capture the experimenter's attention. It is tempting to conclude from this that these chimpanzees have some notion of attention, and perhaps of seeing.

In order to test this, the chimpanzee was presented with two experimenters, one of whom could not see them for various reasons: she was covering her eyes, or was blindfolded, or had a bucket over her head, or had her back turned. If the chimpanzee understood anything about visual attention, even a very rudimentary understanding, it should beg from the experimenter who can see it. The findings of the experiment were therefore very surprising: chimpanzees showed no preference for the two experimenters in the case where one had her eyes closed; nor did they show a preference when one had her head turned away; nor when one had a bucket on her head. In fact, they only preferred one experimenter over the other when one had her entire body facing the other way.

Povinelli and Eddy conclude that chimps have simply learned to gesture towards someone facing forward, regardless of all other attentional cues. The apes were able to learn to use these other cues during the course of the experiment, since they were only reinforced when they begged from someone who could see them. Even then, however, their understanding appeared very shallow. For example, they eventually learned to beg from someone with open eyes if the other experimenter had closed eyes. Also, when both experimenters had their backs turned, they learned to beg from the one looking over her shoulder. After this, the experimenters presented the incorrect option from the first pairing (eyes closed), now paired with the correct option from the second pairing (looking over her shoulder). The chimpanzees were now more likely to beg from the experimenter with eyes closed, the incorrect response. This suggests that the chimpanzees were primarily judging according to whether the person was facing them. If both or neither were facing them, they could learn to discriminate on the basis of other cues, but this learning is very situation-specific; when these cues were put in conflict with the facing versus not-facing dimension, the chimpanzees reverted to using that. Clearly, the chimpanzees had learned nothing about "seeing".

There is some controversy concerning whether chimpanzees can learn to use gaze cues to find food. It seems to be possible in principle, but difficult. Adapting Anderson et al.'s (1995) paradigm, Itakura and Tanaka (1998) found that chimpanzees could learn to find food in one of two locations, even when the experimenter only glanced at it. Povinelli, Bierschwale and Čech (1999) found that their chimpanzees could not do this, although they could use head and eyes cues. These two studies used a very similar procedure, and the different findings may be a matter of the specific characteristics of the chimpanzees: Itakura and Tanaka's chimpanzees were experienced experimental participants, were older, and may have had a higher level of enculturation.

The picture that emerges concerning chimpanzees' understanding of gaze direction is this: They can follow gaze quite effectively, and react appropriately when the other's gaze is obscured by a screen. They can follow head direction. They can follow eye direction when the experimenter only moves her eyes. In other words, they are very good at using others' gaze cues to orient towards or to search for the object the other is looking at. They are not so good at using gaze for anything else, especially when only the experimenter's eye movements are informative. Why this should be remains a mystery.

Chimpanzees have had one conspicuous success involving appreciating what another has attended to. Hare, Call, Agnetta and Tomasello (2000) took advantage of the natural dominance hierarchy of chimpanzees. If a subordinate chimpanzee, a dominant chimpanzee, and a piece of food are put in the same place, there is usually only one outcome: the dominant chimpanzee eats the food. However, what if there were two pieces of food, and one was only visible to the subordinate chimpanzee? In Hare et al.'s experiment, a dominant and a subordinate chimpanzee were looking into a room through opposite doors. Two pieces of food were placed in the room, one in open view and the other obscured by an opaque barrier, such that it was visible only to the subordinate chimpanzee. The doors then opened, with the subordinate chimpanzee getting a slight head start. Subordinates were significantly more likely to go for the hidden food (roughly 75% of times, going for the visible food just under 25% of times). Subordinates did not prefer the hidden food in noncompetitive situations.

In a later experiment, Hare, Call and Tomasello (2001) used a similar setup to see whether the subordinate chimpanzee could remember what the dominant chimp had witnessed. If the dominant chimpanzee had witnessed a piece of fruit hidden, subordinates only approached the food about 80% of the time, compared to 90% when the dominant had not witnessed it being placed, a small but significant difference. In a further experiment more similar to Hare et al.'s (2000) procedure, there were two pieces of food. Subordinates saw both hidden, whereas dominants saw only one. However, in this situation, subordinates were not significantly more likely to approach the food that only they had seen.

Thus, chimpanzees can take into account what the other chimpanzee can see. There is even some evidence that they can take into account what the other has seen previously. Here "see" simply means "is facing", and "has seen" means "has been facing"; the experimenters did not examine the specific cues used to infer perceptual access. Hare et al. suggest that chimpanzees perform well in their paradigm because it simulates natural food competition situations, whereas in other paradigms "they may not understand the cooperative motive of the human communicator" (2001, p. 140). Although this has some plausibility, these chimpanzees are "professional" experimental participants, and spend their entire lives selectively being given pieces of fruit. It would be odd if they had not come to expect humans to give them pieces of fruit. Povinelli and Eddy's (1996b) begging chimpanzees, for example, clearly thought there was a good chance of one of the experimenters giving them food. The question was, this experimenter here, or this one with the bucket on her head?

In fact, the minimum necessary conclusion from Hare et al.'s experiments is the same as from Povinelli and Eddy's: Chimpanzees are sensitive to whether another is facing a target object or not. The distinction is in whether the target is the chimpanzee itself, as in Povinelli and Eddy's experiments, or a target object, as in Hare et al.'s experiment. If the other is facing the target object, she is more likely to give food (Povinelli & Eddy) or approach the target (Hare et al.). Hare et al. (2001) have extended the procedure to examine past perceptual access, and find at least some sensitivity to what another has been facing, as well as what they are currently facing.

Where Hare et al. (2001) part company with Povinelli and colleagues is in their interpretation of their findings. Provocatively, they claim that chimpanzees understand both *seeing* and *knowledge*, i.e., that the dominant chimpanzee cannot see this fruit now, or that he did not see this fruit hidden earlier. By "know", however, these researchers mean something less powerful that our everyday adult understanding of "know": Roughly speaking, they mean to have had previous perceptual access to a state of affairs which has not changed since. A very similar concept has been applied to infants by O'Neill (1996), who called it understanding of *engagement*. Two-year-old children are highly sensitive to what a person is currently involved in (especially relative to the child's current wishes), and also what they have been involved in previously. This is discussed below.

Povinelli and Vonk (2004, p. 11) respond to Hare et al.'s claims (see, for example, Tomasello, Call & Hare, 2003) by arguing that "the experimental results from the kinds of techniques that are currently in vogue cannot add a single bit of evidence in unique support of the conclusion that chimpanzees reason about mental states". Their general point is that any particular understanding of behaviour could be based on learning a specific association between events or situations and behaviour. Here, for example, chimpanzees may have learned about others seeing food and attempting to attain it, and perhaps have noticed they are less likely to do so when an occluding object is interposed between them. Using types of situations familiar to chimpanzees exacerbates the problem, since they are more likely to have learned relevant associations in these situations. A lot can be done with specific associations, and rules learned for particular situations. So much so, in fact, that it becomes potentially difficult to think of tests that would require us to conclude that the participant had concepts of mental states intervening between experience and behaviour. Povinelli and Vonk (2003) suggest that an entirely novel situation might be required, perhaps one where the individual is allowed to have a particular experience, and subsequently has to reason that another individual in the same circumstances would have the same experience. Their particular suggestion is that an individual be allowed to wear each of two helmets. One helmet blocks all vision; the other allows the wearer to see perfectly well. Having experienced this, the participant could then be shown two individuals wearing the helmets, and required to predict their behaviour accordingly. Such a test has not been done, and the debate continues.

In summary, the evidence from nonhuman primates suggests this: Prosimians, such as lemurs, show no sensitivity to others' visual cues. Monkeys can follow head direction, but show little ability to learn to use this cue to find objects. Chimpanzees show superb gaze-following skills, being able to use head direction, or eye direction alone, and can appropriately take occluding screens into account. They can also make use of others' perceptual access to predict behaviour: They know that someone facing them is more likely to give them food than someone facing away, and they can take account of a competitor's visual access when competing for food. However, both of these skills are based on whole-body orientation. Chimpanzees do not appear to be able to use their sophisticated gaze-following skills when required to predict the gazer's behaviour. As I shall argue below, chimpanzees have the gaze understanding of an 18-month-old human infant. The question of whether any of this implies a theory of mind reduces to this: it depends what you mean by "theory of mind". Chimpanzees are sensitive to global perceptual access, probably based on whole-body orientation. They are also able to predict some aspects of behaviour based on this access, and even have some ability to take previous perceptual access into account. Most people would not want to call this a theory of mind: Although chimpanzees understand something about the relation between perception and behaviour, there is no evidence that they think there is any intervening "mind" that mediates this relationship. In fact, the relevant research so far suggests that they do not.

Human infants

Much of the work on infants' understanding of visual attention has concerned their tendency to follow gaze. Scaife and Bruner (1975) first found that when an adult broke off eye contact with an infant and looked elsewhere, infants as young as 3 months looked in approximately the same direction. They referred to this as joint visual attention. Despite this good performance from very young infants, later research has concluded that children cannot reliably follow an adult's head turn until some time later. In early research, the measure used was typically whether the infant looked to the same side as the experimenter. Corkum and Moore (1995) point out that this ignores the number of times infants look to the opposite side. If children looked to the opposite side as often as they looked to the same side, you would not want to conclude that they were following the adult's gaze. In fact, previous joint attention research might just have been measuring infants' increasing tendency to look around.

Corkum and Moore (1995) ran their own study to establish when children can reliably follow different types of gaze cue: either the head and eyes turned together, the head turned while the experimenter maintained eye contact, or the eyes alone moved. The angle of movement was 61° in each case. Corkum and Moore measured the number of times infants looked to the correct side *minus* the number of times they looked to the incorrect side. The only gaze cues infants followed were the combined head and eye turns, and even then, only in the two oldest groups, 15- to 16-month-olds and 18- to 19-month-olds. This shows that infants do not follow eye turns on their own. However, the 18- to 19-month-olds were sensitive to eye direction in some sense, because they were significantly more likely to follow a head and eye turn than they were a head turn alone (unlike younger children).

In a subsequent study, Moore and Corkum (1998) looked in more detail at infants' ability to follow eye turns. They suggest that the earlier study may have masked an ability to follow eye turns because these trials were mixed in with trials involving head turns. Since head turns are much more salient, they may have de-emphasized the eyes-only trials. Another feature of their earlier study was the lack of targets; if infants follow a gaze shift and find nothing interesting, they might not bother the next time. In order to motivate children to follow gaze, they now included animated targets, outside of infants' peripheral vision (about 80° from the midline). During a four-trial "shaping" phase, the experimenter shifted her gaze to a target, and it began to move. In experimental trials, the toys animated if the infant also looked at them. This procedure produced a lot of head turning even in the youngest children, who were 8 to 9 months old: They were obviously aware that something interesting might happen. However, it was not until 18 to 19 months that infants began to consistently turn in the correct direction. The improvement with age appears to be sudden: Over 80% of 18- to 19-month-old infants reached criterion, compared to about 15% of 15- to 16-month-olds.

From this work, it appears that infants do not follow others' head directions until well into their second year, and only follow eye direction from 1½ years onwards. However, there is evidence that younger children may follow head turns to objects if the head and the object are simultaneously visible. D'Entremont, Hains and Muir (1997), for example, had targets (two puppets) either side of the experimenter's head, which she periodically looked at by turning her head through 90° (and talked to the puppets too, which is perhaps more natural). In this case, even 3-month-old infants looked more often to the puppet she was looking at rather than the other one.

D'Entremont et al. (1997) measured infants' eye direction rather than head turns, because of concerns about younger infants having insufficient control of their neck muscles. Hood, Willen and Driver (1998) went one step further by using a measure that does not require the infant to move at all, attentional *cuing*. This involved presenting children with a computer monitor, on which there was a face that made an eye turn in one direction. This kind of cue causes adults to shift their attention in the same direction, even though they do not necessarily make corresponding eye movements. Shortly afterwards, a target appeared to one side of the face, either in the direction looked in or in the opposite direction. If infants' attention had been cued by the eye turn, they would look at the target more quickly if it appeared to the side looked at. This was exactly what Hood et al. found with 4-month-old children, indicating that even at this age, change in eye direction was sufficient to shift infants' attention. However, there was one important proviso: the face vanished before the target appeared. This never happens in real life. When Hood et al. ran a condition in which the face remained on the screen, children continued to look at the face for 61% of trials, only turning to look at the target 26% of the time.

This finding is rather curious, as it seems children have an ability they are not able to use under normal circumstances (when faces do not suddenly vanish into thin air). This could be taken as evidence of an innate ability to follow eye direction. Young infants might be unable to use this ability until other developments take place; in this case they might not have sufficient control of their own attention to disengage from a fixated stimulus (the face). Infants' eye-direction-detecting skills might have to wait until they are able to overcome this "sticky fixation".

However, the idea of an innate eye-direction detector is called into question by subsequent research by Farroni, Johnson, Brockbank and Simion (2000). Their findings suggest that the effect may not be specific to eye movements: Cuing may simply be due to the motion. In their first experiment Farroni et al. replicated Hood et al.'s (1998) finding, with a larger effect size. In a second experiment, instead of the eyes moving to one side, the entire face moved, while the eyes remained stationary; the final configuration of eyes and face was identical, the only difference being in what moved. Farroni et al. found as big a cuing effect as when the eyes moved, but this time in the direction that the face had moved, i.e., in the opposite direction to the eye direction. In a third experiment, the original stimuli were used but the eye movement was masked by a long blink. This time there was no cuing effect, presumably because the motion was obscured. Thus, infants are cued in the direction of whatever moves, eyes or face, and when there is no apparent motion, they are not cued by the eyes. It is plausible that it is simply the motion that cues infants.[1]

Innate gaze detection is a popular idea, but relatively neglected is the idea that the human eye has evolved in order to make gaze naturally easy to detect. As discussed above, we are the only primate with extensive visible sclera, and the rotation of our eye produces the strong impression of the iris and pupil darting to one side (whereas what happens in fact is that the entire eyeball has rotated). Motion naturally captures attention, and at least part of our gaze-following skill may result from the nature of the stimulus rather than specialized brain mechanisms for following gaze. After all, why bother evolving extensive neural mechanisms when you can just change the colour of the sclera? This may also explain why younger infants will follow head turns to objects currently in their visual field: The motion will cause them to move their eyes in that direction, but they may have no concept that people can be looking at things outside their visual field (or that people look at things at all).

However, by the end of the first year, it appears children are starting to do something more conceptual than simply following others' gaze cues. Woodward (2003) used a habituation paradigm, in which an experimenter turned her head to look at one of two objects, both simultaneously visible to the child. This was repeated until the infant became habituated, and then one of two novel trial types was presented. The position of the two toys was reversed and the experimenter either looked at the old toy in its new position, or looked to the original position at the new toy. The trial in which the experimenter looked at the old toy was most different to the habituation trials perceptually. However, the trial in which the experimenter looked at the novel toy was most different to the habituation trials in terms of the *gaze relationship* involved. Woodward found that 12-month-old infants looked longer when the actor looked at the novel toy, suggesting that they were sensitive to the change in the gaze relationship. Younger children did not distinguish between the two trials. All three age groups followed the experimenter's head direction in the test trials, and this did not differ significantly between the age groups or the two types of test trial.

Further evidence that 1-year-olds are beginning to represent a relationship between gazers and objects comes from Butler, Caron and Brooks (2000). They adapted a standard joint attention procedure by adding an occluding screen. In the no-screen condition, the experimenter turned her head to look at one of two peripheral targets, as usual. In the screen condition, the experimenter's line of sight to the targets was blocked by two large screens on either side of her, although she could still see the child. The experimenter turned her head just as before, but of course would not be able to see either target. In the window condition, a large and conspicuous aperture was cut into the screens, allowing the experimenter to see the targets. Eighteen-month-old infants responded appropriately to the experimenter's gaze, following her head turn when there was no barrier or a barrier with a window, but tending not to follow it otherwise. Fourteen-month-olds also looked less often when there was a barrier, but looked less often still when the barrier had a window, perhaps indicating that they did not yet fully understand occlusion. Over a third of the older children leaned forward to try to see what was behind the barrier, compared to only one of the twenty-two 14-month-olds. Dunphy-Lelii and Wellman (2004) replicated this study and found that 14-month-olds performed reasonably well on window trials. However, 18-month-olds were still more likely to lean forward to look around the barrier (about 60%) than 14-month-olds (around 20%) (Dunphy-Lelii & Wellman, 2004, p. 62).

Implications

By 18 months, and perhaps before, children can represent gaze as a spatial relationship between a person and an object. They also understand that this relationship can be impeded by barriers. The 18-month-old infant has sophisticated gaze-following abilities. Just like the chimpanzee. The big question is whether infants have any greater insight into attention than chimpanzees.

Most theorists interpret these findings richly, concluding that by 18 months infants understand that gaze is *referential*. This term is often used without clear definition, but at least some researchers give it a very rich mental state definition. For example, Butler et al. (2000) define *referentiality* as "understanding that all mental states are about or directed to some content (perceptible or representational)" (p. 360). Some theorists assume that rich understanding exists from birth or shortly after. Simon Baron-Cohen's (1995) mindreading system very explicitly does this. Baron-Cohen proposes several modules that start to operate in sequence during the first 4 years of life. The model is illustrated in Figure 7.2. Very soon after birth, an Eye-Direction Detector (EDD) becomes active. This detects eye-like stimuli, and also computes a relationship between the eyes and the object of attention. This relationship is interpreted as seeing. "Seeing" strongly implies an understanding of an internal mental state. Another module, the Intentionality Detector, interprets animate objects as having goals and desires: e.g. intending to go over there, or wanting to have that cheese. These two mechanisms feed their output into the Shared Attention Mechanism (SAM), which becomes active between the ages of 9 and 18 months. Its function is to compute "triadic representations", relationships between three things: the child, someone else and an object. An example of a triadic representation is the typical joint attention episode, in which the child and mother both look at and interact with an object. A special significance to joint attention episodes is built into the architecture of Baron-Cohen's mindreading model. He suggests that the SAM is absent or impaired in people with autism, and this is the root of their mindreading difficulties. In normal individuals, the output of SAM feeds into the ToMM, which comes on line between 18 and 48 months.

The theory is extremely nativist, and implies that even infants' earliest sensitivity to gaze demonstrates an understanding that eyes see things. Although few researchers subscribe to the whole model, the EDD is taken seriously [Hood et al.,

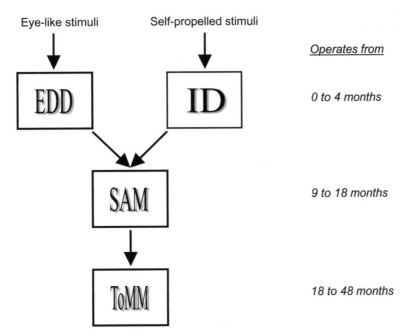

FIGURE 7.2 Baron-Cohen's mindreading system.

(Adapted from Baron-Cohen, 1995.) Notes: EDD, Eye-Detection Dectector; ID, Intentionality Detector; SAM, Shared Attention Mechanism; ToMM, Theory of Mind Mechanism.

(1998) and Farroni et al. (2000), for example, frame their findings in terms of an eye-direction detector]. Infants clearly are sensitive to direct gaze from an early age. However, the fact that they do not follow others' eye movements until roughly 18 months is cause to doubt that they are detecting eye direction before this age.

Other theorists prefer to conclude the minimum from gaze following. Moore and Corkum (1994) argue that children could learn to follow gaze without any understanding of its significance. Once they have learned, however, following others' gaze is their route to understanding the subjective nature of visual experience. Learning could even occur incidentally. For example, during episodes of face-to-face interaction, occasionally the infant's mother will disengage and turn to look at something else. Typically this will be something interesting. The infant, distracted by the lack of interaction, will tend to look around. If the infant looks in the same direction as the mother, he or she will often be rewarded by an interesting sight; this is less likely if he or she looks in the opposite direction. After a number of such experiences, the infant will become conditioned to expect an interesting sight in a particular location, given a particular head movement by the mother. Mothers may also actively "teach" gaze following during episodes of joint attention with objects. The mother attempts to draw the infant's attention to the object, repeatedly alternating gaze from infant to object. If the infant follows the mother's gaze, he or she will be rewarded by interaction with an interesting object.

Once gaze following is achieved, infants have an excellent opportunity to learn about attention. They know something about two types of gaze: that between another person and an object, and their own experience of seeing. In joint attention activities, children's attention is called to both types of gaze simultaneously. At some point they realize that these are the same kind of thing. They realize that their experience of seeing involves a connection between themselves and an object, and can perhaps start to attribute aspects of their phenomenal experience of seeing to others. This allows them to understand the subjective nature of gaze, that they and other people might see (or not see) different things. This is a key step along the way to having a representational understanding of visual attention (Moore, 2006).

Baron-Cohen (1995) and Moore and Corkum (1994) span the range of views of what lies behind infants' ability to follow gaze, from very rich to minimal. Both would agree that 2-year-olds know what people are looking at. But do the gaze-following data really show this?

Gaze judgement

Human children offer one source of information about their gaze understanding that chimpanzees do not: you can ask them. If infants can determine what someone is looking at, then at least by the time they are toddlers, they should be able to say so. This simple judgement would not require a particularly sophisticated conception of looking, but inability to make such judgement would certainly make a sophisticated conception implausible.

Until recently there was little data on the issue. Piaget claimed that until middle childhood (roughly 7 years) children were profoundly egocentric, unable to adopt another person's point of view. Piaget's famous demonstration of this was the three mountains task. The child is shown a model of three mountains and asked to pick from a set of photographs how the mountains would look to a person at a particular point on the other side. Up until the age of about 7 years, children choose the photograph corresponding to their own view, suggesting that they cannot take the perspective of another person. Like a lot of Piaget's experimental designs, this has been justly criticized for posing extraneous difficulties over and above the target ability. As well as having to appreciate that the other person sees the scene differently, the child must engage in complicated mental rotation. It also lacks "human sense" (Donaldson, 1978). Why on earth would one want to know how three mountains look to someone else? Even Piaget's Swiss 7-year-olds had little experience of seeing mountains from opposite perspectives.

However, although most Piagetian tasks can be modified such that considerably younger children can pass them, the tasks nevertheless often address a true conceptual deficit. In this case, children do have problems taking others' perspective, although this ability develops earlier than 7 years. Flavell (1974) distinguished two levels of knowledge involved. Level 1 knowledge concerns what others can or cannot see: perceptual perspective taking. Level 2 knowledge concerns how something looks: conceptual perspective taking. The distinction is illustrated by a study by Masangkay, McCluskey, McIntyre, Sims-Knight, Vaughn and Flavell (1974). An experimenter showed children a card with a picture of a dog on one side, and a picture of a cat on the other. He held the card up between himself and the child, and asked "What do *you* see?", and "What do *I* see?" All of the 3-year-olds and nearly two thirds of 2-year-olds could say that they could see the dog and the experimenter could see the cat. This is Level 1 knowledge. In a further experiment, a picture of a turtle in profile was laid between the child and the experimenter. The child was asked "Do you see the turtle right side up, or do you see the turtle upside down?" The same question was asked about the experimenter. Children had to understand that although the turtle might look upside down to them, it looked right side up to the experimenter. About a quarter of young 3-year-olds, half of older 3-year-olds, and most older children passed this task. This is Level 2 knowledge: understanding not only what someone can see, but *how* it looks to them.

This is the kind of knowledge that Piaget's three mountains task measures. The mountains task has additional difficulties, such as complex mental rotation. However, when suitably simplified, 4- to 5-year-old children can pass this task (Donaldson, 1978; Light & Nix, 1983). The fact that children pass this task around the same time as the false belief task is no coincidence: both measure conceptual perspective taking.

It is intuitively quite plausible that Level 2 knowledge develops out of Level 1 knowledge. It is also plausible that Level 1 knowledge is responsible for gaze following, allowing children to understand that people can see different things based on their head and eye orientations, and the presence of occluding objects. The Level 1/Level 2 distinction would then map smoothly onto the idea that under-standing of mental states develops out of understanding of gaze. However, we do not know whether gaze following is based on Level 1 knowledge. When Flavell introduced the distinction in the 1970s, the fact that children below 7 years could take others' perspectives at all was big news. Little attention was paid to the poor performance of 2-year-olds and younger 3-year-olds on Level 1 tasks.

Masangkay et al. (1974) also included a condition that was similar to the gaze-following tasks used with infants. Instead of measuring children's tendency to follow gaze, however, children were simply asked what the experimenter was look-ing at. The child sat opposite the experimenter, who kept her head facing forward and stared at one of several objects positioned around the child. Just over a third of 2-year-olds passed this task. Level 1 perspective taking may not be the same as gaze following.

The only study to explicitly examine the onset of Level 1 perspective taking is very recent. Henrike Moll and Michael Tomasello (2006) employed a fairly natural situation in which an experimenter enters the room looking for one of the two toys he and the child were playing with a short while earlier. The child can see both toys but one is hidden from the experimenter by an occluding bucket. Having briefly looked round, and with an expression of dissatisfaction, the experimenter asks for "the other toy". Moll and Tomasello reasoned that if children understood what the experimenter could and could not see, they would conclude that the experimenter wanted the unseen toy. Thus the task requires Level 1 knowledge of what can be seen, plus a simple inference based on the knowledge that people do not continue to search for things they can already see. The findings were that 24-month-olds handed the experimenter the hidden toy two thirds of the time. This was better than would be expected by chance, and better than 18-month-old children, who handed the correct toy over less than half the time. Moll and Tomasello conclude that 24-month-old children understand what people can and cannot see, even when this differs from what they themselves can see. Younger children do not understand this.

By the age of 2½ years, children can go further: They understand what people have and have not seen. Daniela O'Neill (1996) demonstrated this using a clever technique. A 2-year-old and an experimenter played with a fascinating toy while the child's parent watched, read a magazine or waited outside the room. Then the experimenter put the toy on a high shelf and left the child with his or her parent. The children all seemed highly motivated to persuade their parents to get the toy down again. However, the children whose parents had not witnessed it being placed there made significantly more gestures towards the object, named it and its location. This indicates sensitivity to the parent's knowledge state: Because their mother did not witness the toy being placed there, the child needs to make more effort to inform her.

It would be natural to assume from these findings that 2-year-olds know what someone does and does not know on the basis of recent experience; subsequent commentators on the study have frequently concluded this. O'Neill (1996) is more careful in her interpretation, introducing the idea of "engagement". Engagement refers to a person's involvement in a situation. Even young infants are sensitive to adults' lack of involvement in their current activities, and increase communication attempts accordingly (Ross & Lollis, 1987). O'Neill's findings suggest that by 2½ years of age children can take into account past disengagement, and increase their communication about what happened during this period. Engagement is thus a rudimentary nonmentalistic concept of attention. Although rudimentary, it works quite well in most situations. The cues children might use are broad stable ones, amongst them: physical presence, apparent distraction (e.g., talking to someone, doing a sudoku), body posture and head direction. Eye direction is not a good cue to engagement, since it is transient and, although it signals what you are attending to *right now*, it is a poor indicator of the general direction of attention over a protracted period. For example, a child's mother may be fully engaged in a child's pretend tea party, but cast frequent glances towards the child's younger sister asleep in the corner. Attention, as understood by adults, is split, but the mother is nevertheless engaged with the game.

This research suggests that Level 1 knowledge may be distinct from gaze-following skills. Although children can follow gaze from 18 months old or earlier, Moll and Tomasello (2006) do not find Level 1 ability until 24 months. Level 1 may involve new conceptual knowledge around the age of 2 years. O'Neill (1996) demonstrates that at least by 2½ years children are sensitive to what people have previously attended to, introducing the concept of engagement. Understanding in terms of engagement plausibly incorporates Level 1 knowledge. However, engagement potentially de-emphasizes eye direction as a cue, because of its fleeting transient nature. The question arises, when can children make the kind of judgements about visual attention when eye direction *is* the necessary cue?

Research suggests that judging eye direction remains hard for 2-year-olds. As discussed above, Masangkay et al. (1974) found only poor performance on their eye-direction task. Lee, Eskritt, Symons and Muir (1998) looked at children's ability to judge gaze, and to infer desire on the basis of gaze cues. Over several experiments, 3-year-olds were above chance at judging gaze direction, but performance was generally poor. Judging desire based on eye direction was below chance at 3 years in the first three experiments. In a fourth experiment children were shown a video in which a clown's eyes moved to one of three targets, and children had to indicate which object the clown wanted. When only the clown's eyes moved, 3-year-olds performed well, but 2-year-olds were at chance.[2] In a further experiment with just eyes-only trials, 2-year-olds performed at chance on one half of six trials, but above chance on the second half. The authors do not say whether overall they were above chance. This study provides little evidence that children younger than 3 years can follow gaze, or attribute desire on the basis of it.

Around the same time, Jim Anderson and I conducted a couple of studies looking at gaze judgement (without the additional factor of desire attribution). We had been interested in seeing whether something like the SAM had psychological reality in chimpanzees. At the time, we had no access to chimpanzees, so we ran the task on the 3- and 4-year-old children in our department's playgroup to see how it worked. We showed them pictures of pairs of people either looking at the same or different balls. The SAM ought to detect the triadic gaze relationship when the people attend to the same ball. We did not expect our young human participants to have any difficulty with this, but they were only correct about 67% of the time, where chance is 50%. Performance on control tasks approached ceiling (Anderson & Doherty, 1997).

In Doherty and Anderson (1999), we followed up this finding by looking at whether 2- to 4-year-olds could say where a single person was looking (a task hypothesized to use the EDD). There were three basic tasks. In the Looking-at-you task, children saw pictures like Figure 7.3a and were asked "Which one is looking at you?" In the Looking-where task, they were shown pictures like Figure 7.3b, and asked "Which one is Sam looking at?" We were concerned about children paying attention (a definite problem with 2-year-olds), as well as their ability to extrapolate from a central stimulus to a peripheral target. As a control we included a Point-direction task, showing stimuli like Figure 7.3c and asking "Which one is Sam pointing at?" Each task had just four trials (because 2-year-olds' attention spans can be really short). The results are shown in Figure 7.4. Performance on the Point-direction task was very good, even for the 2-year-olds, so we can be confident they were paying attention.[3] However, only one child from the younger group managed to pass the Looking-at-you task, and one additional child passed the Looking-where task; both these children were 3-year-olds. In a subsequent experiment, we compared these tasks with a task in which head and eyes pointed to the target. Performance on the original tasks remained poor, but performance on the head-and-eye-direction tasks was near ceiling, and as good as the Point-direction task. So children clearly understood the task demands; it was just the eye-direction stimuli that caused problems. In the remaining experiment of this study we used a real life human gazer (me) and found that children performed no better than on the picture tasks. Children have a specific difficulty in judging eye direction.

These studies suggest that until they are 2 years old children cannot pass tasks that require them to make judgements or conclusions about what someone is attending to. By the age of at least 2½ years, children can incorporate knowledge about what people attended to previously. However, it is not until they are about 3 years old that they can use the specific cue of eye direction. This suggests the

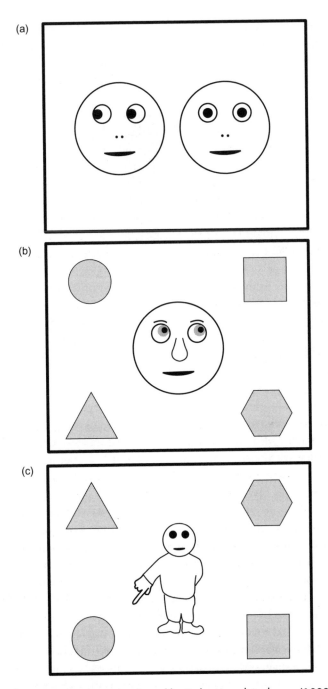

FIGURE 7.3 The gaze-judgement stimuli used by Doherty and Anderson (1999). (a) Looking-at-you task; (b) Looking-where task; and (c) Point-direction task.

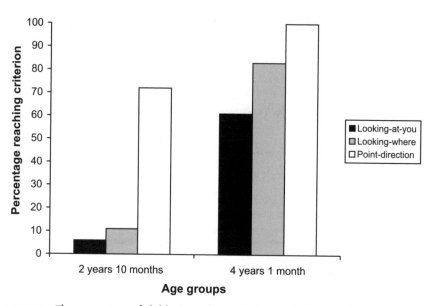

FIGURE 7.4 The percentage of children reaching criterion on Doherty and Anderson's Gaze-direction (Looking-at-you and Looking-where) and Point-direction judgement tasks.

Redrawn from Doherty and Anderson, "A New Look at Gaze: Preschool Children's Understanding of Eye-direction." *Cognitive Development, 14*, 549–571, Copyright (1999), with permission from Elsevier.

possibility that gaze following and judgement of eye direction are completely different abilities. Following O'Neill's (1996) concept of engagement, children's early understanding of attention may neglect eye gaze as the specific cue. Our research, along with Masangkay et al. (1974) and Lee et al. (1998), suggests that this is probably the case. What remains to be determined is what causes children to begin to follow eye direction when they do.

One speculation is that it has to do with their dawning understanding of the representational nature of mental states. As adults we know that eye direction is critical to determining what someone is attending to at any given moment. As such, it also determines what people will know and come to believe, and it can be used to determine desires too (especially if those desires are covertly expressed). Eye direction may only become an interesting cue once the child starts to develop a representational theory of mind. In support of this, Doherty and Anderson (1999) also looked at performance on a false belief task alongside the Looking-where task. The two tasks were significantly associated ($r = .40$, $p = .02$), although this correlation was no longer significant when age had been partialled out. (This suggests that the tasks may be related, or may develop coincidentally, or have an indirect relationship. More research on the issue is needed.)

Summary and discussion

Primates, like many other animals, are sensitive to direct gaze. Chimpanzees can follow human gaze to an object, even when only the eyes point towards the object of attention. Monkeys may not be able to do this. This is not surprising, since in all primates except humans the direction of the iris and/or pupils is obscured (and probably camouflaged) by a pigmented sclera. In other words, nonhuman primates have evolved eyes that are hard to follow. Humans, the exception, have gone the other way, evolving eyes in which the direction of gaze is clearly signalled. This clear signalling may have evolved alongside improved ability to detect eye direction. However, our closest relatives, chimpanzees, also possess this ability when they have been reared by humans.

Human infants are sensitive to direct gaze very early in life. They can follow others' head direction to an object in the first few months of life, if the object is already in their field of view. They cannot follow gaze beyond their current field of view until they are a year old or older. They cannot follow eye direction when it is the only cue until about a year and a half. At around the same time they are able to take into account the effect of occluding screens when following others' gaze. If the gaze direction intercepts an occluder, children seem to expect there to be an object on the visible side of the occluder. This suggests that they are able to represent a relationship between the eyes and/or head of the gazer, and the object gazed at.

Although by this time they use others' gaze to orient their own attention, children do not seem to be able to do anything that requires a judgement of others' visual attention until they are about 2 years old. Chimpanzees may never be able to make a judgement on this basis, although a lively debate continues on the matter. At 2½, children (and perhaps subordinate juvenile chimpanzees) can take into account what another has attended to in the past. This implies a rudimentary understanding of knowledge. O'Neill (1996) characterizes this in terms of engagement; whether or not another was "engaged" with a situation in the past must be taken into account when judging their likely behaviour now. This concept is potentially effective for most everyday situations, but it does not imply an understanding of internally represented mental states. A mental state understanding of attention may only develop when children start to understand other representational mental states like belief and knowledge at the age of 4 years. This may also provide a motive to attend to eye direction, which is a good indicator of what someone is attending to *right now* but a poor indicator of what they are *engaged* or involved with.

An interesting additional question is how we determine what someone is looking at. One possibility is that this skill is based on a more explicit version of the knowledge embedded in gaze following. That is, infants already have good gaze-localization skills, but initially this knowledge can only be used to orient the child's own attention towards the object of gaze; it is not available to the rest of the cognitive system for explicit judgements. Perhaps development consists of this knowledge becoming more generally available. Another possibility is that gaze judgement is based on a completely new skill.

One way of getting at this issue would be to examine the development of gaze-judgement accuracy. If it is based on a new skill, initially children may not be very good at it, getting slowly better. If it is based on a translation of an old skill, however, children should rapidly be able to use their existing competence in a new way. In an unpublished study, Doherty et al. (2007) looked at how good 3- to 6-year-old children were at judging smaller gaze deviations. We knew that 3-year-olds could say whether the experimenter was looking to the left or to the right, but would they be able to say which of three targets to the left she was looking at? Targets were small toy animals at 15°, 30° and 45° from the midline (or 10°, 20° and 30°). The experimenter looked at one of the targets and asked the child which. Three-year-olds were at chance when the experimenter only moved her eyes. Even when she moved her head in the same direction, they were only better than chance at the 15° trials, not the 10° trials. Children got steadily better with age at these tasks, but even 6-year-old children were not at the adult level (and adults were not perfect at the eye-direction tasks).

This apparent improvement of accuracy from chance at 3 years to near-adult levels a few years later suggests that gaze judgement is an entirely new skill that appears at 3 or 4 years old and slowly improves. This new skill may be prompted by a dawning mental state understanding of attention. [See Doherty (2006) for speculation about the nature of these two potential gaze detection systems.]

Chapter 8

Developmental interactions 1: Executive functioning and theory of mind

Introduction

E XECUTIVE FUNCTIONS ARE PROCESSES relating to self-control. This includes the control of actions, or control of thoughts and attention. Many theorists argue that executive functions play a critical role in the development of theory of mind. Self-control is necessary to decide on and achieve a goal, especially in the face of distractions. Children become increasingly able to think flexibly and to control their own behaviour at the same time that they become able to ascribe beliefs and other mental states to others. This is not a coincidence. However, the nature of the relationship is hotly contested. Having an insight into your own mental states plausibly is necessary for a certain level of self-control; theory of mind may be necessary for or enhance executive functioning. Alternatively, directing attention away from reality towards invisible, hypothetical mental states may require executive functioning; executive functions may be necessary for or enhance theory of mind. Both proposals are plausible; both may be true. This chapter discusses the theories in more detail, and the evidence that currently fails to properly decide between them.

To make things concrete, consider the children's game "Simon says". An adult gives children instructions, such as "put your hands on your head". The game has two rules: If the instruction is preceded by the words "Simon says", players have to follow the instructions as quickly as possible; if the instruction is not preceded by the words "Simon says", players must do nothing. This game illustrates several distinct executive abilities. First, children have to hold in mind the rules of the game, which requires some *working memory*, particularly when the game is new. They must also be able to switch behaviour according to which rule is relevant, i.e., *set shifting*. Typically the adult will give several "Simon says" instructions in a row, after which children will have greater difficulty *inhibiting* the tendency to do what was said regardless.

The three factors of inhibition, working memory and set shifting cover what are intuitively felt to be the important executive functions. They can be more formally defined as follows:

(1)   Inhibition of prepotent responses. This is the ability to deliberately inhibit powerful or automatic responses (prepotent = more powerful). A typical example of this is the Stroop task (Stroop, 1935). Participants are shown colour words such as "Red", "Green", and so on. Their task is to name the colour of the ink the words are written in, which is usually different to the word. The normal response to a word is to read it, and this response has to be inhibited. For adults this is difficult, and leads to longer reaction times than when the word and the colour of the ink are the same (see MacLeod, 1991, for a review). Since preschool children usually cannot read, a similar task has been developed in which they are told to say "night" to a picture of a sun, and "day" to a picture of a dark sky with stars and moon (Gerstadt, Hong & Diamond, 1994; note that this is not strictly analogous to the Stroop, because it does not involve switching dimensions, e.g., from naming the word to naming the colour. There is also no pre-existing link between the responses and the stimulus pictures; the task relies on the mismatch between the picture and the word).

(2)   Updating and monitoring of working memory representations. This involves temporarily holding in mind information relevant to the task at hand, and altering it as appropriate. A typical task measuring this is the backwards digit span task. The experimenter reads out a sequence of numbers, and the participant has to repeat it backwards. This requires both recalling the list and altering it mentally by reversing the sequence. With small children, the numbers can be replaced by nouns.

(3)   Shifting between tasks or mental sets. This involves producing different types of response to the same stimuli. A typical task involves sorting objects according to one dimension (e.g., colour) then switching sorting criterion (e.g., to shape), a well-known example being the Wisconsin Card Sort Task (Berg, 1948).

Most executive tasks tap one or more of these abilities, and many tap more than one to some extent (the "task impurity problem": it is very difficult to devise tasks that test only one of the three factors). Studies suggest that the three dimensions are related, but to some extent separable (Miyake, Friedman, Emerson, Witzki, Howerter & Wager, 2000).

Historically, research on executive function has been mainly neuropsychological. Damage to the frontal part of the brain is particularly common, both because we are more likely to smack this part of our head into something, and because the inside of the skull is unfortunately shaped such that any kind of blow can cause some frontal damage. The physicist Holbourn (1943) first demonstrated this by constructing models of brains out of jelly. Subjecting them to violent rotational jerking inside model skulls produced most damage to the lower part of the frontal lobes and to the forward part of the temporal lobes. Nowadays, of course, there are more sophisticated ways of investigating brain injury.

People with frontal damage typically show executive function difficulties. One classic test is the Wisconsin Card Sort Test, a test of set shifting and presumably inhibition. Participants have to sort a set of cards into separate piles according to a particular attribute. The cards differ in colour, and in the type and number of the shapes printed on them. Participants are not told which dimension is relevant, but each time they place a card in a pile they are told whether that is right or wrong. Patients with frontal lobe damage often have no difficulty inferring and using the first rule, for example that cards should be divided into piles according to colour. However, when the rule changes to another dimension (e.g., from colour to shape), patients continue to sort according to the old dimension. They do this despite corrective feedback from the experimenter. This *perseveration*, along with other executive difficulties, is so characteristic of frontal lobe damage that often researchers have treated frontal lobe tasks and executive function tasks as synonymous.

Young children also are known to show executive function deficits. The frontal lobes develop slowly throughout childhood (Stuss, 1992), and go through a growth spurt between the ages of 4 and 7 years (Thatcher, 1992). During this period there are marked improvements in executive function. For example, Jones, Rothbart and Posner (2003) gave 3-year-olds a simplified version of "Simon says" using two toy animals. Children had to do what Elephant said, but not do what Bear said. Children from 3 years 0 months to 3 years 2 months were very poor at this game. They happily did what either character said, and did not inhibit the action, or even seem to be aware of having made an error. Children from 3 years 3 months to 3 years 5 months successfully inhibited their actions on 76% of trials. They also reacted much more slowly if they had made an error on the preceding trial. Slightly older children performed almost perfectly. Failure to inhibit was correlated with the ratings given by children's caregivers for attentional shifting and inhibition accuracy ($r = .48$, $p = .005$). This suggests that the "Simon says" game was picking up on skills children use in normal life. Interestingly, the middle group tended to use physical strategies, such as sitting on their hands, to control impulsive responding. The older children presumably had no need; the younger children may have been unaware of the need to do so. This suggests that awareness of the need to inhibit actions may precede the ability to do so, which is a contested theme discussed below.

Theories

So, there is a rapid increase in executive function ability between the ages of about 3 and 4 years and a similar increase in performance on theory of mind tasks. There are several reasons why this may be more than a coincidence. In the last few years, investigating the link has become one of the most active areas of developmental research—and a particularly confusing one. Before looking at the data, it is useful to summarize theories that attempt to explain the relationship between them.

Theory of mind tasks have executive components

Children may fail the false belief task because the executive demands of the task are too high. They may nevertheless have the necessary conceptual understanding. Any cognitive task measures two factors: the conceptual competence that is being tested, and performance factors required to take the test. If the test is a valid one, children will have no trouble with the performance factors and will pass or fail the test depending on whether they possess the target ability. The false belief task measures understanding that behaviour is based on an agent's mental representation of the world. To perform the task children must also be able to follow a simple narrative and remember the key events, and use this information to make an inference. This requires some working memory. Working memory may also be needed to consider a second perspective on a particular situation. Switching between the child's own and another person's perspective on a situation may involve set shifting. Children may also have to inhibit their own representation of reality, which is likely to be more salient than their representation of the other's belief. Thus all three main categories of executive function may be involved in the false belief task, and to varying degrees in other theory of mind tasks.

In the 1990s, there were numerous claims that lowering one or more of the executive demands of the false belief task led to a dramatic improvement in performance, as discussed in Chapter 2. Claims that executive function deficits mask existing theory of mind have been termed "expression theories" (Moses, 2001), since they hold that children simply have difficulty expressing what they know. For example, Mitchell (1996) proposed the *reality masking* hypothesis: Young children have a bias to attend to current reality, and this bias is so strong that it makes attending to beliefs very difficult. Children nevertheless understand beliefs, so manipulations that make beliefs more salient should improve performance. Mitchell and Lacohée (1991) attempted to show this by adding a "posting" procedure to the Smarties task. When children first saw the Smarties tube, they were invited to post a picture of what they thought was inside into a toy postbox. When they discovered the real contents was a pencil, they were asked about their prior false belief. The belief still had a real counterpart in the form of the picture of Smarties. Even though this counterpart was invisible, children performed much better on the posting task than they did on the standard version. [This result is difficult to reproduce, however. See Mitchell (1996) for a discussion of replication attempts.]

Despite its appeal, this sort of account became difficult to hold after Wellman et al.'s (2001) meta-analysis of false belief research. If understanding of false belief was masked by executive difficulties, lowering executive demands should improve performance. Wellman et al. found that both increasing the salience of belief and using a task in which the target object is absent (thus decreasing its salience) improved performance. However, the improvement was modest, and was not more marked in younger children, as would be predicted if their theory of mind ability was masked by performance factors. Furthermore, another finding that appeared to support the Reality Masking hypothesis does not seem to replicate. Several studies suggested that children's ability to explain behaviour based on false belief was superior to their ability to predict it. As discussed in Chapter 2, these findings seem to be largely the result of methodological artefacts. Subsequent research that removed these artefacts, for example by applying suitable guessing baselines, suggests that explanation is about as difficult as prediction. Explanation is based on real actions, so does not require children to inhibit current reality. It should therefore pose much lesser executive demands. If explanation is as difficult as prediction, it is hard to argue that children simply have difficulty expressing their theory of mind understanding.

Executive functioning is necessary for the development of theory of mind skills

Developing theory of mind skills in the first place may require a certain level of executive functioning. There are two possible types of *emergence* theory of executive function. First, children may possess mental state concepts but lack the framework needed to properly employ them. In Harris's Simulation Theory (1992), for example, children must alter default settings: In order to simulate, children must temporarily alter their own representation of reality and of their own current mental states, to correspond with those presumed to be held by other people. This process sounds like it would make heavy executive demands: Temporarily overwriting default settings may require inhibitory abilities; holding both sets of default settings in mind may require working memory; switching between them may require set-shifting abilities.[1] Cognitive Complexity and Control (CCC) theory, discussed in detail below, is a more specialized version of this kind of theory.

The second type of emergence theory holds that executive function is necessary to develop mental state concepts. For example, Russell (1996) argues that the abilities to monitor one's own actions and act at will are necessary for proper self-awareness, which is a prerequisite for understanding mental states: "executive accounts are (or at least can be) the bedrock" (p. 262). Carlson and Moses (2001) take up this idea, suggesting that some capacity to distance oneself from current stimuli is required to reflect on representations of these stimuli. "Some degree of inhibitory capacity would thus seem to be necessary to form mental state concepts (and any other abstract concepts for that matter)" (Moses, 2005, p. 19).

Theory of mind is necessary for the development of executive function

Perner (1991) argues precisely the opposite: that metarepresentation is necessary for certain kinds of executive function. Simple actions and cognitive operations are carried out by mental entities known as schemas (Norman & Shallice, 1986). For example, in a card-sorting game a schema will be created to encode the action of putting a red card in the left pile. When a red card is presented, this schema becomes most active, and the action is carried out. Schemas inhibit each other so that typically, given environmental input and the contents of working memory, the most appropriate schema is activated. This kind of automatic inhibition is mastered by the end of infancy.

In some situations, the correct schema may not be selected automatically. For example, in a card-sorting game, say the rule changes to sorting on the basis of shape. A red square is presented, which activates both the new "square to the right box" schema and the "red card to the left box" schema. These two schemas inhibit each other, but the previously used schema is still highly activated. It therefore wins out over the novel schema and causes the participant to incorrectly put the red square in the left-hand box.

To stop this happening, the old schema must be inhibited by a higher-level system. Inhibition involves examining the contents of active schemas, and inhibiting those schemas whose contents are currently undesirable. This requires a sharp distinction between schemas (the things that must be inhibited) and their contents (the action sequences represented by the schema). It must also be understood that the relationship between a schema and its content is that the schema causes the action specified by the content. In other words, children have to:

(1)   Represent the relationship between a schema and its representational content, i.e., metarepresentation.
(2)   Understand that mental entities—schemas—cause action.

This is very similar to what is required for the false belief task. Children must represent the relationship between a belief and the situation it represents, i.e., metarepresentation. They must also understand that mental entities—beliefs—cause action. The two requirements are not identical: They differ in the types of mental entities involved. However, it is plausible that belief reasoning and the ability to inhibit schemas based on content both involve common developments in metarepresentation and the understanding of the causal nature of mental entities. They should therefore develop at around the same time, and correlate with each other.

Lang and Perner (2002) looked directly at children's understanding that their own mental states cause actions. In a cute procedure, they used the knee-jerk reflex, the involuntary leg kick that happens when part of the knee is tapped. This reflex was elicited in 3- to 4-year-old children, and they were asked whether they had meant to do that. Faced with the stark evidence that they had in fact just moved their leg, 3-year-olds happily assented that they had meant to. Older children, however, realized that it had been involuntary. This suggests that older children can monitor their own intentions. They judge the act to be unintentional because they were unaware of any relevant intention. Performance on this task was strongly related to false belief performance, much more so than two measures of executive function. Since the task itself does not make any obvious strong executive demands, it seems a fairly pure measure of self-monitoring.

It is possible to speculate that theory of mind evolved as a self-monitoring mechanism, allowing much greater self-control and therefore more complex behaviour. Such a mechanism could be readily applied to others' behaviour, because everyone's behaviour has similar causes. The key difference is that you can be aware of your own intentions by introspection, whereas the intentions of others have to be guessed at. (No one has yet argued this, however.)

Cognitive complexity and control

This theory is that the false belief task is difficult because it involves a particular complexity of conditional reasoning. It is framed in terms of the task designed to test it, the Dimensional Change Card Sort (DCCS) task. The DCCS is a highly simplified version of the Wisconsin Card Sort Task. Children are shown two target cards, for example a blue rabbit and a red car, as in Figure 8.1. The test cards to be sorted are blue cars and red rabbits. In the colour game, children have to sort the blue things to the blue card and the red things to the red card. Children typically happily put the blue cars to the blue rabbit and the red rabbits to the red car. After a few trials of this, the experimenter announces a new game, the shape game. This time all the cars go to the car card, and all the rabbits go to the rabbit card, so children have to sort in the opposite way to before. Three-year-old children find it difficult to switch, typically continuing to sort by the original criterion; most older children are able to switch between the rules and sort correctly.

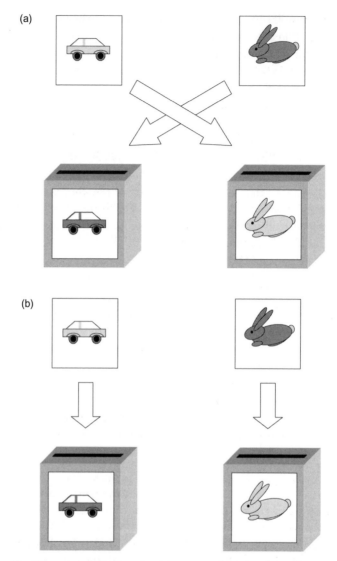

FIGURE 8.1 The Dimensional Change Card Sort procedure. (a) The colour game. Things are sorted to the card of the same colour. (b) The shape game. Things are sorted to the card of the same shape.

This apparent difficulty in shifting mental sets has been explained by the CCC theory (Zelazo & Frye, 1997). They conceive of the card-sort task as involving embedded if–then rules as follows:

If setting condition 1 THEN
    IF antecedent 1 THEN consequence 1
    IF antecedent 2 THEN consequence 2
If setting condition 2 THEN
    IF antecedent 1 THEN consequence 2
    IF antecedent 2 THEN consequence 1

Setting conditions are the particular games, the colour game or the shape game. Antecedents are the cards, blue cars and red rabbits; consequences are which target locations cards are sorted to, marked by the blue rabbit and red car. So in the colour game (setting condition 1), the blue cars (antecedent 1) go to the blue rabbit (consequence 1); whereas in the shape game (setting condition 2), the blue cars (antecedent 1) go to the red car (consequence 2).

So far so good. The theory is weaker on its analysis of the false belief task. The proposal is something like this:

If me (setting condition 1) THEN
    IF *looking for724;chocolate*   THEN *there* (condition 1)
    IF ... antecedent 2   THEN *here* (condition 2)
If Maxi (setting condition 2) THEN
    IF *looking for chocolate* (antecedent 1) THEN *here* (condition 2)
    IF ... antecedent 2   THEN *there* (condition 1)

There is no plausible antecedent 2 in this case. This is not particularly problematic, but it does pose the question whether a simpler structure would be sufficient. Perner and Lang (2000) suggest the following rule structure:

IF *I am looking for chocolate* (antecedent 1)   THEN *there* (consequence 1)
IF *Maxi is looking for chocolate* (antecedent 2) THEN *here* (consequence 2)

The problem can clearly be represented in more than one way. There is no principled reason to choose between the two proposals, except perhaps to choose the simplest adequate one. Perner and Lang (2000) also point out that the same analysis can be applied to developmentally much earlier reasoning tasks. Repacholi and Gopnik (1997) found that by about 18 months children understand that people can have different food preferences (see Chapter 4). This understanding can be represented thus:

If me (setting condition 1) THEN
    IF *wanting to eat* (antecedent 1)   THEN *choose crackers* (consequence 1)
    IF ... antecedent 2   THEN ... consequence 2
If other (setting condition 2) THEN
    IF *wanting to eat* (antecedent 1)   THEN *pick broccoli* (consequence 2)
    IF ... antecedent 2   THEN ... consequence 1

It is also not clear that the child needs to be able to navigate the whole rule structure in the DCCS task. The task is sequential: Children have to use two antecedent–consequence rules, then a short while later learn and use another two. There is typically no need to remember the previous rules. In fact, failing to inhibit the memory of previous rules may be the reason the task is difficult. However, although the way the theory is framed seems arbitrary, the predicted relationship between the false belief task and the DCCS task is strong (e.g., Frye, Zelazo & Palfai, 1995; Perner et al., 2002a). As a result, it has generated a considerable research effort, which is reviewed later in this chapter.

Evaluation of theories linking theory of mind and executive function

There is little doubt that executive functioning and theory of mind are related developmentally, possibly in a complex interdependent way. Perner's (1991) argument that theory of mind is necessary for executive inhibition seems theoretically sound; Carlson and Moses's (2001) argument is also compelling, that the ability to distance oneself from current experience is necessary to reflect on alternative perspectives. However, a clearer theoretical specification of how much ability, and of what sort, is necessary. The argument is most plausible for hypothesizing about others' mental states; introspection on one's own schema may not require distancing.

Evidence

Inhibition: The "Windows" task

The idea that theory of mind development may primarily involve the development of executive functioning was first suggested by Russell, Mauthner, Sharpe and Tidswell (1991). Their aim was to develop a test of deception: novel, so it could not be solved using learned strategies, but simple for children who understood mental states. They devised the "Windows" task; a potentially cruel procedure in which children had to point to one of two boxes in order to win a chocolate. The child had to tell an experimenter which box to look in. If the experimenter looked inside the box with the chocolate, she kept it; otherwise the child could have it. Each box has a small window so that the child, but not the person opposite, can see what is inside. To get the chocolate, children should point to the empty box.

On the first trial almost all the 3-year-olds pointed to the box with the chocolate inside; most 4-year-olds pointed to the empty box. The experiment did not stop at one trial: There were a total of 20 windows trials, and despite losing the chocolate on each trial, most 3-year-olds continued to point to the baited box for all 20 trials. No 4-year-old did this. Younger children's perseverative responses seem similar to those made by neuropsychological patients with frontal lobe damage. This very much looks like an executive function deficit.[2]

Russell, Jarrold and Potel (1994) suggest that the false belief and Windows tasks both require inhibition of reference to a salient object. The false belief task is difficult because reality is more salient than knowledge of "mental reality". To pass it requires suppression of knowledge of the true state of affairs. Specifically, "executive development makes possible a level of mentalizing in 4-year-olds which was not possible earlier" (p. 312): A certain degree of mental self-control is required to reflect upon mental states.

However, performance on the Windows task was only weakly related to a false belief task. Sixty-two percent of children passed a transfer task in which a deceptive motive was given for moving the object. The Windows task was harder, with 48% and 34% passing under liberal and conservative criteria, respectively. The two tasks were only related if liberal criteria were used (although in this case the correlation was a healthy $r = .524$, $p < .001$), and neither age nor verbal mental age were statistically controlled for. Subsequent research with the Windows task has not included false belief tasks.

It may be that manipulation of others' beliefs is not the reason why the Windows task is difficult. The task only really requires children to influence the experimenter's behaviour, and the behaviour is entirely predictable: The experimenter always looks where the child tells him or her to. Russell, Jarrold and Potel (1994) examined this by removing the competitor altogether. A single experimenter and child sat side by side, both able to see through the window. The child could not deceive the experimenter, since they could both see the chocolate. Results showed that the task was just as hard as when the experimenter could not see which box contained the chocolate.

It seems clear that the Windows task is not a measure of deception. However, it remains unclear exactly what it is a measure of. The standard task may be difficult because it requires children to inhibit the "prepotent" response (i.e., more powerful response) of pointing to a desired object. Hala and Russell (2001) found that if children pointed with an artificial pointer rather than with their finger they were much less likely to perseverate, although they performed as badly on the first trial. Pointing emerges early and is used often, so may be difficult to inhibit compared to using a novel, artificial pointer (a cardboard hand). Hala and Russell also had a cooperative condition, in which the experimenter and the child shared the chocolates if the child managed to deceive another opponent. This also led to less perseveration. Hala and Russell argue that having the experimenter as an ally reduces children's natural unwillingness to deceive an adult (the second experimenter). However, another condition, in which the child instructed the experimenter where to point before the opponent had entered the room, was as hard as the standard task. Instead, the critical manipulation may be the sharing of the reward. The authors suggest that this encourages a third-person perspective on what the child has to do, causing a "distancing" between the goal and the means of achieving it. A less abstract possibility is that having an experimenter as ally gives children a greater sense of control over the game, allowing them to try novel strategies.

Sense of control may also explain Russell, Hala and Hill's (2003) findings with an automated version of the task. The boxes were replaced by a machine with two transparent cylinders, one of which contained chocolate. There were trapdoors beneath each cylinder, and two buttons. Pressing the button next to one cylinder caused the trapdoor beneath the other to open, so to get the chocolate children had to press the opposite button. This version of the task removes the elements of deception and of social apprehension. It was relatively easy; most 3-year-olds were correct even on the first trial. A version in which children had to instruct an opponent by pointing to which button to press was only slightly harder. Superficially, the inhibitory demands of the automated version seem to be the same as the standard version. These results are hard to explain in the context of previous Windows task studies. Russell et al. (2003) speculate that pressing a button does not require executive inhibition, and that pointing to a button requires less inhibition than pointing to a salient state of affairs.

Simpson, Riggs and Simon (2004) suggest that the standard Windows task is difficult simply because children have to infer the rule, "point to the empty box". They simply told children that if they pointed to the empty box, they would get the chocolate. The child and experimenter sat together, opposite the opponent who (oddly) was a toy dog. When children were told the rule, the task seemed easy, with a mean success rate of 94%, compared to 58% over 16 trials of the standard Windows task. It may be that the standard Windows task does not measure inhibition or perseveration, but difficulties in inferring a nonobvious rule.[3]

In summary, Russell et al.'s (1991) Windows task introduced the idea that executive inhibition may be critical to the development of theory of mind. However, subsequent research with the task has not convincingly established the reason why children find it difficult.

General relationships between inhibitory control and theory of mind

One way to get round the task impurity problem is to not worry too much about what any one task measures. Several studies have given children batteries of tests thought to measure particular aspects of executive function. Carlson and Moses (2001), for example, gave 3- and 4-year-old children several tasks presumed to measure inhibitory control. They had two types of task. Conflict tasks involved a prepotent response that had to be inhibited. These included the day/night Stroop, the card-sort task and the simplified version of "Simon says", all mentioned above.

The other kind of task was delay tasks, in which children had to withhold a response for a given period. For example, they had to pull back a plunger on a pinball toy and only release it when the experimenter said "Go!" The experimenter waited varying times, up to 25 seconds. Another delay task involved building a tower, with the child and the experimenter supposed to take turns placing blocks. Performance on this battery was compared with performance on a set of theory of mind tasks, including transfer and contents false belief, appearance–reality and a deceptive pointing game.

The findings were that overall the theory of mind and inhibitory control batteries were strongly correlated ($r = .66$, $p < .001$) and remained so when age, gender and verbal ability were partialled out ($r = .41$, $p < .001$). Many of the correlations between individual tasks also remained significant. The three standard theory of mind tasks were strongly intercorrelated, even after age, gender, verbal ability and performance on the executive function battery were partialled out. This suggests that there is more to theory of mind development than development of executive function. Nevertheless the two types of ability are developing in the same period and are related.

From a cross-sectional finding like this, it is difficult to know what the causal relationships between the two abilities are. There are longitudinal studies which address the issue, but in my opinion they are inconclusive. Hughes (1998) examined the relationship between a battery of executive function tasks and a battery of false belief tasks with children of mean age 3 years 11 months, and the same children 13 months later. In contrast to Carlson and Moses's (2001) findings, the theory of mind tasks in this study were not strongly related to the executive function tasks. Roughly speaking, once age and verbal ability were statistically controlled for, early theory of mind did not correlate with anything very much: not later theory of mind, nor with most of the early and later executive function measures.

By contrast, early executive function significantly predicted later theory of mind. This result has been used to argue that executive function abilities pre-date theory of mind, since early executive performance predicts later theory of mind performance, but the reverse is not true. However, only one of the executive tasks showed a significant independent relationship with later theory of mind performance. This was Hughes and Russell's (1993) detour-reaching box task, presumed to be a test of inhibition. Children had to inhibit the natural tendency to reach directly for a marble, and instead flick a switch first, then reach. An arrangement with an infrared beam and a photocell meant that an immediate reach would cause the marble to drop down a trapdoor before it could be grasped. Furthermore, a second-order theory of mind task was added to the later theory of mind battery: Perner and Wimmer's (1985) ice-cream-van story (the 5-year-old participants were probably at ceiling on the first-order measures). This task probably has significant executive demands over and above its theory of mind demands: Children have to follow a complex story and coordinate the perspectives of two other people. These executive demands may account for the correlation with the earlier executive battery (and the lack of correlation with the earlier theory of mind battery). At best, the evidence for a predictive relationship between executive functioning and later theory of mind is tenuous.

Carlson, Mandell and Williams (2004) further explored longitudinal relations with younger children. They constructed batteries of plausible theory of mind and executive function tests that could be taken by 24- and 39-month-old children. The executive function batteries comprised mostly conflict and delay tasks. These batteries were strongly related across the time periods ($r = .51$, $p < .001$). The early theory of mind battery included tests of whether children can recognize others' intentions, Repacholi and Gopnik's (1997) discrepant desires task, a Level 1 visual perspective task and one of Harris and Kavanaugh's (1993) pretence comprehension tasks. The later theory of mind tasks included false belief, appearance–reality, Level 1 and Level 2 visual perspective tasks and a pretend–reality task (Frye et al., 1995). Since the batteries comprise different tasks it is hard to be sure they measure the same abilities at different time points. As it turned out, there were only weak relationships within each theory of mind battery, and no overall relationship between them.

As was the case with Hughes's (1998) study, early executive performance predicted later theory of mind, but early theory of mind did not predict later executive performance. However, again, the predictive relationship rested on a single nonstandard task. Early executive function performance did not predict later performance on false belief, appearance–reality or visual perspective-taking tasks. This counts against the hypothesis that executive inhibition is required for theory of mind development. In fact, early executive function performance only predicted performance on a pretend–reality task (Zelazo et al., 1995). In this task the child and experimenter pretended, for example, that a piece of string was a snake. Children had to say what the object really was and what they were pretending it was. What this task measures is unclear. Even 2-year-olds can distinguish between pretend and real states of affairs. However, the requirement to switch repeatedly between pretence and reality may be a form of set shifting, requiring inhibition of both pretend and real situations. Thus the relationship with the early executive battery may be because of the executive components of this task.

In summary, both of these studies have prominently been used to claim that early executive functioning is causally responsible for later theory of mind development. However, in each study, performance on only one task from one battery correlated over time with the composite scores on the other battery. Furthermore, these correlations are plausible because some of the theory of mind tasks used make substantial extra executive demands. Carlson et al. (2004) in fact found that early executive function performance did *not* predict performance on any of their standard theory of mind tasks.

Although executive measures of inhibition clearly *are* related to theory of mind skills, the direction of the relationship is impossible to determine from studies to date. This may be because the relationship between the two is more complex than a case of one causally influencing the other. Interestingly, Carlson et al. (2004) also found that children's use of internal state language at 24 months was related to both early and later executive function performance, even after later theory of mind performance was partialled out. This suggests a role for early mental state talk in later executive functioning, and would be worth further investigation.

Working memory

Davis and Pratt (1995) suggested that children may perform poorly on false belief tasks because they cannot simultaneously represent all the premise information— the facts about what happened and where Maxi was at the time. This is a form of expression account, although the child's mental state understanding is not masked by trivial task factors. Instead, children simply do not have the memory capacity to employ their concepts of belief. Davis and Pratt measured preschool children's working memory capacity using a backward digit span task: The experimenter reads out a list of digits, and children have to repeat the list backwards (starting from lists 2 digits long). This is a test of working memory because the information has to be manipulated in the mind—the list must be reversed.

Davis and Pratt gave 3- to 5-year-old children the backwards digit span task along with two false belief tasks and a "false" photograph task. This task was included because it was assumed to have the same working memory demands as the false belief task. When asked to repeat a string of digits forwards, children were able to repeat on average lists up to 4 digits long. Their mean backwards digit span, on the other hand, was just over 1: Roughly half of children could reverse two numbers, and the other half could not (a "list" containing a single number cannot be reversed, obviously). Performances on the photograph and false belief tasks were both significantly associated with performance on the backwards digit span task ($r = .48$ and $r = .46$, respectively, $p < .01$); entering backwards digit performance into regression analyses explained small but significant amounts of variance on both the false belief and "false" photograph tasks. These tasks were not themselves associated.

Gordon and Olson (1998) performed a similar experiment. Instead of a backwards digit span, they had two tasks that required children to do two things at once. In one task, children had to tap their finger continuously while naming three objects. Younger children had problems remembering to keep tapping after naming an object. The other task required children to update information in working memory: They had to simultaneously count and name three objects, for example, "one is a penny, two is a key, three is a frog". These were compared with performance on a contents false belief task and an appearance–reality task. Preschool children performed about equally well on the theory of mind and working memory tasks, and all tasks were significantly correlated, even after age was partialled out. The counting and labelling task was harder than the finger-tapping task, and more closely associated with the false belief tasks. In fact it remained so if performance on the finger-tapping task was also partialled out. Children had difficulty updating the number while they named objects, saying instead "One is a penny, one is a key, one is a frog".

So, working memory tasks clearly correlate with false belief tasks. There are at least three possible reasons why this may be. First, the working memory tasks considered all require some element of inhibition. In the backwards digit span task, children have to inhibit the tendency to repeat the list verbatim. In the counting and labelling task, two normal activities—counting several objects, or naming them—have to be alternated, so the natural tendency to carry on counting or to carry on labelling must be inhibited. Since children also clearly have inhibition difficulties, this could account for poor performance on the working memory tasks.

Carlson, Moses and Breton (2002) compared performance on working memory and inhibition tasks. Conflict inhibition tasks, such as the simplified "Simon says", were strongly correlated with a working memory battery comprising the counting and labelling task, backwards digit and backwards word span tasks. This relationship held even when age and verbal and nonverbal IQ were partialled out. The two types of executive function task are clearly strongly related. This is consistent with the idea that the difficulty in both types of task involves the need to inhibit responses.

The second possibility is that a certain amount of working memory is required either to take false belief tasks, or to develop concepts of belief in the first place. Gordon and Olson (1998) favour such an emergence account: "Our suggestion is that the concept of false belief itself is acquired when the child has the computational resources to represent, that is to hold in mind, a previously created representation even when a new representation is created by a new perceptual situation" (p. 81). These two representations can then, for example, be ascribed to different people. They can also be given different truth values. In other words, a certain minimum working memory capacity is required in order to metarepresent. Until children are capable of holding in mind two representations, they cannot even begin to frame concepts about the representational relationship.

This idea is interesting, but is not sketched in detail. One obvious difficulty with accounts relying on working memory limitations is with pretence. From 18 months onwards children are capable of holding in mind the real situation and the pretend version of the same situation. Their ability to follow pretend transformations (e.g., Harris & Kavanaugh, 1993) show that they are able to manipulate the information held in memory. That suggests they have the necessary working memory capacity for false belief understanding. Furthermore, the false photograph task appears to mimic the memory demands of the false belief task, yet is considerably easier—so long as the test question makes clear whether it is the real situation or the situation in the photograph that is being asked about. [Davis and Pratt's (1995) study was carried out before this finding was published. See Chapter 5.] Any working memory account would have to explain why the false belief task makes more working memory demands than tasks with apparently similar loads.

A final possibility is worth considering. In order to manipulate information represented in working memory, it must help to realize that the information is mentally represented. This is particularly true for novel tasks, such as those used in the above experiments. Some behaviours that require the manipulation of your own mental representations, like pretence, are heavily scaffolded by adults and practised over an extended period. This allows children to come up with a way of conceiving of pretence that does not require them to understand that the pretend scenario is mentally represented (see Chapter 6). With the backwards digit span task, however, children only have a few minutes to become familiar with the procedure, so no alternative route is possible. In this task, information is not simply recalled, but rearranged mentally. There is no tangible counterpart to support this rearrangement. Working memory tasks, because they rely on the manipulation of mentally represented information, may require children to understand that information can be mentally represented. The link with theory of mind might therefore be relatively direct.

Set shifting

This section concerns the DCCS task. There have been frequent demonstrations of a relationship between false belief tasks and the DCCS, and these usually remain once age and verbal ability have been partialled out (e.g., Frye et al., 1995, Experiment 2; Kloo & Perner, 2003, Experiment 1; Muller, Zelazo & Imrisek, 2005; Perner et al., 2002a, Experiment 1), although this is not always the case (e.g., Carlson & Moses, 2001; Perner et al., 2002a, Experiment 2, only the explanation task remained correlated). The debate over the task concerns why it is difficult.

There have been at least four different accounts put forward to explain this: (1) as discussed above, Zelazo and Frye (1997) argue that the complexity of the task's underlying structure is the source of difficulty; (2) the task may be difficult because children are unable to inhibit previously appropriate action schemas; (3) alternatively, children may be unable to inhibit previously appropriate attentional biases; and (4) finally, the task may be difficult because it requires one stimulus to be described in different ways. The evidence presently favours the last two options: executive inhibition of attention, or an inability to understand that one thing can be described in two different ways.

(1) Cognitive Complexity and Control

Possible theoretical objections to this approach were noted above. There are also empirical difficulties. Several studies have shown that the task can be made considerably easier by alterations that leave the embedded rule structure exactly the same. For example, Perner and Lang (2002) removed the target cards. Usually the two sorting locations are marked by cards that have the same dimensions as the test cards, but crossed. If the test cards are red rabbits and blue cars, the target cards will be blue rabbits and red cars. To CCC theory, this feature of the task is incidental; removing the cards should not alter the overall pattern of results. Perner and Lang asked children to sort according to the preference of two puppets: Donald likes red things, Mickey likes black things. Later, Donald likes snakes, Mickey likes cats. Children had no difficulty with this task, either with remembering the rule in the preswitch phase, or in implementing the new rule in the postswitch phase (see also Towse, Redbond, Houston-Price & Cook, 2000). This is difficult for CCC theory to explain, since the IF–IF–THEN rule structure is the same: IF the colour game, then IF a red thing, THEN put it over by Donald—and similarly for Mickey, and for the shape game.

Perner and Lang also found that children were good at a *reversal shift* card-sorting game: Instead of the criterion changing to the other dimension (e.g., from colour to shape), it changed within the same dimension (e.g., from "red things here" to "red things over there"). Children found this easy, even though this game can also be described in the embedded rule structure suggested by CCC theory. This finding has been replicated by Kloo and Perner (2003) and Brooks, Hanauer, Padowska and Rosman (2003). [Brooks et al. found that the game could be made considerably more difficult simply by varying the colour of the cards, even though colour was never mentioned, and even when the target and test cards were different colours—green or yellow for target, red or blue for test. This finding is difficult to account for, and has largely been ignored. In fact, it may not be reliable. Recently Kloo, Dabernig and Perner (2007) attempted to replicate it, but found that varying the colour in a reversal shift task did not make the task harder.]

(2) Inhibition of inappropriate action schemas

The above findings are also bad news for the second theory—that children are unable to inhibit previously appropriate action schemas that now cause children to respond in the wrong fashion (e.g., Perner, Stummer & Lang, 1999). According to this theory, children form an action schema in the preswitch phase that must be inhibited when the rule changes. However, this should also be the case in tasks without target cards, and for tasks involving only reversal shifts, yet these are not difficult.

One striking piece of evidence favouring this theory had been the fact that children can report what the rules are, yet do not follow them in their sorting behaviour (Zelazo, Frye & Rapus, 1996). This appeared to be a dissociation between knowledge and action: Children know what the rule is, but it does not guide their behaviour. Plausibly what guides behaviour instead is an outdated action schema. However, Munakata and Yerys (2001) point out that when asked to sort a card, children are faced with conflicting cues of colour and shape. When asked to report the rule, however, children are asked (e.g.) "Where do trucks go in the shape game?" This is not the same as having to decide where to put a *red* truck. When sorting, the previously used dimension of colour conflicts with the currently relevant dimension of shape. By contrast, the explicit question makes no reference to the conflicting dimension. The dissociation may therefore be because the source of conflict is omitted from the explicit question. Munakata and Yerys altered the questions to include both dimensions, for example, "Where do the red trucks go in the shape game?" When the questions were phrased this way, children performed as poorly as they did in the postswitch sorting. There was no longer an apparent dissociation between knowledge and action.

(3) Inhibitory control of attention

Other researchers have suggested that inhibition difficulties may exist at the level of attention, not at the level of action schemas. For example, Kirkham, Cruess and Diamond (2003) suggest that children suffer from "attentional inertia". In the preswitch phase, they think of objects in terms of their colour (for example). Having adopted this mindset, they find it difficult to switch to thinking of them in terms of another dimension—their shape. To do this requires inhibitory control of attention. This theory fits the evidence discussed so far quite well. Kirkham et al. further tested their theory by asking children to label cards according to the currently relevant dimension just before sorting each card. This is usually done by the experimenter: If the colour game is being played in the postswitch phase, the experimenter will announce, "Here's a blue one. Where does it go?" Instead, Kirkham et al. asked the child, "What colour is this one?" This minor change in procedure directed attention towards the relevant dimension, and was sufficient to improve 3-year-olds' performance from 42% correct in the standard game to 78% in this label condition. In another condition, cards were sorted face up into trays and left there. This made it much harder to sort correctly in the postswitch phase. This could be because it increases the salience of the previously relevant dimension, thus increasing the inhibitory requirements.

(4) Understanding redescription

Perner and Lang (2002) and Kloo and Perner (2003) suggest a conceptual basis for "attentional inertia". This is based on the observation that the switch in rules involves redescribing objects: "Children's inability to understand redescription, we suggest, is the common denominator underlying children's difficulty with the standard DCCS task and their failure to understand false belief" (Kloo & Perner, 2003, p. 1835). Children certainly have problems understanding that objects can be redescribed. They have a bias against referring to one object with more than one word, the Mutual Exclusivity bias (Dockrell & Campbell, 1986; Markman & Wachtel, 1988).[4] The ability to acknowledge that objects can be referred to by different names develops about the same time as children pass the false belief task (Doherty & Perner, 1998; Perner et al., 2002b; see Chapter 5). Kloo and Perner extend this analysis to the DCCS.

To test this theory, Kloo and Perner (2005) used cards on which the dimensions were separated: Instead of a blue banana, a card would have an uncoloured drawing of a banana next to a blue circle. This relatively minor change improved performance considerably. If the dimensions were separated only on the target cards, not on the test cards, there was little difference. However, if the dimensions were separated on the test cards (the things requiring redescription), then performance rose from about 50% correct to more than 80%. Performance was better still if the target cards also had separated dimensions. In subsequent experiments, the dimensions were completely separated by using cut outs of the animal shapes and cut outs of the coloured circles. These were presented on a paper plate; children had to select the appropriate item from the pair and put that into one of the sorting boxes. This task was easy, with even young 3-year-olds correctly sorting 80% of the time, compared to less than 20% of the time on the standard task.

These results strongly support the redescription theory. They also support the attentional inertia theory: Separating the dimensions should make it easier to disengage attention from the no longer relevant dimension. Both theories can explain the evidence considered so far. There is more at stake here than the DCCS, of course: If Kirkham et al. (2003) are correct, then children's difficulties with false belief, alternative naming and other metarepresentational tasks may be explained by their immature executive functioning.

Diamond and Kirkham (2005) attempted to resolve the issue by looking at adult performance on a computerized version of the DCCS. Apart from the mode of response, the game was the same as for children: The dimension to sort by was displayed at the bottom of the screen. To either side of it were the two target stimuli, a red truck and a blue star. Test stimuli appeared in the centre of the screen (red stars or blue trucks) and participants had to press buttons below the target stimuli according to which dimension was relevant. For example, if the dimension was colour and the test stimulus was a red star, participants had to press the key below the red truck. The dimension changed after the first 10 trials.

Naturally, the adults involved made few errors. The measure of interest was reaction time. When the dimension changed, the reaction time suddenly increased. Curiously, when it reverted to the original dimension 10 trials later, the reaction time decreased to almost its original level. Thus there was a reaction time cost to switching, and participants showed a bias to sort faster by whichever dimension they had sorted by first. Diamond and Kirkham (2005) argue that this demonstrates that adults have the same inhibitory problems as children, but to a lesser degree. Since adults certainly have the conceptual competence required to redescribe the stimuli, this cannot be the difficulty for children.

This argument does not preclude the possibility that children have both inhibitory and conceptual problems with the task. After the necessary conceptual development, additional inhibitory problems might persist into adulthood. It also assumes that the inhibitory difficulties faced by children and adults are the same. Recently Kloo, Aichorn and Perner (2007) have examined this. They also looked at adult reaction times, but this time the dimensions were separated on screen. In children, this reduces the inhibitory demands—children do not have to inhibit the way they initially think about an object; they simply have to switch from one object (e.g., a shape) to another (e.g., a coloured circle). If adults and children have the same inhibitory abilities, simply to a different degree, then adults should show little difficulty on a computerized version of the separated dimensions card-sort task.

The procedure matched that of Diamond and Kirkham (2005), except that the test stimuli consisted of a colourless line drawing next to a coloured circle—for example, a colourless cup and a blue circle rather than a blue cup. Again, after the first 10 trials, the criterion changed. The reaction time cost of switching was significantly *larger* in the separated dimensions task than in the standard DCCS: Separating the dimensions hinders adults in the task, whereas it helps children. This suggests that adults' difficulties with the DCCS are not the same as children's.

Summary

The relationship between executive functioning and theory of mind is a hot topic, and with good reason. There are two best candidate theories for why executive function and theory of mind are related: Executive functions require understanding of one's own mental processes and theory of mind requires inhibitory ability. Both have been suggested since at least 1991 (Perner, 1991; Russell et al., 1991), and the present evidence is not strong enough to dismiss either.

"Expression" accounts of executive function are no longer plausible, in view of the data. These theories hold that children possess a theory of mind, but cannot express what they know (at least in psychological tests) because of poor executive function. These accounts predict that measures to decrease the executive demands of theory of mind tests should improve performance dramatically. Wellman et al.'s (2001) meta-analysis, discussed in Chapter 2, shows that only moderate improvement is possible, and not selectively of younger children. The idea that younger children have a functioning theory of mind that psychologists have largely been unable to uncover is almost certainly wrong.

Emergence accounts (e.g., Moses, 2001) are much more promising. These theories hold that a theory of mind is initially absent, and requires a certain level of executive functioning to develop. Emergence accounts are also possible in which mental state concepts are innately specified; development could involve working out how to use them effectively. Such accounts are difficult to evaluate at present because no detailed one has been suggested. Diamond and Kirkham's account is an expression account: Abilities are expressed as soon as there is sufficient inhibitory ability to do so. This works well for the DCCS: Small alterations to the procedure such as removing the target cards produce large improvements in task performance. No similar manipulation reliably improves performance on false belief tasks. In my opinion, however, the evidence in general favours conceptual change. Children pass a whole range of tasks at the same time: false belief (prediction and explanation, for self and for others), appearance–reality, alternative naming, DCCS, knee-jerk reflex attribution, and the working memory and inhibition tasks discussed above. It is very unlikely that these tasks all make very closely matched demands on inhibitory abilities. However, there is no reason why conceptual change should not be explained in terms of underlying executive development, in the form of an emergence account. It could also simply be explained in terms of conceptual change.

The other candidate theory for the executive function–theory of mind relationship is that of Perner and colleagues. This puts the emphasis on conceptual change driving developments in executive function. The logic of the theory seems basically sound: In order to inhibit inappropriate actions or attention, you must be aware of your tendency to perform such actions or to attend inappropriately. Opponents of the theory would have to explain how effective action and attention is possible without the ability to reflect on one's own mental states. On the other hand, being aware of one's inappropriate tendencies does not automatically mean they can be controlled. For this, some measure of inhibitory ability is required. It therefore seems likely that development involves a complex interplay of conceptual change and executive function.

Chapter 9

Developmental interactions 2: Language and theory of mind

Introduction

THEORY OF MIND AND language are arguably the two main abilities that distinguish humans from other species. It would be strange if they were not intimately related. Apes have neither the ability to learn language nor appreciable theory of mind, yet we may have separated from chimpanzees only 4 million years ago (Hobolth, Christensen, Mailund & Schierup, 2007). This is very recent in evolutionary time. Humans and chimpanzees are extremely closely related. The difference between human and chimpanzee genomes is little more than 1% (F. C. Chen & Li, 2001). As a result, it seems highly unlikely that humans have evolved two fundamental independent changes in mind—theory of mind and language. Furthermore, theory of mind is typically expressed verbally, and effective language use relies on monitoring the probable mental states of the listener, and making inferences about the mental states of the speaker. It may make little sense to consider them as separate abilities. How they are related developmentally remains controversial. Do children need language to represent and learn about mental states? Does theory of mind allow children to learn and use language? The cause–effect relationship between the two is potentially very complex.

151

Language is conventionally subdivided into pragmatics, semantics and syntax. Pragmatics relates to the appropriate use of language. For example, if I say "the pub will be open by now", it is probably not just to inform you about the opening hours of our local. If you then look out into the Scottish drizzle and say "nice day for it", you might be being sarcastic. Pragmatics involves going beyond literal meaning to work out what speakers really mean by what they say, and what listeners are likely to infer by what speakers say. This requires keeping track of everyone's mental states: I know that you already know when the pub opens, but I want to plant the idea of going for a drink. You know that I can see it is raining; you want to express an opinion about it, possibly in relation to the proposed pub trip. Pragmatics *is* theory of mind, applied to language.

How useful would language be without a theory of mind? Some of our communication has the aim of directly changing another person's behaviour: "stop", or "give me that", for example. This does not seem to need a theory of mind. However, most of our communication involves exchanging information, mainly to change each other's mental states. Without a theory of mind, there would be little point to most conversation. It is hard to see how a language of any complexity could evolve or develop without understanding of others' mental states. It seems likely that a population of people who had no pragmatic understanding would have little use for language, or at least would largely say things that were not useful to others. This may be illustrated by the case of autism, which is characterized by impaired theory of mind. Many people with autism do not develop language; those who do tend to have characteristically odd speech. Their speech may be too loud, too quiet, or too fast, repetitive, and of no clear relevance: Generally it fails to meet listeners' informational needs. People with autism also often do not recognize the intentions behind speech, responding to indirect requests, such as "Can you pass the salt?" by simply answering the question at face value, "Yes", without passing the salt. See Chapter 10 for discussion.

Semantics concerns word meanings. Its most direct relevance to theory of mind concerns the meanings of mental state terms. Having labels for mental states may help children focus their attention on them, and help distinguish between related mental states. The behaviours produced by pretending and being mistaken, for example, may look much the same to a 3-year-old—action that does not seem to make sense in terms of the current situation. Hearing *pretend* and *think* referred to by distinct words may alert children to the fact that nonsensical behaviour falls into two distinct categories, and helps them identify the characteristic differences. Furthermore, children hear the same words applied to their own mental states and those of others. This may help children to compare their own subjective experience of thoughts and feelings with other people's behaviour. The idea that learning mental state words helps children learn mental state concepts is empirically plausible because children start to use mental state terms appropriately around the same time they pass theory of mind tasks (e.g., Moore, Pure & Furrow, 1990). However, it is also plausible that children acquire the concepts first, and only then learn to use associated words appropriately. Which causes which is difficult to determine.

Semantic ability may affect theory of mind development beyond the learning of mental state terms. Children's vocabulary development consistently relates to their theory of mind understanding. It is common to use a test of vocabulary in theory of mind experiments to control for the effects of verbal mental age. Often some ability is associated with theory of mind ability: metalinguistic awareness, or executive functioning, for example. The association may simply be because children with higher mental age perform better at most tasks. With a measure of mental age, however, the shared effects of mental age can be extracted statistically. If the association remains, it may indicate a more specific relationship between the two abilities. The British Picture Vocabulary Scale (BPVS) is the most popular test of verbal mental age in Britain, a version of the Peabody Picture Vocabulary Scale used in the United States, similar to the Picture Vocabulary Test used in Japan. Happé (1995) found a strong relationship between BPVS score and performance on false belief tasks in both normal children and children with autism. The normal children passed the tasks when their verbal mental age was around 4 years; children with autism did not do so until their verbal mental age was about 9 years. As well as being an indicator of general intelligence, then, vocabulary development may have a more specific contribution to the development of theory of mind.

Finally, syntax is the part of grammar that concerns language structure. Complex grammatical ability might be necessary to represent states that differ from current reality. In particular, mental state expressions usually have a complex form, with propositions embedded within sentences. Mastering this form may be necessary to mentally represent other people's mental states. Another possibility is that the ability to keep track of word order is related to the ability to keep track of mental states in relation to reality. Syntactic development may reflect or promote this ability.

Children's use of mental state terms

An obvious area of interest is the age at which children begin to use mental state terms. Children's ability to use words like "know" and "think" appropriately could be the first indication of some grasp of these concepts. One of the earliest uses of the phrase "theory of mind" in the developmental literature was by Inge Bretherton and Marjorie Beeghly (1982). They looked at references to internal states by 2-year-old children. This was mainly based on mothers' reports of which words their 28-month-old children used. Words for physiological states such as "hungry", "thirsty" and "tired" were used by most children, as were perceptual words like "see", "look" and "hot/cold". They also frequently used emotional terms ("happy", "sad", "scared"). Children tended to use internal state terms more often of themselves, except for terms implying moral judgement; words like "bad", "naughty" and "supposed to" were much more likely to be used of other people. Of particular interest were references to the core elements of a theory of mind: desire and belief. The 2-year-old children frequently used desire terms (probably because they are useful for getting things you want). However, references to cognitive states like belief were rare, and significantly less frequent than to other internal states. So, whereas almost all children said that they wanted things, only a third of children made comments about their own or another person's thoughts.

Although cognitive terms were not used frequently, they were still used by some. Does this indicate a theory of mind? That depends on what children meant when they used these words. Mental state terms are used in a variety of ways, and frequently do not make genuine references to mental states. For example, "Do you know what?" clearly uses the mental state term "know", but usually functions simply to get someone's attention. In Bretherton and Beeghly's study, two thirds of children reportedly used the word "know", but it was typically within the phrase "I don't know". This is a useful formula for avoiding a topic, not offering an opinion or filling a pregnant pause when nothing else comes to mind. In these cases it does not need to be interpreted as a comment on a mental state. Similarly, a third of children used "think". As well as referring to mental states, "think" can be used to express a possibility, a disagreement or uncertainty. The example the authors reported, "I think Mommy is beautiful", could be interpreted in any of these senses.

To draw firm conclusions from children's use of mental state terms, knowing the context that words were used in is essential. Bretherton and Beeghly (1982) relied largely on mothers' judgement of whether or not their child used a given word, so do not have details of specific uses. More recently, Wellman and Bartsch (1994) examined utterances from the speech of 10 children aged 2 to 5 years. The utterances are from the CHILDES database, a collection of transcripts of child speech (MacWhinney & Snow, 1985, 1990). Wellman and Bartsch looked for uses of belief-related terms such as *think, know, expect, wonder, believe* and *dream*, and desire-related terms such as *want, wish, hope, afraid (that)* and *care (that)*. Using the context in which these terms were used, they classified them as genuine references to mental states, or uses that could serve some other function.

When context is taken into account it is clear that genuine references to desire are already in the speech of children at the end of infancy. Genuine references to belief, however, only begin to appear as children turn 3 years. For example, take the following exchange with a child aged 3 years and 3 months:

Abe: I didn't get you a surprise.
Adult: You didn't. I'm sad.
Abe: No, don't be sad. I thought I would, 'cept I didn't see one for you.

Here, the isolated phrase "I thought I would" could be used as a politeness marker or as a request (for example, "I thought I'd take a biscuit" as an indirect request for a biscuit). However, the context suggests that Abe really is talking about a plan he had had.

Genuine references to belief rise steadily until children are about 5 years old. Although the samples end around this age, the percentage of genuinely psychological references to belief seems to have stabilized at about 25% (and we do not know the proportion of adult uses of belief terms that are genuine). Similar age trends occurred with statements in which children contrasted beliefs or desires with reality, or with other beliefs or desires. These contrastive uses of mental state terms included phrases like "I thoughted it was busted", or when told not to push a button, "I want to push on this one". Here, children seem to be making a clear distinction between mental states and reality. For beliefs, this type of contrastive statement also appears at the age of about 3 years and rises very rapidly during the next year. Contrastive desire statements, however, are again already present at the end of infancy.

Children's use of mental state terms in natural conversations mirrors findings from experimental studies of their understanding of mental state concepts. Children understand and refer to desires, even contrastively, from a very young age. Children only begin to make genuine reference to beliefs and similar mental states from the age of 3 years, roughly the age from which children start to pass the false belief task. The four children who provided the most data for Wellman and Bartsch's analysis all produced some belief references by the age of 3½ years. They might therefore be a little precocious, but are not beyond the normal range. Furthermore, it is not hard to think of reasons why the children of linguists and psycholinguists should have precocious conversational skills. It is also worth recalling, however, that even many 2-year-olds use mental state terms like "know" and "think": Younger children know the appropriate words, but nevertheless use them in very limited ways.

The effect of language on theory of mind development

Mental state distinctions in different languages

Is it necessary to learn mental state verbs in order to think explicitly about mental states? This question cannot be directly answered at present, but some cross-linguistic data are relevant. Languages differ in the extent to which they make mental state distinctions explicit. Perner (1991) discusses work by Aksu-Koç (1988) on Turkish evidential verb markers. When discussing a past event in Turkish, the verb is given a different ending according to whether the speaker saw the event ("-di"), or were told about or inferred it ("-miş"). Thus the language explicitly encodes information about how knowledge came about. Does this enhance children's ability to understand sources of knowledge? Aksu-Koç showed children simple events, like the popping of a balloon, in which they either saw the popping event, or inferred it from the final, popped state of the balloon. When asked to relate the events, even 3-year-olds showed some ability to use the appropriate endings, "-di" when they saw the balloon pop, and "-miş" when they had to infer it. This tendency markedly improved just after 3 years 8 months. Only the 4-year-olds could judge whether a doll, reporting an event with "-di" or "-miş", had seen the event or was told about it.

These Turkish-speaking children seemed to demonstrate an understanding of the relationship between evidence and knowledge at roughly the same time as English-speaking children. Thus the fact that this relationship is explicitly marked in their language does not substantially enhance their understanding of it.

Lee, Olson and Torrance (1999) took advantage of a similar linguistic feature of Chinese to compare performance on theory of mind tasks. In Standard Chinese (a form of Mandarin), there is more than one verb commonly used in situations when English speakers would use "think". These differ in connotation. *Xiang* (想) roughly corresponds to "think". *Yiwei* (以為) is more similar to "assume" (literally: "take something/someone to be"), and thus when used about someone else can imply that his or her belief is or may be false. *Dang* (當) is only suitable for describing beliefs that are false. Lee et al. gave a transfer, a contents and an appearance–reality false belief task to Chinese preschoolers, varying which of the three words for (false) belief was used in the test questions. They found considerable differences in performance. In the contents and transfer tasks, for *yiwei* and *dang* about half of 3-year-olds passed, compared to about 20% or 30% for the more neutral *xiang*. By contrast, there were no significant differences in children's ability to report whether the protagonist knew the object had been moved, or predict where he would search first in the transfer task.

Thus, although younger Chinese preschoolers show poor understanding of false belief, this understanding may be enhanced by the connotations of the mental state verb used in the test question. However, this understanding seems very local, not extending to the search question used later in the same task. Shatz, Diesendruck, Martinez-Beck and Akar (2003) found similar results with speakers of Turkish and Puerto-Rican Spanish. Like Chinese, these languages have verbs for belief that explicitly mark the belief as false. They compared children speaking these languages with children speaking Brazilian Portuguese and English, neither of which explicitly mark the truth or falsity of beliefs. In this study there was also an advantage of explicit false belief questions in a false belief task. However, the advantage was small, and only evident in the 4-year-olds; 3-year-olds performed slightly worse on the explicit question. Again, there was no advantage on the search question. Furthermore, Shatz et al. found that Turkish and Puerto-Rican children were actually worse at explaining why the protagonist looked in the wrong place.

In a second experiment, Shatz et al. (2003) compared Puerto Rican Spanish speakers and English speakers, split according to socioeconomic status (based on parental education and occupation). Again they found the Spanish speakers had an advantage for the explicit false belief question, but this was again local, conferring no advantage for the subsequent search question. By contrast, socioeconomic status had a more general influence (this is discussed in more detail below).

Clearly, linguistic markers that indicate the truth or falsity of beliefs enhance children's performance on false belief tasks. However, this enhancement is only local: Children are only able to make the distinction when it is encoded in the question used to test them. In other words, when asked "where does Maxi falsely believe his chocolate to be", 3-year-old speakers of Turkish or Chinese are more likely to answer correctly than when the "falsely" is not specified. Oddly, despite better performance on the belief question, they do not do better on the search question, which is asked immediately afterwards. If the explicitly marked belief questions had alerted children to the falseness of the character's belief, why could they not correctly predict or explain his search?

One possible explanation is that children do not understand these belief terms in the way that adults do. When a language explicitly marks the falseness of a belief, the explicit false belief term will consistently be associated with actions that do not match the situation—as is also the case for pretence. Also like pretence, a similar parallel situation can often be imagined in which the action would make sense. In both cases, this is a situation where certain properties are altered; in the case of the false belief task, the properties simply match the situation that held a minute or two ago. Young speakers of these languages may therefore understand these words in a similar way to which they understand the word *pretend*. This would explain why they give the right answer to the false belief question, and the wrong answer when asked to predict or explain where someone will look, since the look question is a request to predict behaviour that aims to be effective in the real situation.

Generally, cross-linguistic research on belief terms has so far shown that different ways of referring to belief, knowledge or evidence do not substantially enhance general understanding of these concepts. Being able to refer to mental state terms at all may be necessary for theory of mind development, but specific features of these terms do not appear to affect the rate of development.

Syntax

Psycholinguistic data suggest that genuine belief references appear between the ages of 3 and 4 years. The appropriate use of mental state words also requires particular forms of syntax. It is possible that the development of mental state syntax is at least as important as the development of mental state vocabulary. One hypothesis is that in order to represent mental states children must develop the ability to use and understand the grammar of *sentential complementation*. Roughly speaking, this is a fancy way of referring to putting propositions after the word "that" in sentences like "Maxi thinks *that* the chocolate is in the cupboard" or "Sally says *that* the marble is in the box". Complements such as "the chocolate is in the cupboard" are propositions in their own right. Embedding them in a sentence produces a syntactically complex statement. This complexity is necessary to express propositional attitudes, and therefore to report mental states. de Villiers and de Villiers (2000) suggest that it may not be possible to represent propositional attitudes at all without this syntactical ability. If true, theory of mind development could not proceed before children master this aspect of syntax.

This is a plausible idea, but it is obviously difficult to prove that the syntactic ability develops first. Instead, the syntax may develop to express what is already understood. de Villiers and Pyers (2002) examined the issue longitudinally. They looked at children's ability to remember false complements, involving brief illustrated stories that relied on verbs of thinking or communication. For example, children were told, "He thought he found his ring, but it was really a bottle cap". They were asked "What did he think?" Any reference to ring, rather than bottle cap, was considered correct. Of interest was whether the ability to report the complement in this task preceded false belief ability.

An obvious concern is that this memory-for-complements task looks very much like a form of false belief task: Children are being asked to remember and report a description of a false belief. Any developmental similarities to other false belief tasks might be trivial as a result. de Villiers and de Villiers (2000) claim that this measure does not require the ability to attribute false beliefs. The sentences children hear already contain the attribution, and they need only remember what was said. This could make the task less demanding. Nevertheless, it is likely that children have to represent the character's belief in order to extract the appropriate object (or the whole complement) from the sentence. Furthermore, children may require an understanding of false belief in order to reconstruct the mistaken proposition in memory. Thus the suspicion remains that the memory-for-complements task is a covert false belief task.

Children's performance on the complements task was measured three times over the course of about a year, beginning when they were aged 3 years 4 months. Children also received a battery of false belief tasks. The battery was unusually verbal. It involved the unexpected contents task, which requires children to verbally express the contents of a false belief, and the false belief explanation task. The unexpected transfer task, the least verbal of the commonly used false belief tasks, was used. However, in this study children only passed it if they could also explain why the character would look in the empty location. Children's performance on this battery was slightly poorer than their memory for false complements. Early complements ability predicted later false belief performance; early false belief performance did not predict later memory-for-complements performance, at least once general language ability had been accounted for.

de Villiers and Pyers (2002) conclude that understanding of complementation develops before false belief understanding, and contributes to false belief understanding. However, a different conclusion is possible if the data are analysed using only children's answers to the unexpected transfer belief question—without requiring them to explain or justify their answers. In this case, false belief performance was consistently better than performance on the memory-for-complements task. Early performance on either task predicted later performance on the other, but early transfer performance was a stronger predictor of later complement performance. Basic false belief competence seems to precede or arise at the same time as memory for false complements.

There is no good reason to discount performance on the transfer task as a measure of false belief understanding (after all, most criticisms of the false belief task are that it underestimates competence). Instead, these results suggest that developing the syntax of complementation is not the main driving force behind false belief understanding. However, it may be useful in the more slowly developing ability to talk about beliefs. This is an important skill, and probably enhances more complex theory of mind development.

A further problem with the complementation theory is that children only seem to have problems when complements are linked to belief or communication verbs (e.g., think that, know that, say that). Children appear to have few problems using the grammar of complementation with mental state verbs that do not require understanding of misrepresentation. Custer (1996) read children sentences such as "Charlie is pretending that his puppy is outside" or "Charlie thinks that his puppy is outside", and asked them to pick which of two pictures was "in his head". This is similar to de Villiers and Pyers's task, the main difference being that pretend complements were also included. Children were significantly better at selecting the content of someone's pretence than someone's belief. The difference was not large, but nevertheless suggests that children's difficulty with belief tasks is more than just with the grammar.

Perner, Sprung, Zauner and Haider (2003) looked at complementation in German, in which it is possible to express some kinds of desires using "that" constructions (in German, "dass"). For example, children were asked about what one character wanted another to do. In German, the grammatically correct way of expressing this uses a complement: "What does the puppet want that the rabbit does?" ("Was will die Puppe, dass der Hase tut?").

In other conditions children were asked about what the puppet said or thought that the rabbit was doing, e.g., "What does the puppet think that the rabbit is doing?" ("Was glaubt die Puppe, dass der Hase tut?") In German, these sentences have identical syntax, differing only in the mental state term used. If poor understanding of the grammar of complementation was responsible for children's failure to remember complement statements, they should find both kinds of sentence equally difficult. In fact, children did well on the desire sentences, with two thirds of a 2- to 3-year-old group correctly reporting the puppet's desires. Performance on the belief sentences was no better than performance on standard false belief tasks, nearly at floor for the 2- to 3-year-olds. This finding suggests that the grammar of complementation is not the source of children's difficulty with false complement statements. Instead it seems to be the falsity and the nature of the mental state verb used: Specifically, verbs that make a claim about the state of the world.

Effects of training

Nevertheless, although failure to understand complementation is not the immediate cause of children's difficulties understanding belief, experience of complementation might help false belief understanding to develop. Lohmann and Tomasello (2003) conducted a false belief training study to see whether experience in the language of complementation advanced children's false belief understanding. Three-year-old children had several sessions in which they and the experimenter played with deceptive objects, such as a pen that looked like a flower. They discovered the identity of the object, chatted with the experimenter about it and interacted with a puppet who also initially had a false belief about the object. Children were split into three groups according to the type of language the experimenter used. For one group, the experimenter commented throughout using mental state verbs in sentential complement syntactic constructions; for another group, the experimenter commented on the objects but did not use mental state verbs or complementation; for the third group, the experimenter did not make informative comments. There was also a group that did not find out the real identity of the objects. Instead, the experimenter told them a story involving the object, and talked about the story characters' mental states. They heard the same number of mental state verbs and complement sentences as the full training group, but the mental states were not contrasted with reality (naturally, since children did not realize they had a false belief about the nature of the object).

The children who did not hear informative comments did not improve on an unexpected contents false belief task. The group who had heard mental state verbs contrasted with reality using sentential complement structures improved considerably. The other two groups improved slightly. Thus, mental state talk paired with appropriate false belief experience can enhance children's false belief understanding. Mental state talk that is not in the context of false belief experience, or false belief experience with nonmental state talk had only a modest effect.

It should be noted that in this experiment, each use of a sentential complement also involved a mental state or communication verb ("think", "know" or "say"—performance did not differ between the two types of verb). The effects of training could therefore have been due to the use of verbs that explicitly mention mental states, rather than the syntactic structure they contributed to. In practice it is difficult to distinguish between the two, but Perner et al.'s (2003) findings of good performance on desire complements give grounds for caution. If training with sentential complementation was given with only pretend or desire verbs, would performance on false belief tasks improve? This has not been tested yet.

Another possibility is that neither the syntax of complementation nor the use of mental state verbs was directly responsible for improvement. Instead, mental state language may have been effective because it directed children to think about mental states (in this case, about the mental states produced by deceptive objects, rather than about the deceptive objects, which are quite interesting in themselves). This interpretation is suggested by a study by Peskin and Astington (2004), in which they compared storybooks with and without mental state language. Surprisingly, the books *without* mental state talk were more effective in improving children's false belief understanding.

Six children's books were adapted so that either the text was full of metacognitive terms, or they were completely absent. The metacognitive stories included words like "know" and "think", as well as less frequent words such as "decide" and "expect". (Naturally, mental state terms were typically used with sentential complements.) The nonmetacognitive books had the same story, but the characters' mental states remained implicit. Children were read one of the sets of books at home and at school numerous times over a 4-week period: On average children heard the stories more than 70 times. After 4 weeks, children were tested on batteries of false belief prediction and explanation tasks. They were also tested on their comprehension of metacognitive verbs: They were told a brief story and were given a choice of two metacognitive verbs describing a character's state of mind (e.g., "Does Kate really *know* it's a yellow one, or is she just *guessing*?"). Lastly, children were encouraged to tell stories with props to see how many metacognitive verbs they used.

Both the group who had heard the metacognitive stories and the group who had heard the control stories improved on the false belief prediction tasks. Similarly, performance on the explanation tasks improved after the stories. However, explanation improved considerably more in the control group, who had not heard the metacognitive stories. Children's understanding of metacognitive terms had not improved in either group, but the experimental group used more different metacognitive terms, and used them more often.

The finding of superior explanation performance in the control group was not expected. Peskin and Astington suggest that this group had to work out for themselves the mental states of story characters. The group who heard the metacognitive terms, on the other hand, had this done for them. Perhaps the extra effort required on the part of the control group resulted in deeper understanding. Finally, it is interesting to note that although the experimental group used more metacognitive terms, they did not appear to understand them any better than before. This study suggests that mental state language is not as important as the opportunity it can provide to think about mental states. Indeed, explaining things to children may not be as beneficial as creating the opportunity for them to work things out for themselves.

General language development

Specific aspects of mental state language, such as mastering the grammar of sentential complementation or learning mental state terms, do not appear to drive theory of mind performance. However, they may enhance it, either directly or by calling children's attention to mental states. More convincing claims have been made about the effects of the general development of language on the acquisition of theory of mind. Astington and Jenkins (1999) compared general syntactic and semantic language development with theory of mind development. They saw children three times over a 7-month period, beginning with children aged 3 years 4 months. They gave children a theory of mind battery comprising transfer and contents false belief tasks and an appearance–reality task. Children were also given the Test of Early Language Development (TELD; Hresko, Reid & Hammill, 1981). This test was subdivided into items assessing syntactic and semantic skills. They found that early theory of mind did not predict later language ability. However, early language ability did predict later theory of mind performance; only to an extent, however: Language ability at the first session predicted later theory of mind, but language ability at the second session did not. Furthermore, only scores on the syntax items predicted later theory of mind performance. Scores on the semantic items did not predict subsequent theory of mind scores at all.

On these findings, Astington and Jenkins concluded that theory of mind depends on language and, specifically, on syntax. They speculated that syntactic abilities are necessary to represent the spatial arrangements of objects in the real world, and separately in a character's mental representation of it: For example, to keep track of the location of Maxi's chocolate both in reality and within Maxi's belief. Astington and Jenkins do not favour the sentential complementation theory, partly because they observed children using sentential complements in their speech but failing theory of mind tasks.

The conclusion that it is syntax rather than general linguistic development that is important rests on the assumption that the syntax items of the TELD constitute a relatively pure test of syntactical ability. Ruffman, Slade, Rowlandson, Rumsey and Garnham (2003) suggest that they do not. It is obviously impossible to have a completely pure test of syntactical ability: Semantic skills are always also necessary to understand the words in a sentence, amongst other things. The critical question is whether children fail TELD *syntax* items because of *semantic* difficulties. Some of the items clearly could be challenging for semantic reasons. One of the two TELD examples Astington and Jenkins mention requires children to describe the relative positions of a dog and a chair. In three pictures, the dog is on, under and behind the chair. This tests children's understanding of the semantics of preposition (what "on", "under" and "behind" mean). It certainly does not seem to be particularly about word order. Ruffman et al. argue that most of the TELD syntax questions are heavily dependent on semantic knowledge. Thus the relationship with theory of mind abilities may depend on the semantic rather than the syntactic demands of the questions. In fact, the current version of the TELD is no longer divided along semantic and syntactic lines. It is simply divided into receptive, expressive and spoken language (Hresko, Reid & Hamill, 1999).

What is required to test Astington and Jenkins's (1999) specific conclusion is a test of word order. Ruffman et al. (2003) used questions from another standard language test, the Sentence Structure subtest of the preschool Clinical Evaluation of Language Fundamentals (CELF) test. They selected items that tap an understanding of word order (such as "Mom showed the dog the cat"), and compared them to items from the same subtest in which word order was not crucial to sentence understanding (for example, "He will eat the apple", selecting pictures from a man walking away from an apple, a man with an apple in front of his face and a man with an apple core on a plate). Performance of children at 3 years 7 months on these language items was compared with later performance on a variety of theory of mind tasks, including the standard transfer and contents tasks, and later the second-order false belief task. Children were tested on four occasions over 2½ years. The findings extended Astington and Jenkins's findings by showing that language around the age of 3 years predicted belief understanding over the next 2½ years. However, syntax did not predict performance. Instead, semantics and overall language performance predicted later belief understanding (and the effect was largely the result of semantic ability; syntactical ability did not add much).

The specificity of Ruffman et al.'s (2003) test suggests that Astington and Jenkins's (1999) syntactic hypothesis is not correct. Other elements of syntax might predict belief understanding, but word order does not. Ruffman et al. conclude that language in general is important for belief understanding.

Milligan, Astington and Dack (2007) have recently published a meta-analysis confirming this. They included 104 studies that had standardized or experimental tests of English language ability and of first-order false belief performance, comprising data from 8891 children. The analysis confirmed the findings of studies discussed so far, that language ability and false belief are strongly associated, independently of children's age. The size of the effect varied significantly from study to study, but on average was moderate to large.

The analysis covered tests of general language, semantics, syntax, memory for complements and receptive vocabulary. There was only one significant difference between these five measures: Receptive vocabulary measures were less strongly related to false belief performance than were the other more general language measures. This is consistent with the idea that many aspects of language relate to theory of mind. Receptive vocabulary measures may be more weakly related because they are designed to measure a narrow, specific aspect of language ability. The type of false belief task used made no difference, suggesting that they do not differ in their linguistic demands. This supports Wellman et al.'s (2001) conclusions that the different types of false belief task and different forms of test questions were equivalent. Studies that compared language and false belief longitudinally showed bidirectional relationships between them, although there was a stronger effect of early language on later false belief. Thus Milligan et al.'s (2007) analysis suggests that false belief understanding develops as a result of general language development. False belief understanding also promotes further language development. The exact mechanisms of these effects remain a matter for research, but there is good evidence that conversation plays a role.

Talk about belief

One group of children have less opportunity than most to talk about mental states: deaf children with nonsigning parents. About 90% of deaf children are born to parents who are not deaf. As a result, these children typically do not master sign language until they go to school. These late-signing deaf children are severely delayed in passing false belief tasks. For example, Peterson and Siegal (1999) compared the theory of mind skills of deaf children from deaf and hearing parents. Both groups were at school and were judged by their teachers to be of average verbal ability or better (although the children with signing parents were judged as more competent). The children were between 5 and 13 years old, with a mean age of 9 years. They were given transfer and contents false belief tasks, and while the children with signing parents performed at least as well as normal 4-year-olds, the children with hearing parents performed poorly: 38% passed the transfer task and 47% passed the contents task. This was slightly worse than a group of children with autism, who had a mean verbal mental age of about 8 years. A number of studies have replicated the finding of theory of mind delay in late-signing children, even when nonverbal or low-verbal tests are used (Schick, de Villiers, de Villiers & Hoffmeister, 2007; Woolfe, Want & Siegal, 2002). Some studies have found the delay to be substantial: Russell et al. (1998) gave a transfer task to groups of deaf children, mean ages 6, 10 and 15 years. Only in the 15-year-old group did a majority of children pass.

There are a number of potential explanations for this delay. It is difficult to rule out the possibility of associated neurological impairments. Deafness is often a consequence of rubella or meningitis, and is often not the only consequence. In the studies mentioned, however, participants had no known learning difficulties. Peterson and Siegal (2000) also suggest that deaf children's neurological development may be different as a result of their hearing difficulty. However, the most probable cause of the delay is the lack of language experience. An early lack of linguistic input may have pervasive effects: Less experience with mental state words or syntax; an absence of conversation relevant to mental states (which are otherwise unobservable); and also consequent limitations on social interaction, including activities like pretend play. The delay in theory of mind ability may be due to any or all of the above. Peterson and Siegal favour a lack of conversation about mental states

Whether or not this is the primary cause of deaf children's delayed theory of mind development remains in question. However, there is good reason to think that conversation plays a role in normal theory of mind development. Research on this issue began with the seminal work of Judy Dunn and colleagues. Dunn, Brown and Beardsall (1991a) examined 36-month-olds' conversations with their mothers and siblings. They found that the causes of feelings were most often discussed during disputes, suggesting that social conflict promotes the development of social under-standing. The importance of discussing feelings was confirmed by a test of emo-tional understanding more than 3 years later. Children were asked to judge the emotions of characters in a recorded conversation, whose emotions changed during the exchange. Success on this task was strongly related to the amount and diversity of talk about feeling at 3 years old. Dunn, Brown, Slomkowski, Tesla and Youngblade (1991b) also found that family talk about feelings and causality when children were 33 months old predicted false belief performance when they were 40 months old. However, because false belief performance was virtually at floor even by the end of the study, this finding must be interpreted cautiously. [This data set was also used in Youngblade and Dunn (1995), discussed in Chapter 6.] Nevertheless, subsequent studies have confirmed the finding that earlier family language is related to later false belief understanding.

Most research has focused on maternal language, naturally. Liz Meins, Charles Fernyhough and colleagues have found that the way mothers talk to their children in early infancy predicts theory of mind performance at 3- to 4-years-old. Meins, Fernyhough, Wainwright, Das Gupta, Fradley and Tuckey (2002) video-taped mothers playing with their 6-month-old infants. They were interested in mothers' "mind-mindedness". This is the tendency to treat the infant as an indi-vidual with a mind, rather than simply as something whose needs have to be satisfied. Mind-mindedness was measured by the appropriateness of mental state comments used while playing with the child. These mainly referred to the child's mental states (since only the child and the mother were present, this is not surpris-ing). Appropriateness was judged according to whether the mother accurately read the child's apparent mental state, and whether her comments were relevant, clear and assisted the ongoing interaction. The children were given a battery of theory of mind tasks (false belief and appearance reality tasks) several years later, when they were aged between 3 years 9 months and 4 years. The strongest predictor of false belief performance was children's verbal mental age at the time of testing, but maternal mind-mindedness, measured at 6 months of age, came a close second.

This is good evidence for a long-term effect of mother's appropriate mental state talk in fostering children's theory of mind development. Ruffman, Slade and Crowe (2002) looked in detail at mothers' talk to children during their fourth year, as theory of mind is emerging. Three times during the year mothers were asked to describe pictures to their children. The pictures showed people interacting in typical situations (a woman bathing a child, a man and a child at the beach, and so on).

The researchers were interested in mothers' use of mental state talk, and how it related to theory of mind development. Children were also given a series of theory of mind tasks at each point.

Mothers used mental state terms much more frequently than children did, giving a sense that mothers were trying to support children's mental state understanding. The more mothers used "think" and "know", the better children did later at the theory of mind tasks. Another good predictor of theory of mind performance was the use of "modulations of assertion": expressions of uncertainty or possibility. For example, "I wonder what that is? It could be a cat" expresses uncertainty about what an object is. This focuses attention on what is known and unknown, so it may well relate to the understanding of knowledge and thought.

A key question is which comes first: Do mothers adjust their mental state talk to the child's current level of understanding, or do they pitch their talk at a higher level? This can be thought of in terms of Vygostky's (1978) concept of a "Zone of Proximal Development". This describes a level of performance beyond the child's current level of ability, but which the child can achieve with assistance. Mothers may be sensitive to what the child can manage, and adjust their mental state talk to a level just outside the child's "comfort zone". Ruffman et al.'s (2002) results suggest this. Mothers' mental state utterances predicted their children's later theory of mind performance and mental state talk. However, neither children's theory of mind performance nor their mental state talk predicted mothers' use of mental state terms. As it is only the mothers' behaviour that predicts the child's later behaviour, mothers seem to be driving development rather than following their child. Overall, even when controlling for early theory of mind, early child mental state talk, early language ability, mothers' education and age, mothers' mental state talk correlated with children's later theory of mind, with an impressively high average partial correlation ($r = .36$).

More recent research suggests that mothers scaffold their children's mental state understanding from much earlier, as Meins et al.'s (2002) findings suggest. For example, Taumoepeau and Ruffman (2006, in press) looked at the mental state language used by mothers to their infants. They asked mothers to describe pictures to their children when they were 15, 24 and 33 months old. Children's theory of mind understanding was assessed using an emotion judgement task, in which children were shown a short picture story and asked to choose the facial expression of the protagonist. For example, in a story in which a lion chases a boy, children had to choose whether the boy had a happy or fearful expression. Mothers mostly used desire talk to the youngest children, focusing on the child's own desires. As children got older, mothers increasingly used belief and knowledge terms, and used them about both the child and other people. For the youngest children, only desire terms related to later mental state talk and emotion task performance. For the oldest children, however, mothers' use of belief terms at the earlier time point was more important. Again, earlier child mental state language was not related to later mothers' mental state talk; mothers were driving development. The only exception to this concerned children's use of personal pronouns. Their use of words like "I" and "you" at 24 months was related to mothers' subsequent tendency to refer to their own mental states.

Taumoepeau and Ruffman (2006, in press) again interpret their findings in terms of mothers adjusting their talk to the child's zone of proximal development. Initially, mothers concentrate on children's desires. These are naturally very salient to the child. If children learn to label these states, this will help them to realize that other people have these internal states too. At around 2 years, children are already talking about desires; mothers, probably realizing this, begin to use more belief talk. Another cue mothers have to their children's understanding of mental states is their personal pronoun use. Appropriate use of "I" and "you" requires children to realize that the appropriate pronoun depends on who the speaker is. This can be seen as a primitive understanding of perspective (from my point of view, you are "you" and I am "me"; from your point of view, it is the opposite). Once mothers realize that children understand this, they start to use more belief terms, and they use them about themselves, the child and about other people, indicating to the child that belief states, like desires, are also the same in themselves and others.

Family and parenting effects

The evidence suggests that the way mothers talk to their children, at least as measured in laboratory free-play situations, promotes children's understanding of mental states and mental state terms. Moreover, mothers modify their language to the child's level of understanding, and play an active role in helping the child develop a theory of mind. These findings help explain other research findings about the relationship between theory of mind, family structure and parenting style.

For example, Ruffman, Perner and Parkin (1999) looked at the effects of parents' discipline style on false belief understanding. They asked parents of 3- and 4-year-old children what they had done or would do in a set of situations in which their child misbehaved. For example:

> Can you remember a time recently when your child teased or hit another child? What did you (would you) say or do?

Parents gave various types of response. One type encouraged children to reflect on the emotional perspective of the victim, for example by asking "How would you feel if he did that to you?" Another type of response was to involve children in a general discussion of what they had done wrong, without referring to the victim's feelings. Parents also simply reprimanded their children without discussion.

The likelihood of parents using these different response types was related to their children's false belief understanding. If parents emphasized the victim's feelings, children tended to do better at false belief tasks. However, if parents used a lot of reprimands, their children performed poorly. Disciplinary situations provide an ideal situation for children to consider others' mental states, if prompted to do so. Parents who take advantage of the opportunity may promote their children's theory of mind. This complements Dunn et al.'s (1991a) finding, discussed above, that in discussion with 3-year-olds, reference to feelings was most common during disputes.

There was also a marked sibling effect in Ruffman et al.'s (1999) study. A number of studies have found that having siblings improves children's theory of mind performance. Perner, Ruffman and Leekam (1994b) found that the more siblings a child had, the earlier they passed the false belief task. Ruffman, Perner, Naito, Parkin and Clements (1998) reanalysed the data and found that only older siblings fostered false belief understanding. Further experiments showed that the effect was stronger for older children, and did not hold for children younger than about 3 years 2 months. This suggests that having older siblings is only of benefit after a certain stage of development. Exactly why having older siblings helps false belief understanding is not yet clear. It may be a combination of several effects. Older siblings may stimulate pretend play, which in turn fosters false belief understanding. Possibly more important are the linguistic opportunities having an older sibling presents. Children will hear language with more complex reference to mental states, both directly from the older sibling, and from the parent to the older sibling.

This social influence is not limited to siblings, of course. Lewis et al. (1996) examined Greek and Cypriot preschoolers. These children lived in small communities, and often had more opportunities to interact with adults and older siblings than is usual in the Anglo-American nuclear families that most theory of mind participants come from. False belief performance was strongly predicted by the number of adults and older children interacted with daily. Lewis et al. suggest that the children are effectively apprentices, learning social skills from a variety of older tutors—the more the better.

Sociocultural differences

There is growing evidence that social relations play a major role in theory of mind development. Language, or at least the social interactions it allows, is a major factor in this relationship. This has implications for theories that postulate an innate theory of mind. According to Modularity Theory, for example, theory of mind reasoning is handled by a specific set of brain mechanisms that are innate. They start to operate after a period of maturation. Their operation can be triggered by the environment, but other than that the environment has little influence on core theory of mind development. Similarly, some executive function explanations of theory of mind development heavily emphasize frontal lobe maturation. These also envisage limited scope for environmental influence. Major social influences on fundamental theory of mind development would be hard for strongly nativist theories to account for.

Two potential sources of large social effects have received little attention until recently: comparisons across different socioeconomic backgrounds, and comparisons across cultures. In each case, there are potentially very large differences in the kind, quality and amount of social interactions children are involved in. These differences should have an effect if social relations are important to theory of mind development. Somewhat surprisingly, the effects of background seem stronger than those of culture.

Social background

Theory of mind research is typically done by middle-class intellectuals, with middle-class child participants, often attending university-run preschools. The researchers and children usually come from Britain, North America and a few other countries we typically think of as "Western" (Austria, Australia, Germany, and so on). The extent of the middle-class bias is hard to determine, since information about children's backgrounds is rarely given—and rarely measured, since asking parents about their and their spouses' occupation and educational experience is awkward and can potentially cause offence.

Holmes, Black and Miller (1996) avoided this issue by selecting schools which took part in the Head Start programme. This is a US programme that provides resources to help counteract the negative effects of growing up poor. Holmes et al. found that disadvantaged children of mean age 4 years 3 months passed transfer and contents task between a quarter and half the time, and children of 5 years 3 months between 52% and 84% of the time. Performance was somewhat worse than might be expected from other studies. For example, Wellman et al.'s (2001) meta-analysis found that children began to perform above chance when they were approximately 4 years old. In Holmes et al.'s sample this may have been about a year later. There was no middle-class comparison group however, so it is hard to assess how much background affected success.

A more systematic study was carried out by Cutting and Dunn (1999), comparing working-class and middle-class children in London nursery schools. Classification was based on parental occupation and education. Children were of mean age 4 years 2 months. The middle-class children scored on average 50% on a battery of false belief tasks, whereas the working-class children scored 31%, a significant difference. Working-class children also did less well on tests of language ability, as well as on tasks assessing emotional understanding. Language ability was related to false belief performance, and contributed independently of family background.

Hughes, Jaffee, Happé, Taylor, Caspi and Moffitt (2005) conducted the largest relevant study to date, looking at 1116 pairs of twins at 60 months of age. They deliberately included a higher proportion of children from low socioeconomic backgrounds; roughly half the mothers were teenagers (Hughes, personal communication, 5 November 2007). Children were given a battery of first- and second-order false belief tasks and a test of verbal ability. Examining twins allows an estimate of genetic and environmental influences on theory of mind. Monozygotic twins develop from the same egg, and therefore are genetically identical. Dizygotic twins develop from different eggs and are only as genetically related as normal siblings, sharing roughly half of the genes that vary between humans. Both types of twin will have similar amounts of common experience.

The correlations of theory of mind performance between the pairs of twins were identical for monzygotic and dizygotic twins ($r = .53$ in each case). This suggests that genetic influences on differences in theory of mind ability were negligible, but that shared environment had a strong influence. For both types of twin, theory of mind scores, socioeconomic status and verbal ability were all significantly inter-correlated. Genetic and shared environmental factors that influenced verbal ability influenced theory of mind to the same degree. The fact that language and theory of mind differences covary is strong evidence that language influences theory of mind, and specifically that theory of mind differences between children from different backgrounds are mediated by language. Hughes et al. (2005) suggest that the frequency, content and form of conversations between children and parents may be the major cause of differences in children's theory of mind development.

Performance of the children on theory of mind tasks was highly variable. Even though children were 5 years old, there was no evidence of a ceiling effect on the first-order false belief tasks: 18% of children failed all four tasks, 28% passed all and the remainder were fairly evenly spread between. Given the size of the study, covering a broad social spectrum, this is good evidence that the idea that children typically pass the false belief task by the time they are 4 years old is an over-estimation of the general population.

Taken as a whole, research on theory of mind and social background suggests that the socioeconomic background children grow up in is a major determinant of the rate at which their theory of mind develops. This is probably largely mediated by language. It is plausible that the frequency and quality of parent–child conversations differ across social class, possibly also influenced by different beliefs about parenting style. There are some comparable findings concerning social differences in pretend play. As discussed in Chapter 6, middle-class children may pretend more and have more complex forms of pretence than children from more disadvantaged backgrounds (Howes & Matheson, 1992, Experiment 2). Whether this contributes separately to theory of mind development, or is also a function of language, remains to be seen.

Cross-cultural differences

Although there are clear differences within a culture based on socioeconomic background, similar differences between cultures have proved difficult to find. This is particularly surprising given dramatic claims by anthropologists about very different views of the mind in some non-Western cultures. For example, Lillard (1998) discusses research on the Illongot in the Philippines. They are said to have a concept of *rinawa* that has elements of mind, heart, soul and life force, while not being quite any of these. Historically, concepts of mind may have changed. For example, ancient Greek mental state terms do not translate easily into modern-day English terms (Astington & Vinden, 2000).

These differences may simply reflect philosophical ideas about the nature of mind; people from different cultures and periods may nevertheless still use the same belief–desire psychology as we do. After all, in our culture our talk about the mind suggests a number of rather confused notions. We make a slightly vague distinction between the head and the heart: the heart governs emotions, drives and desires—but perhaps not all of them; desires relating to ambition or the pursuit of power, for example, may be more readily attributed to the head; anger on the other hand may come from the spleen. In any case, we use these terms metaphorically, and they do not seem strongly to relate to our basic judgements of behaviour.

However, some claims about different theories of mind would involve quite different everyday belief–desire reasoning. Julian Jaynes (1976) made the intriguing claim that until about 3000 years ago, humans were not conscious in the way they are now. Instead, they acted on commands heard from "gods". These commands in fact emanated from the right hemisphere of a person's own brain, and reflected their own desires and knowledge. However, the commands were perceived as coming from outside. This organization of the mind changed as a result of mass human migrations and increasing social complexity. Jaynes supported his argument with literary analysis of, amongst other ancient texts, the *Iliad*, which has little reference to introspection, and the *Odyssey*, which appears to reflect a view of consciousness similar to our own.

However, that was a long time ago, and difficult to assess (and possibly, to take seriously). A modern examination of false belief understanding in a distinctly non-Western culture has been taken to indicate that, in contrast to the dramatic claims of some historians and anthropologists, theory of mind development may follow a universal timetable. Avis and Harris (1991) examined the Baka, a pygmy hunter-gatherer people in the Cameroonian rainforests. Clearly, semi-isolated, unschooled, nomadic hunter-gatherers differ vastly in culture and experience from the middle-class Western preschool children who have participated in most false belief research. In fact, it proved impossible to get local Baka adults to act as experimenters, because the idea of exact repetition of apparently pointless test questions was completely alien to them. Instead, two Baka who had returned to the camp from a more sedentary lifestyle were recruited as experimenters. The adolescent Mopfana cooked wild mango kernels over a fire. He placed them in a bowl with a lid, and announced to a watching child he would be back shortly to eat them. He then went to the male meeting place for a smoke. While he was away, the other experimenter persuaded the child to play a trick on him, moving the mango kernels to a pot. Children were then asked where Mopfana would look on his return: in the bowl or in the pot?

The ages of children had to be estimated. The younger group had an approximate mean age of 3 years 6 months, and most of them—12 out of 17—correctly predicted that Mopfana would look in the bowl. An older group of nearly 6 years were almost perfect. Children were almost as good at predicting that he would feel happy before he looked in the bowl. This may be better than Western children, who are poor at predicting the emotional consequences of false beliefs (Harris et al., 1989; see Chapter 5). However, this is an uncertain conclusion, because the children were no better at a final question about how Mopfana would feel *after* looking in the bowl, which does not require an understanding of belief.

Nevertheless, Avis and Harris's (1991) findings suggest that Baka children have as good a grasp of false belief as Western children. Given the difference between the cultures, this supports the idea that belief–desire reasoning is a universal feature of human development, taking place on a similar timescale in diverse settings.

Not all cross-cultural research has reached the same conclusion. Penelope Vinden (1996) found apparently delayed false belief understanding among Quechua-speaking children in the Andes. These children also come from a "pre-literate" society, although some of them had attended school for short periods. Interestingly, their dialect of Quechua refers to mental states indirectly. For example, rather than asking "What will she think?", they would ask "What will she say?" They do have words for appearance, however. Vinden therefore compared performance on two appearance–reality tasks and two unexpected contents tasks. Despite having clear vocabulary for one and not the other type of task, children were poor at both. Children of about 5 years failed the appearance–reality tasks half the time, and even the children who were nearly 7 years old were not perfect on these tasks. They performed more poorly still on the unexpected contents tasks: Most younger children and about half the older children failed. However, it is difficult to be confident in the findings because of poor performance on control tasks. For example, 5 of the 15 older children were excluded for failing a control version of the contents task in which the *expected* contents were actually inside, and a transfer task was not even reported because most children failed the control questions. It may be that Quechua children with little formal schooling are puzzled by this kind of formal experimental situation, and do not interpret the questions in the way the experimenter expects.

Vinden (1999) went on to look at theory of mind understanding in several other cultures, using an adapted version of Avis and Harris's (1991) deception procedure (which involves a situation that presumably occurs universally). This time, there was little evidence that children from non-Western cultures performed differently to Western children. For example, 5-year-old Mofu children, from Northern Cameroon, correctly predicted where someone with a false belief would look between 64% and 83% of the time, depending on whether they went to school. This compared favourably to 5-year-old schooled Western children, who scored 77%. Further study of the Mofu showed good performance, with 4-year-olds scoring over 8.5 out of 12 on a composite measure of theory of mind (Vinden, 2002). Again there was a modest advantage of attending school.

A more recent study across five different cultures also found no major differences in basic theory of mind development. Callaghan et al. (2005) gave a false belief task similar to Avis and Harris's (1991) to children from five different cultures: Canada, India, Peru, Samoa and Thailand. Apart from the Samoans, all children came from towns or cities and were in schools or preschools, so the samples were not as exotic as before. They found that most 5-year-olds from each group passed the task, and most 3-year-olds failed. Performance of 4-year-olds was mixed. Less than a third of the Samoan 4-year-olds passed. (There were no Thai 4-year-olds.)

Thus, it has typically been concluded that basic theory of mind has a common timescale. However, it may be worth taking into account plausible and testable claims about adult cross-cultural differences between East Asian and Anglo-American cultures. Nisbett and Miyamoto (2005), for example, argue that East Asians have a cognitive style that is holistic, in which context is taken heavily into account. By contrast, people in Western cultures are more analytic and detail-focused. Many of the differences they discuss involve attention and object perception, but there is evidence of more social differences that may be directly relevant to theory of mind development. For example, Morris and Peng (1994) analysed English-language and Chinese-language US newspaper reports of the same multiple murders. The English-language reports made more mention of the personal disposition of the murderer: He had a bad temper, a sinister edge to his character, was disturbed and had internal problems. The Chinese-language reports made more mention of situational factors and relationships: he did not get along with his advisor, he had a rivalry with one of the victims, he was socially isolated.

This suggests a general tendency for East Asian adults to attend more to environmental causes of behaviour. Growing up amongst people with this tendency might affect theory of mind development. Theory of mind tasks are usually deliberately designed so that the context is uninformative. The actual position of Maxi's chocolate does not help you work out where Maxi will search: One must consider factors internal to Maxi. Thus East Asian children may be less successful at this kind of task, but better able to predict behaviour that has more direct environmental causes. This is very speculative, of course, but the data suggest that East Asian children may pass false belief tasks later than their Western counterparts.

An early indication of this came from Chen and Lin (1994), who found that Beijing 3- and 4-year-olds were very poor at contents and transfer tasks, with even the older children getting no more than half the questions right. However, the tasks were not standard, with the questions embedded in Eastern and Western fairy tales, and there was no Western control group. Lee et al. (1999), discussed above, found performance amongst Mandarin-speaking preschoolers was similar to that typically found in Western samples. Tardif, Wellman and Cheung (2004), on the other hand, found that in a sample of Cantonese-speaking preschoolers, most 4-year-olds failed the typical false belief tasks.

Like most cross-cultural studies, these studies did not include a comparison group of Western children, matched on language ability or social background. As discussed in the previous section, there remains uncertainty about the average age at which Western children pass false belief tasks, and this is clearly related to language ability and social background. Thus it is difficult to know whether participants in previous studies would have differed in theory of mind performance had they been compared with matched children from Western societies. However, some East Asian research suggests there is a measurable variation between cultures, perhaps of similar magnitude to social class variation found within Western cultures. Naito and Koyama (2006) examined performance in Japan, finding that middle-class Japanese children of average verbal mental age performed more poorly on false belief tasks than would be expected from Western false belief studies. Haruo Kikuno and I directly matched Japanese and Scottish children on age, verbal mental age and social class, and gave them the same battery of false belief and appearance–reality tasks (Doherty & Kikuno, 2005). We found that the Japanese children's false belief performance was delayed by about a year. Further research is needed to establish this, and determine its cause.

Summary

Language is intimately related to theory of mind development. Children's speech is a good source of evidence about when they grasp concepts such as desire, and later, belief. The age of acquisition of mental state language largely supports experimental studies: Children have a working understanding of desire from infancy, but only start to understand belief around the age of 4 years. Acquisition of language seems to promote theory of mind development. Suggestions that specific aspects of language, particularly the syntax of mental state language, are required for theory of mind development are not supported by the existing data. Similarly, differences in the explicitness with which languages make mental state distinctions do not seem to have much influence on the rate of theory of mind development. Instead, it seems likely that it is the acquisition of language as a whole that helps children to acquire a theory of mind. This may be because it provides a system for talking and thinking about mental states.

Discussion of mental states clearly seems to promote theory of mind development. This may explain why late-signing deaf children are delayed on theory of mind tasks. They had adequate language by the time their theory of mind understanding was measured, but had not had as much opportunity to talk about mental states, especially with family members. Although the case of deaf children is unusual, there is clear evidence from normal development that mothers can drive children's theory of mind development through their mental state talk. Mothers are often sensitive to what their children can understand, and tailor mental state talk to a level just beyond the children's current ability. Children also benefit from other family interactions, both when being told off using appropriate emphasis to mental states, and through having older siblings. It remains an open question how conversation about mental states improves theory of mind: Is it specifically through acquiring mental state language, or more generally through experience of attending to and thinking about the desires, beliefs and emotions of others?

There are clear within-culture variations in the rate of theory of mind development, linked to socioeconomic status. This implies strong social influences on theory of mind development. Hughes et al.'s (2005) large twin study found that theory of mind differences covaried with language differences, suggesting that differences between socioeconomic groups may be the result of the linguistic interactions children have (and thus may also be influenced by factors such as parenting style and maternal mind-mindedness). Despite clear within-cultural differences, cross-cultural studies have in general found few differences. This is particularly surprising given the fact that these studies typically do not control for the factors that influence theory of mind development within a culture. Two studies that have attempted to control for these factors, comparing Japanese and Western children, have found a significant delay in Japanese theory of mind development. This may be accounted for by differences in East Asian and Anglo-American cognitive style: East Asian theory of mind may focus more on the environmental influences on behaviour; Anglo-American theory of mind may emphasize the intrapersonal factors. This remains speculative.

Chapter 10

Autism

Introduction

WHAT WOULD IT BE like to lack a theory of mind? Your early experiences might have been something like this:

> As it was a long time before I realized that people might actually be speaking to me, so it was a long time before I realized that I too was a person—if somewhat different from most others. I never thought about how I might fit in with other people when I was very young because I was not able to pick people out from objects ... Objects are frightening. Moving objects are harder to cope with ... Moving objects that make a noise are even harder to cope with ... Human beings are the hardest of all to understand because not only do you have to cope with the problem of just seeing them, they move about when you are not expecting them to, they make varying noises and along with this, they place all different kinds of demands on you which are just impossible to understand.
>
> (Joliffe, Lansdown & Robinson, 1992, p. 16)

This quote is from a personal account of growing up with autism. Autism is one of the most debilitating developmental disorders. One of its principal characteristic features is a profound lack of social understanding. Simon Baron-Cohen, Alan Leslie and Uta Frith (1985) first made the connection between this symptom and the emerging interest in theory of mind by asking the question "Does the autistic child have a theory of mind?"[1] This question has spawned an amazing quantity of research, which has improved our understanding of this strange disorder immeasurably.

Characterization

Autism has a peculiar fascination. One reason may be that extreme lack of social understanding is sometimes paired with extreme talent. Roughly 10% of people with autism have some special, usually very specific talent. These individuals are known as "savants". (This term has replaced the phrase "idiot savants". Although this nicely expressed the contrast between mental handicap and special ability, the word "idiot" has changed from a medical term to a term of abuse.) Savant abilities are very rare in people with other forms of learning difficulty. Autistic savants can show remarkable ability in areas such as art, music or mathematics. A common savant skill involves immense knowledge of calendar dates. Some individuals would be able to tell you accurately without delay what day it will be on 14 August 2048—or any other day you care to mention. One savant could pair days and dates over a period of 40,000 years (Hermelin, 2001).

A well-known fictional portrayal of savant abilities appeared in the film *Rainman* (Levinson, 1988). In this film, Dustin Hoffman plays an adult with autism. His behaviour is typically autistic: He is socially inept, highly literal and insists on routine in what he does and wears. However, he is also capable of remembering an exact sequence of cards, a skill which his manipulative brother uses to his advantage in a casino. Raymond, however, does not understand the concept of money, and has no idea he is being exploited. A more recent fictional character with autism is Christopher Boone, in Mark Haddon's (2003) *The Curious Incident of the Dog in the Night-time*. This engaging first-person account gives a plausible idea of what it is like to be at the high-functioning end of the autistic spectrum. Despite finding social life deeply puzzling, Christopher studies for his maths "A" level several years early and is an excellent chess player.

Someone with autism can excel at something most of us find difficult, like mathematics, but be completely unable to fathom something that seems simple, such as realizing what someone else wants or intends to do. The symptoms of the disorder can be very specific. However, it should be borne in mind that both the fictional characters mentioned, and the individual quoted at the beginning, are all part of the small minority of high-functioning people with autism. Recently, such people tend to be diagnosed with Asperger's syndrome. Asperger's syndrome is diagnosed when autistic symptoms occur in people whose intelligence is within the normal range (IQ above 70), and whose language development initially proceeds normally. Whether or not this should be considered a separate category remains controversial (see Klin, Pauls, Schultz & Volkmar, 2005). Mild Asperger's syndrome may even shade into normality. Because intelligence is normal or even high, especially in certain areas, the disorder can even remain undiagnosed.

Interest in people with high-functioning autism can obscure the fact that most people with the disorder have moderate to severe learning difficulties. In classic autism this may be about 75%, and more than half of those affected develop no appreciable language. This means that theory of mind deficits in autism have only been examined in a fraction of sufferers; typical experiments include only children with verbal mental ages of above 4 years. Most experimental participants are children, since they tend to attend special schools and are easier for experimenters to find and get access to. This can give the impression that autism is restricted to childhood. However, sadly the disorder is life-long.

Most individuals with autism are male. Proportions vary from study to study, but the ratio is roughly 4:1. The ratio varies with IQ: For very low IQs, it approaches 1:1, whereas for higher IQs and particularly for Asperger's syndrome, there may be 15 boys for each girl. The reasons for this are not known. Frith (2003) speculates that autism in girls may be less likely to be detected, possibly due to better language and more compliance in educational settings. Another possibility is that it is related to high foetal testosterone levels, which have differential effects on boys and girls (Knickmeyer, Baron-Cohen, Raggatt & Taylor, 2005).

Simon Baron-Cohen (2002) suggested that autism may be an extreme case of the "male brain". According to this speculative theory, male brains are characterized by a greater tendency to "systemize"—to be interested in a variety of predictable systems. Examples include machines, maths and sports. Women, on the other hand, are more inclined to empathize—to understand and react appropriately to the thoughts and feelings of others. Most people have a balance of these two ways of making sense of the world. Some people, however, develop very good systemizing skills, but are very poor at empathizing: individuals with autism.

The idea that autism is the result of an extreme form of the male brain goes back to Hans Asperger (1944, quoted in Baron-Cohen, 2002): "The autistic personality is an extreme variant of male intelligence . . . In the autistic individual, the male pattern is exaggerated to the extreme". Although this is an intuitively appealing way of describing some of the differences between people with autism and ordinary people, currently the evidence for this theory is not compelling. Girls have been found to have a slight advantage on false belief tasks, but this only usually becomes apparent in very large samples. For example, Charman, Ruffman and Clements (2002) found a sex difference in subsets of samples of 375 and over 1000 children. However, the difference was very small. Hughes et al. (2005) in their study of 1116 twin pairs found a small advantage for girls on a battery of first- and second-order false belief tasks. Ruffman (personal communication, July 2006) suggests that the difference evident in large samples may be due to an increased likelihood of the sample containing a small number of children with undiagnosed Asperger's syndrome; these will be predominantly boys.

History

Autism is not new. Ancient fairy stories occur worldwide in which children are stolen away and strangely beautiful but remote changelings are left in their place. These stories may well have been attempts to explain the behaviour of children with autism. Frith (1989, 2003) identifies several cases of possible historical autism. These include Victor, the "Wild Boy of Aveyron". This child was found naked at the age of about 12 years in a forest in central France in the late 1800s. From the reports of Itard, the Chief Physician at the National Institution for Deaf-Mutes in Paris, it is clear that Victor had many of the characteristic features of autism. He was socially indifferent, and even after a long period living in civilization developed little comprehension of language. It seems likely that Victor was abandoned to his feral life by parents who could not cope with his autistic behaviour.

Autism was not diagnosed as a separate disorder until the 1940s, coincidentally by two Austrian psychiatrists who both chose the term "autistic" to describe their patients. Leo Kanner (1943), working in the United States, identified "early infantile autism" in a group of children. These children were aloof and indifferent to other people, which Kanner called "autistic aloneness", and had a strong desire for sameness and elaborate routine: "obsessive insistence on sameness". Hans Asperger (1944) in Vienna similarly diagnosed a group of patients with "autistic psychopathy". Asperger survived the allied bombing raids that destroyed his clinic, but his work was little known in the English-speaking world until after his death in 1980. The term Asperger's syndrome was coined the following year by Lorna Wing, building on Asperger's intuition that even children with normal or high intelligence can be autistic.

Diagnosis

Figure 10.1, published by the National Autistic Society, gives an idea of the range of symptoms shown by people with autism. After its discovery, autism was initially diagnosed using Kanner's criteria of autistic aloneness and obsessive insistence on sameness, which had to be present by 24 months at the latest. The most

Autism is...

a complex life-long disability which affects a person's social and communication skills. It is a spectrum disorder occurring in varying degrees of severity and affects more than 500,000 people in the UK today. Not all people with autism will need life-long support but the first step towards progress is recognition of the condition.

These pin people illustrate some ways in which autism is displayed.

Early diagnosis is essential if people with autism are to achieve full potential. It is only when their disability is understood that they can be helped to maximise skills and minimise problems.

For more information contact:

The National Autistic Society, 393 City Road, London EC1V 1NG Tel 020 7833 2299

Graphic design based on illustrations used by Prof J Rendle-Short, Australia and National Society for Autistic Children, USA.

The National Autistic Society is a company limited by guarantee. Registered in England No 1205298. Registered Office: 393 City Road, London, EC1V 1NG. Registered as a Charity No 269425.

FIGURE 10.1 Poster produced by the National Autistic Society, illustrating some of the characteristics of autism. Reproduced by kind permission of the National Autistic Society.

significant development in diagnosis since then has been Wing and Gould's (1979) introduction of the concept of a triad of impairments. These are in:

(1) Social interaction.
(2) Social communication.
(3) Imagination. For the purposes of diagnosis, imagination is now replaced in the triad by a repetitive and narrow range of interests and activities.

In addition to explicitly including an impairment in communication, the triad also allows diagnosis according to "a wider autistic spectrum". Autism proper is now defined using precise criteria by the two main systems of classification of mental impairments: the World Health Organization's *International Classification of Diseases* (ICD-10, 1993) and the American Psychiatric Association's *Diagnostic and Statistical Manual* (DSM-IV, 1994). Both systems incorporate the triad, but restrict autism proper to a disorder with a narrower range of symptoms that corresponds well with Kanner's original idea of the disorder. However, many more people do not meet Kanner's criteria but show symptoms from the triad. These can be manifested in different ways and to varying degrees. In other words, it is becoming more common to think of autism as part of a disorder that is much broader and more varied than its strict psychiatric classification. At one end it blends into the normal population; at the other end individuals have severe learning difficulties.

Asperger's syndrome is at the upper end of this spectrum, and is now commonly recognized as a separate disorder (but see Klin et al., 2005). Both DSM-IV and ICD-10 restrict the diagnosis to individuals without delay in language or cognitive abilities. Nevertheless, they have autistic social impairment, pedantic speech, and they usually have intense but circumscribed interests. Clumsiness is also common. However, some experts claim that Asperger's can be seen *with* language or cognitive delay. This difference in opinion has led to large differences in the estimated incidence of Asperger's syndrome.

Prevalence: Is there an autism epidemic?

Autism was considered a rare disorder until relatively recently. In the last 15 years, however, there have been claims of a dramatic increase in occurrence. Although seized upon for scare stories by the media, this is probably due to changes in diagnostic practice and an increasing awareness of the disorder, rather than a genuine increase in the prevalence autism.

The first attempts to estimate the number of people with autism in the population were in 1966 (Lotter, 1966; Rutter, 1966). These found 4 to 5 children out of 10,000 had the disorder, or about 4.5 hundredths of a percent. Wing and Gould (1979) found the number to be 4.9 per 10,000, with an additional 16.3 showing social impairments similar to those seen in autism (i.e., on the spectrum). Numerous other studies up until 1991 confirmed these findings, with estimates of roughly 4.4 cases per 10,000. In the 10 years from 1992 to 2001, however, the observed rate increased to 12.7 per 10,000 (Fombonne, 2003). Fombonne suggests that on the basis of current data a reasonable estimate is about 10 per 10,000. (For Asperger's syndrome, the estimate is 2.5 per 10,000, based on DSM-IV, rather than looser criteria used by a number of researchers.)

This certainly looks like a dramatic rise in the prevalence of autism. Recently, there has been considerable public debate and media scaremongering about the combined measles, mumps and rubella (MMR) vaccine, following suggestions of a link with autism by one group of researchers (Wakefield et al., 1998). The lead author, Dr Andrew Wakefield, was at the time being paid by the Legal Aid Board to investigate the case of a group of parents who claimed that their children had been damaged by the vaccine. It was later discovered that several of these children were among the eight children in *The Lancet* study whose parents associated the onset of symptoms with the MMR vaccination. Parental report of the onset of symptoms was a key piece of the data. There was an obvious conflict of interest here: The lead author and about half of the parents stood to gain financially if the link between the MMR vaccine and autism was supported by the data.

Once these facts were realized, 10 of the 13 authors of this study took the unusual step of retracting this suggestion, and the journal, *The Lancet*, publicly announced that it should never have printed the study. Subsequent studies have concluded that there is no link between the MMR vaccine and autism (R. T. Chen & DeStefano, 1998; Fombonne & Chakrabati, 2001). However, the harm was already done, and the possibility of a link between the vaccine and autism has become firmly lodged in the public's mind. The number of parents having their children vaccinated has dropped dramatically, and the risk of measles, mumps and rubella, all of which can be serious diseases, has increased. (At the time of writing there is a measles epidemic in Japan, which will kill 1 in 1000 of those infected.) Ironically, one of the consequences of congenital rubella can be a form of autism (Chess, 1977).

So, the MMR scare seems to have been unfounded. How else could the apparent increase in cases of autism be explained? A number of factors could cause more cases to be reported without a true increase. Wing and Potter (2002) consider these in detail. It is unlikely to be caused by changes in diagnostic criteria, but may be influenced by how these criteria are being interpreted by professionals. Recently there has been increased awareness of autism and of the possibility of milder forms of the disorder, and this probably leads to more cases being diagnosed. Some cases will now be diagnosed much earlier. Others would formerly have been diagnosed as other disorders or given a general label of "learning difficulties" or "mental retardation". For example, in California between 1987 and 1994 there was an increase of

9.11 cases of autism per 10,000. Over the same period there was a *decrease* of 9.24 cases per 10,000 of mental retardation of unknown causes. The similarity in these numbers is unlikely to be a coincidence. It is possible that much of the recent apparent increase in autism results from people being moved from one category to another.

It has also been recognized that autism can occur alongside other disorders, or severe mental retardation. Thus a number of cases will have autism added to another classification. It is also accepted that even children with average or high intellectual ability can have autistic symptoms, as well as an increasing acceptance of the existence of Asperger's syndrome. Improvements in the specialist services for autism have also made professionals and parents more willing to accept diagnoses of autism, since this will make appropriate help available. For example, the beginning of the apparent rise in autism in the United States coincided with autism being included in the Individuals with Disabilities Education Act, which guarantees free appropriate education to children with disabilities.

Overall, there are a number of plausible reasons why the apparent increase in autism may not represent a true increase in incidence, but simply changes in type and probability of classification. It is still possible that the incidence of autism is on the rise, but at present there is no compelling evidence for this.

Causes

Kanner originally thought that autism was biological in origin, and perhaps genetic. However, in the United States at the time, psychoanalysis was extremely influential, and Kanner briefly came to believe that the disorder resulted from cold, clinical parenting. He coined the phrase "refrigerator mother" for women who just happened "to defrost enough to produce a child". The idea was taken up and spread by Bruno Bettelheim, particularly in his book *The Empty Fortress: Infantile Autism and the Birth of the Self* (1967).

This theory is very distressing for parents of children with autism. Not only do they have to cope with the difficulties of bringing up a child with autism, they find themselves blamed for their child's condition. The refrigerator parent theory is now completely discredited in Britain (although it still seems to have some currency in Europe), but at the time there were suggestive pieces of evidence. Parents of children with autism often do show emotional abnormalities. Much of this may result from coping with a child with a particularly disturbing disorder. However, there is also a tendency for some parents of children with autism to have mild symptoms themselves (Baron-Cohen & Hammer, 1997; Briskman, Happé & Frith, 2001). It is now recognized that autism is at least in part a genetic disorder, and closely related individuals may share some autistic traits. This is not necessarily a bad thing: Fathers of people with autism tend to have jobs in engineering, computing and other technical or numerical fields (Baron-Cohen, Wheelwright, Stott, Bolton & Goodyer 1997; but see also Jarrold & Routh, 1998). It may be that a "little bit of autism" can be a good thing: People with autism have characteristic strengths as well as impairments (see the discussion of weak central coherence, below). In addition to the well-known savant abilities, a strength of individuals with autism is the ability to attend to and isolate detail. People with autism may also be very good at collating and systemizing information (Baron-Cohen, 2002). Relatives of people with autism may have some of these strengths without the weaknesses, at least not to a serious extent.

In any case, psychiatrists may have misinterpreted mild autistic traits in parents as being the cause of their offspring's autism. Instead, this simply reflects the genetic nature of the condition. Extreme mental and social neglect *can* lead to autistic-like symptoms. This was shown in the case of children found in Romanian orphanages. After the communist dictator Ceausescu was deposed in 1989, children in orphanages were found in conditions that varied from poor to appalling. They were undernourished, usually confined to cots or even kept in isolation and received virtually no social contact from their "caregivers". Subsequently many were adopted abroad. Rutter et al. (1999) studied 111 of these children who had been adopted in Britain. Of these, 11 children showed autistic-like symptoms. Apart from one child who spontaneously recovered, all had been in the institutions for at least a year, significantly longer than the nonautistic Romanian orphans. Five of the eleven children had severe developmental delay.

At 4 years old, these children showed several typical autistic-like features: They had difficulty forming normal social relationships, but tended to cling to their adoptive parents; they had communication difficulties; and they had markedly narrow but intense interests in things like new £10 notes (but not £5 or £20 notes, nor old £10 notes), watches and vacuum cleaners. However, by 6 years old, these autistic features had diminished markedly. This is not normal in autism, where autistic symptoms tend to increase in this age range. The sample also had an equal sex ratio, again not typical in autism.

The Romanian orphan study shows that autistic-like symptoms *can* arise from extreme deprivation. However, the deprivation was not just social: Children were also poorly nourished and lacked normal experiences, such as the opportunity to interact with objects, wander about and see different things. This makes the refrigerator mother theory of autism completely implausible: Not even the coldest of parents could match the extreme deprivation experienced by the Romanian orphans, and despite this extremity, symptoms were only seen in a small minority of the orphans, and diminished when proper care was given.

Genetic origins

Evidence for the genetic nature of autism comes mainly from studies of twins. Identical twins have the same DNA. If one identical twin has autism, then the other twin has about a 60% chance of also having this disorder. Moreover, in about 90% of cases the other twin has some autistic symptoms, so is on the autistic spectrum (e.g., Bailey et al., 1995). Fraternal twins develop from different eggs, and therefore are only as related as normal siblings. The chance of a fraternal twin of an autistic child also having autism is only about 6%. This is low compared to identical twins, but much higher than in the general population. As mentioned above, family members of people with autism are also more likely than the general population to show autistic-like traits; they may be more anxious, impulsive, aloof, shy, oversensitive, irritable or eccentric (Murphy, Bolton, Pickles, Fombonne, Piven & Rutter, 2000), although some of these traits may also be accentuated by the responsibility of caring for a child with autism. The search for which particular genes increase the risk of autism continues (Rutter, 2005).

Environmental causes

The best known and most easily preventable cause of autistic symptoms is phenyl-ketonuria. This is a condition with a well-understood genetic cause. Children with the condition are unable to metabolize phenylalanine, an amino acid common in food. It is also a neurotoxin. If undiagnosed, children can suffer subtle brain damage, giving rise to learning difficulties and autistic symptoms. Fortunately, if it is diagnosed damage can be avoided simply by feeding children a phenylalanine-free diet.

Other than phenylketonuria, there is limited evidence of infections or intra-uterine toxins (including drugs and alcohol taken by the mother) giving rise to autism (Rutter, 2005). As has been discussed, there is no reason to take seriously the major scare of this kind, the MMR vaccine. For the time being, apart from there being a clear genetic element, the cause of autism remains unknown.

The theory of mind hypothesis

Two new pieces of terminology, "theory of mind" and "triad of impairments", entered the literature around the same time. Baron-Cohen et al. (1985) hypothesized that the two may be related. The theory of mind hypothesis of autism is simple: Autism is the result of an absent or impaired theory of mind.

For the hypothesis to be accepted, several conditions are necessary:

(1)   It must be shown that each feature of the triad of impairments can result from an impaired theory of mind.

(2)   All individuals with autism must show theory of mind impairment.

(3)   Most individuals with nonautistic clinical diagnoses should not show theory of mind impairment.

Impairment is defined relative to mental age. So, if an autistic child of mental age 12 years only had the theory of mind abilities of a normal 8-year-old, that would be evidence for the hypothesis. On the other hand, an individual with a different disorder, with a mental age of 5 years, should have at least the theory of mind abilities of a 5-year-old. If theory of mind impairment occurred in other developmental disorders, a lack of theory of mind could not be responsible for the very specific impairments seen in autism.

Impairments in social interaction

The first test of the hypothesis involved giving a sample of autistic children a false belief task. Baron-Cohen et al. (1985) adapted Wimmer and Perner's (1983) unexpected transfer task, removing the context story (about cake making and chocolate) and presenting just the basic facts of an object being moved without someone's knowledge. This version has since become common.

The 20 autistic children in the study were between 6 and 16 years old, with a mean age of nearly 12 years. In measuring the theory of mind skills of children with autism, it is important to choose children whose mental age is at least as high as that of ordinary children who would pass the tests. This should ensure that children can understand the task, remember the story and make the necessary inferences. The children in this study had an average verbal mental age of 5½ years, and a nonverbal mental age of over 9 years (typically people with autism have higher nonverbal than verbal mental ages). All children passed the control questions. Only 4 of the 20 children with autism (20%) passed the false belief question. These children did not differ from the others in terms of chronological and mental age.

A control group of ordinary 4-year-olds performed well on the task (85% correct), as would be expected. A group of children with Down's syndrome, a genetic disorder associated with developmental delay, also performed well (86% correct). This group was included to ensure that the poor performance of children with autism was not just due to learning difficulties. Given that the symptoms of Down's syndrome are quite different to those of autism, if both groups had performed poorly it could not be argued that a lack of theory of mind causes autistic symptoms.

The conclusion was clear: Most children with autism fail a standard false belief task, and therefore may be unable to represent mental states. This study spawned an astonishing amount of research. An initial legitimate concern was with the use of dolls and toys. Children with autism do not typically engage in pretend play. Their failure to attribute beliefs to dolls could be because they do not treat the dolls as surrogates for people, rather than indicating a lack of theory of mind. Leslie and Frith (1988) heroically stood in for Sally and Ann, with Leslie moving a coin while Frith was outside the room. Most children still failed to predict where Uta Frith would look for the coin on her return: only 5 out of 18 children with autism passed the task, despite having a mean verbal mental age of 7 years. The use of dolls was not the source of difficulty.

Children with autism also typically fail the unexpected contents task, for both self and for other (Perner, Frith, Leslie & Leekam, 1989), and the appearance–reality task (Baron-Cohen, 1989a). Their mental state vocabulary is also poor. For example, few children could pick, from the following list, which words were things the mind could do: Letter, Car, Dream, Think, Tape, Horse, Want, Computer, Know, Flower, School, Remember, Pretend, Cover, Idea, Understand. Only 4 of 15 children with autism correctly picked at least six of the eight mental state terms and rejected at least six out of eight distracters, compared with all of a matched group of children with moderate learning difficulties. Children with autism also produce fewer mental state words in everyday speech, particularly words referring to belief and knowledge (e.g., Tager-Flusberg, 1992).

Of course, a minority of children tested passed theory of mind tasks. Could it be that these children have a normal functioning theory of mind? This is a serious concern, since the children with autism who fail the false belief task are only a minority of all children with autism. Most do not have the intellectual or linguistic ability to take standard theory of mind tests. Of those who are sufficiently able, some pass the tests. If these children had an unimpaired theory of mind, the theory of mind hypothesis would only describe the minority of individuals who are able enough to take the tests but not able enough to pass them.

However, success on the standard false belief task does not mean that children have an unimpaired theory of mind. Children who pass first-order theory of mind tasks often fail second-order tasks (Baron-Cohen, 1989b). Happé (1995) looked at the relationship between success on standard false belief tasks and verbal mental age in a large sample of children with autism (70 children). She found that whereas ordinary children have a 50% chance of passing standard tasks at the verbal mental age of 4 years, children with autism have to have a verbal mental age of 9 years or over before they are 50% likely to pass. Thus, children with autism are delayed on false belief tasks relative to their verbal mental age.

This suggests two main possibilities: children with autism may eventually acquire a normal theory of mind, but more slowly than normal; alternatively, children with autism of sufficient intelligence may be able to work out how to pass theory of mind tasks, but do so by another route. Happé suggests that their theory of mind may be effortful, verbally mediated and involve explicit calculation. The theory of mind of normal children or adults, by comparison, typically seems effort-less and automatic.

I encountered an example of this while doing my PhD at Sussex University, supervised by Josef Perner. A student with autism was doing a Psychology conversion MSc at the department. Naturally, she was very interested in the theory of mind deficits in autism. While a child she had taken part in numerous theory of mind experiments: Autism is rare, but research on autism is common by comparison, and able children with autism are very much in demand by researchers. (This is something of a problem with autism research: Any of the participants may have taken part in numerous studies before, including theory of mind training studies. The assumption that the participants are naïve may well be unwarranted.) She and Josef played around with a few versions of the false belief task. She passed the standard transfer task with ease. However, in a task with a third location not involved in the story, she failed. She had worked out that the correct answer was always the empty location; when there were two empty locations, she could only guess.

Note that this was a woman with a Bachelor's degree, studying for a Master's degree. Her coursemates were not aware that she had autism (although they had noticed some social symptoms), and she did not come across in casual interaction as particularly unusual. Over the following year, and presumably long after, she asked about and learned more and more about social rules. One puzzle concerned holding doors open. In Britain, it is considered polite to hold a door open if someone is following you. However, if they are too far away, holding the door becomes socially odd and burdensome to the other person. The question is, how far away do they have to be? You probably have never had to think about this, but the student wanted a rule. This is characteristic of high-functioning people with autism or Asperger's syndrome: They like social rules and will follow them precisely. (The best rule I could come up with: If the door would close naturally before the other person reached it, you do not have to hold it.)

So, there probably is something in Happé's idea that some people with autism work out theory of mind the hard way, and sometimes their theories pick out irrelevant features of theory of mind tasks. However, in her "Strange Stories Task" Happé (1994) found that a few children with autism could explain complex behaviour in situations for which they were unlikely to have learned specific rules. These were short stories involving mental states. For example, the Double Bluff story goes like this:

> During the war, the Red army captured a member of the Blue army. They
> want him to tell them where his army's tanks are; they know they are either by
> the sea or in the mountains. They know that the prisoner will not want to tell
> them, he will want to save his army, and so he will certainly lie to them. The
> prisoner is very brave and very clever, he will not let them find his tanks. The

tanks are really in the mountains. Now when the other side asks him where his tanks are, he says, "They are in the mountains."

The participants were asked the following questions:

Is it true what the prisoner said?

Where will the other army look for his tanks?

Why did the prisoner say what he said?

The main measure used was the last question, requiring participants to explain actions or statements. There were two examples from each of 12 types of story of varying difficulty. In the simplest story someone told a lie to escape punishment; more complex stories involved sarcasm, persuasion or the double bluff described above.

These stories were told to people with autism, grouped according to whether they could pass second-order false belief tasks, just first-order or failed all false belief tasks. The second-order passers did well on the stories, giving appropriate justifications on 20 out of 24 stories. This was not significantly worse than a group of ordinary 8-year-olds and a learning difficulties comparison group, although it was worse than ordinary adults, who scored almost perfectly. First-order passers could explain only about half the stories, and those who failed the false belief tasks could explain less than a third of stories.

These slightly more natural stories, then, seem to reveal a range of performance in children with autism that roughly approximates their performance on first- and second-order false belief tasks. The most able participants almost make it into the normal range—but not quite. The Strange Stories Task suggests that even second-order passers have some impairment of their theory of mind. This supports the theory of mind hypothesis of autism: There is always *some* theory of mind deficit. However, it also suggests that these impairments are not always severe. People with high-functioning autism may well have theory of mind ability similar to, if not at quite the level of, typical adults. Stories like the Double Bluff above are novel, presenting a situation that is easy to grasp, but not in the direct experience of most people. It also may involve a third-order attribution: The prisoner *knows* that his captors *think* that he will try to make them *believe* the wrong thing.

Impairments in communication

There is no doubt that people with autism have characteristically odd communication. The most obvious abnormality is that roughly half of those with classic autism do not have language. This group is largely neglected by the theory of mind hypothesis. Their lack of language may simply be caused by their developmental delay. However, a contributory factor may be a lack of the normally irrepressible motivation children have to communicate with others. Most of those who do learn to speak show a number of characteristic oddities that are consistent with poor theory of mind. Speech may be too loud, too quiet or too fast. Most children with autism show some echolalia, that is repeating the speech of others word for word, either immediately or much later. It is not clear why this is, but it demonstrates a detachment of language from its communicative use. Another common phenomenon is pronoun reversal, where the child will substitute "I" for "you" and vice versa, and also reverse "teach" and "learn", "borrow" and "lend", and so on. This may indicate confusion about social roles and difficulty taking the perspectives of others (Frith, 1989, 2003). Other common problems include failure to distinguish between new and old information. We typically mark a new topic with tag phrases, such as "by the way . . ." and "speaking of which . . .". People with autism may not use such phrases when introducing a new topic, but use them inappropriately at other times. This may be because they do not understand why these phrases are used. Autistic speech is also frequently repetitive, and can be disjointed.

All this suggests a failure to understand the informational needs of the listener. The pervasive comprehension problems of people with autism relate to the *pragmatics* of language use. Pragmatics concerns the appropriate use of language, and the difficulty in autism seems to concern the gap between what a speaker said and what a speaker meant. This gap can be very large, but typically listeners are very good at bridging it, so that we often fail to notice there is a gap at all. We bridge the gap by inferring what the speaker means, intends or believes. Consider the following example from Pinker (1994; cited by Baron-Cohen, 1995):

Woman: I'm leaving you.
Man: Who is he?

In order to understand this exchange, one has to infer the thought process of the man: He thinks she must be leaving him for another man. Without the ability to attribute this belief, the dialogue makes no sense; the man's question appears unconnected to the woman's statement.

This particular exchange is especially hard (especially since we are presented it without knowing anything of the context). However, in much of everyday speech, gaps between what was said and what was meant are frequent. The philosopher Paul Grice (1957) proposed a set of rules for conversations that capture what listeners expect: For effective communication, utterances should be true, clear, relevant and provide the appropriate amount of information. When an utterance does not appear to conform to these maxims, listeners usually assume that there is a hidden meaning such that the utterance does conform to the maxims. In other words, when it is not immediately obvious, listeners try to work out what the speaker intended to convey. For example, I say that Charlie is not here, and you say there's a train strike. This appears to violate the requirement to be relevant, but I assume that you are trying to be cooperative, so that it must be relevant in some way. I therefore infer that Charlie was trying to get here by train.

Effective normal communication therefore relies on bridging the gaps between what was said and what was meant via inferring the beliefs and communicative intentions of the speaker. This is bound to be difficult for someone who has difficulties inferring the mental states of others. Several studies have looked at comprehension of nonliteral speech in autism. Happé's (1994) Strange Story Task discussed above included several stories involving nonliteral speech, such as sarcasm, or someone joking that a large dog was not a dog, it was an elephant. Children's theory of mind performance predicted their ability to explain these stories, suggesting a direct link between theory of mind and the ability to comprehend nonliteral speech. Similarly, Surian, Baron-Cohen and Van der Lely (1996) produced pairs of sentences, one of which violated a Gricean maxim. Children with autism had difficulty saying which of the sentences was funny or silly. They were at chance in exchanges like the following:

"Do you have any brothers?
Doll 1: Yes, I have 500 brothers.
Doll 2: Yes, I have two brothers."

This violates the Maxim of Quality, to be truthful. Children with autism were also at chance when exchanges violated other maxims by including too little, too much or irrelevant information, but somewhat better when one of the sentences was impolite. For example:

"Do you want to play with me?
Doll 1: No, you are too stupid.
Doll 2: No, it's too cold to play outside."

Overall, only three of the eight participants passed this task, and they were also the only three to pass a standard false belief task. Conversational pragmatics and false belief understanding seem to be intimately related in the development of children with autism.

Impairments in imagination

Children with autism famously do not engage in pretend play. Whether or not this is predicted by the theory of mind hypothesis depends on which theory of theory of mind you subscribe to. According to Leslie's (1987) theory, a single mechanism is responsible for both pretend and belief computations. Damage or abnormal development of this mechanism would account for problems both with pretend play and theory of mind abilities. Most other theorists view pretend play and understanding of belief as separable abilities. Pretend play may well be a precursor to belief understanding, and involve parts of the same ability. However, Simulation Theory (e.g., Harris, 1992) and Theory Theory (e.g., Perner, 1991) are both consistent with children being able to pretend play yet having theory of mind deficits. After all, this is the case for the average 2-year-old.

Thus it was not a disaster for the theory of mind hypothesis when it turned out that children with autism can exhibit pretend play. Vicky Lewis and Jill Boucher (1988) distinguished between spontaneous pretend play and elicited play. Although children with autism do not show pretend play, is this because they can not? Lewis and Boucher observed children with autism left for 5 minutes with a set of toys and junk objects. There was not much evidence of symbolic play, although the comparison group of ordinary children did not show much evidence either, probably because they had novel toys, so functional play was more fun. However, when handed a toy and a piece of junk and asked "What can these do?", children with autism produced as much pretend play as the ordinary 4-year-old children. Each child with autism produced some pretend play. For example, one child, when handed a doll and five sticks, stood the sticks up in a row, and mimed the doll rolling a nonexistent ball, saying "skittles". Another child, given a car and three bricks, arranged the bricks into a bridge, drove the car part of the way across, then pushed it off, saying "London Bridge, car fell in the water".

This study is fairly convincing. Both examples involve object substitution and invention of nonreal objects. Kavanaugh and Harris (1994, Experiment 3) probed the ability of children with autism to follow pretend transformations, using a picture selection task similar to the one discussed in Chapter 6. Some unfortunate toy animal got covered with a nonexistent pretend substance (tea, paint, and so on) and children were asked which of three pictures the animal looked like now. The pictures showed it as it really was, as it would look after having the relevant substance poured on, or after some irrelevant transformation. Children with autism answered correctly over 70% of the time, much better than mental-age-matched children with other forms of developmental delay.

Children with autism are capable of pretending and of following the pretence of others. Thus the theory of mind hypothesis does not have to explain why children with autism cannot pretend play—because in fact they can. It remains a mystery why they do not do so spontaneously. Kavanaugh and Harris speculate that children may simply be disinclined to put aside known reality for some reason, despite being capable. Rutherford and Rogers (2003) looked at generativity, "the ability to generate novel acts to explore new materials or to solve problems" (p. 295). A lack of this particular executive ability might explain why children are disinclined to do something novel with an object, unless externally prompted. Their sample included very young children with autism, between 2 and 4 years old, as well as ordinary children matched for overall mental age. Children were handed toys, such as a brightly coloured slinky, and the number of different behaviours they produced over a 60-second period was taken as a measure of generativity. In another task, children were encouraged to pretend play with various toys. A graded series of prompts was used if children did not spontaneously pretend. In this task, even after prompting, children with autism did not produce many examples of pretend play. Interestingly, for the whole sample including control groups, generativity significantly predicted the amount of pretend play. Thus, the more generative children were, the better they did at the pretend play task. However, children with autism did not differ on the generativity task from the normal children or the children with other developmental disorders.

Generativity therefore does not explain the lack of play in autism. The issue remains open; children with autism may not pretend play simply because they do not want to. Pretend is a very social activity in ordinary children, initially scaffolded by adults, and later typically done in cooperation with other children. To a child unwilling to interact with others, pretence might not have any appeal.

Evaluation

Whether or not the theory of mind hypothesis can successfully explain the symptoms of autism may depend whether the disorder has a single psychological cause. The assumption driving much research on psychological cause hypotheses, such as the theory of mind hypothesis, is that a single psychological deficit is fundamental, and gives rise to most of the problems associated with autism. Only "most of the problems", because some problems experienced by people with autism are certainly caused by the associated brain damage or abnormality. For example, people with autism often experience excessive thirst (Carruthers, 1996), which is probably caused either by physical brain dysfunction (probably in the hypothalamus) or metabolic abnormality. Although explaining autism in terms of a single psychological deficit would be elegant, the ultimate cause of autism is probably physical, either through acquired brain damage or genetically influenced brain abnormality. A single physical cause can produce multiple distinct psychological effects that could together give rise to autism. Even the search for a single physical cause may be misguided if autism is not a unitary disorder. Presently, two distinct subtypes, autism and Asperger's syndrome, are recognized for diagnostic purposes. Other subtypes could potentially be distinguished based on severity of symptoms. If autism turns out to be a disorder comprising genuine subtypes, rather than a continuum of severity, then each subtype will have different physical causes, and perhaps different psychological effects. [See Boucher (1996), for a thoughtful consideration of these issues.]

Happé, Ronald and Plomin (2006) have recently argued cogently that the search for a single explanation for autism is futile and misleading. They report studies looking for autistic-like traits in 7- to 9-year-old children in the general population. In the children who have some autistic-like traits, these traits do not cluster as strongly as might be expected from the triad: Many children showed evidence of only one aspect of the triad. Furthermore, within children diagnosed with autism, rigid and repetitive behaviour and narrow interests usually emerge later than the other two triad impairments. If the cognitive deficits are dissociable, at least in children within the normal range, and develop at different rates within the clinical population, it is plausible that they have different causes. It is not possible to assume that a single cognitive theory can explain all autistic symptoms.

If autism *did* result from a single psychological cause, the theory of mind hypothesis might have problems. The hypothesis explains two of the impairments in the triad very neatly. There is little doubt that people with autism have an impaired theory of mind. This would explain their social impairments, and given the central role of mental state understanding in communication, it would also explain the characteristically odd communication of people with autism. However, the hypothesis is less good at explaining the third element of the triad.

The third element of the triad was impairments in imagination, in Wing and Gould's original formulation. Arguments in favour of the theory of mind hypothesis have usually been made on this basis. Children's lack of pretend play and poor theory of mind could readily be explained by postulating a single mechanism responsible for pretend play and belief reasoning; abnormality of or damage to this mechanism would impair both abilities. Leslie's (1987) theory of theory of mind was the first suggestion of this kind and it has been very influential in autism research.

However, it is now clear that children with autism *can* pretend and even follow events in the pretend world of other people. It is therefore far from clear that their imagination is impaired. In any case, impairments in imagination have been replaced for diagnostic purposes by repetitive behaviour and narrow, restricted interests. These are not as easily explained in terms of poor understanding of mental states. However, plausible speculation is easy. Many normal interests have strong social components. Even solitary activities such as watching TV derive much of their interest from the voyeuristic pleasure of watching other people's social lives. People with social impairments will not be able to take part in many of the activities that make up normal routines, or simply not enjoy them; what is left is already a much narrower range of possible activities. Furthermore, the puzzling and frightening nature of social life from the point of view of someone with autism might make things that are comparatively easy to understand and master very attractive: Train timetables, calendars or chess may give a reassuring sense of control that is lacking in social areas of life. This might result in intense interest in some topics that could contribute to the remarkable savant skills of some people with autism. So the theory of mind hypothesis can provide a plausible speculative explanation of narrow, restricted interests and to some extent savant skills. It seems less likely that repetitive behaviour can be smoothly explained in this way.

However, some of the stereotyped behaviours such as hand-flapping and rocking backwards and forwards presumably are a form of self-comforting, in response to anxiety. The anxiety may be exacerbated by social incomprehension, but more importantly, people with autism are unlikely to realize the social inappropriateness of these behaviours: "I used to, and still want to, put a big dark blanket over my head. This desire increases when I am with unfamiliar people and in unfamiliar surroundings. Doing this makes me feel much safer, but I used to get hot and run out of air and if I do it now I get told off" (Joliffe et al., 1992).

Thus although many consider the third element of the triad to be the hypothesis's fatal weak point, it is possible to explain the associated symptoms in terms of the theory of mind hypothesis [see Carruthers (1996) for a concerted attempt]. Attempting to explain all three elements may in practice be overambitious or unnecessary, but the theory of mind hypothesis can do a reasonable job.

Executive function impairments

The main rival to the theory of mind hypothesis is the executive function hypothesis of autism. As was discussed in Chapter 8, the relationships between theory of mind and executive function may go either way (or both ways): A theory of mind may be necessary for certain types of self-control; equally, certain types of self-control may be necessary to develop a theory of mind. The issue is complex in the case of typical development, and it may turn out that both hypotheses are partially correct. The same issues arise in the same way in the case of autism, with the added complexity of the effects of brain abnormality.

People with autism certainly do have executive function impairments. This was noted by Russell et al. (1991), who gave the Windows task to a group of children with autism. In the Windows task, children can see into two boxes, one of which has a piece of chocolate inside. Their task is to point to the one they want an opponent to open; the opponent will eat the chocolate if it is in the indicated box, otherwise the child receives it. Participants with autism performed similarly to normal 3-year-olds, giving the wrong response on the first trial, and continuing to do so over 20 trials. They appeared unable to inhibit the powerful learned response of pointing to a desired object.

Around the same time, Ozonoff, Pennington and Rogers (1991) looked at the performance of individuals with autism on the Towers of Hanoi and Wisconsin Card Sort Test. The Towers of Hanoi is a test of planning in the form of a game. In a simple version, there are three poles and three discs, as shown in Figure 10.2. The discs start on the leftmost pole and must be moved to the rightmost pole. The rules are that discs must be moved one at a time and that a disc cannot be placed on a smaller disc. This means that seven moves are necessary to complete the three disc problem. The Wisconsin Card Sort Task was discussed in Chapter 8. It

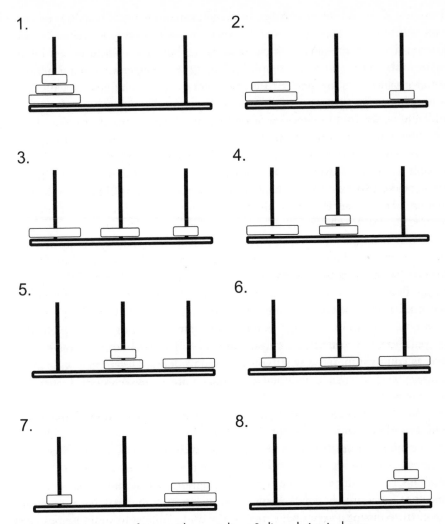

FIGURE 10.2 The Towers of Hanoi. The most direct 3-disc solution is shown.

involves sorting cards into piles according to one dimension, such as colour. At some point the sorting dimension will change, for example to shape, and participants must sort according to the new dimension. Both of these tasks are difficult for people with frontal lobe damage. Ozonoff et al. found that their autistic sample was good at first-order false belief tasks, but performed poorly on second-order tasks. They also performed poorly on the two tests of executive function, and performance on these was what distinguished children with autism most from matched controls. Moreover, theory of mind and executive function scores were correlated.

In the last 15 years, an enormous literature has developed on executive function deficits in autism that I cannot do justice to here. Hill (2004) provides a good review of the literature. A few points are worth noting in particular. People with autism have difficulty with planning tasks, but their difficulties are relatively greater with longer and more complex planning tasks, suggesting that general intellectual impairments are partly to blame. Perhaps more characteristically, people with autism have problems inhibiting prepotent (i.e., more powerful) responses. Oddly, however, they are good at Stroop tasks, which are the classic test of adults' difficulties with inhibiting habitual responses. They are poor at set shifting, both at the Wisconsin Card Sort Task and its simplified cousin, the DCCS task. For example, Colvert, Custance and Swettenham (2002) found that children with autism performed badly on the DCCS, and performance was highly correlated with a battery of first-order theory of mind tasks, after partialling out age and intelligence ($r = .79$, $p < .001$).

Thus, people with autism have clear problems with theory of mind and executive function, and these problems are related. Just as with preschool children, the direction of causality is hard to judge: Are executive function problems primary, causing difficulties in reasoning about the mind? Or is a lack of insight into one's own mind a cause of difficulties in self-control and complex behaviour? An executive account has the advantage of more plausibly explaining the third element of the triad—narrow restricted interests and repetitive behaviour. Novel behaviour requires you to stop doing what you are used to doing. Developing wide interests requires you to disengage with one topic and embrace new ones [see Turner (1997) for a discussion].

However, if a general psychological theory of autism is required, the theory of mind hypothesis and the executive function hypothesis will be difficult to disentangle because both are likely to be true, as cause and consequence. Working out which one is cause and which is consequence is likely to be harder in the case of autism because of the attendant mental retardation, which may cause independent difficulties on certain tasks. A further complication is that studies are conducted with participants of a very wide range of IQs and abilities: In some studies participants have normal intelligence; in others they are severely retarded. The only thing uniting participants is a diagnosis of autism, and it is questionable how comparable different participant groups are. It seems likely that the issue of causality will be easier to work out in normal development first, before being applied to a clinical population.

Weak central coherence

Frith (1989) suggested that the thought of people with autism has a particular character. Normally we strive to extract or impose meaning onto things. When we see a picture, we want to know what it is of; when we hear a story, we want to

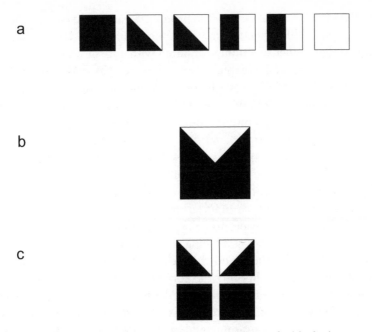

FIGURE 10.3 Wechsler's Block Design subtest: (a) the six faces of a block; (b) a typical target pattern; (c) a presegmented target pattern.

know what it is about; when we enter a meeting, we want to know what is going on. We attempt to pull higher-level meaning from what our senses tell us and put everything in context. In doing so, we tend to lose sight of the details. We do not notice the brushstrokes on the picture or remember the particular words used in the story or meeting. This tendency to focus on "meaning in context" Frith calls central coherence. Her suggestion is that autistic thought is characterized by weak central coherence: People with autism have difficulty seeing things as a whole, but may be very good at focusing on the parts.

This idea is interesting because it offers the possibility of not only explaining autistic deficits, but explaining the surprising strengths shown in autism. As well as the occasional autistic savant, people with autism generally are good at certain things. For example, although their recall of a set of related items is poorer than normal, their recall of unrelated items is relatively good (Tager-Flusberg, 1991). This is the opposite of the normal pattern, and may be because people with autism are focusing just on the items in both cases, so are not assisted by any relationships between them.

The performance of people with autism on intelligence tests also shows an unusual profile. Although they are poor at verbal parts of the tests, on some parts they can perform very well. This is particularly the case on the Block Design subtest of the Wechsler scales. Children are given four blocks. The six faces of a block are shown in Figure 10.3a. The task is to reproduce a pattern given on a piece of card by arranging a set of blocks. One example is shown in Figure 10.3b. Shah and Frith (1993) found that higher functioning children with autism were faster than typical adolescents at this task. However, when the target patterns were given presegmented as shown in Figure 10.3c, the reaction time advantage shown by children with autism disappeared. The aspect of the task that people with autism excel at is in breaking down the design into its constituent parts; when this is done for them, they are no better than controls. Shah and Frith argue that the enhanced ability to segment a pattern is a consequence of weak central coherence: Their perception of the target stimulus was less dominated by its overall pattern.

Happé (1997) looked at the ability to read homographs. These are words with one spelling and two distinct pronunciations, such as *tear* (in your dress) and *tear* (in your eye). Choosing the appropriate pronunciation requires you to take the rest of the sentence into account, something that may be difficult for someone with weak central coherence. She found that relative to normal 7-year-olds, children with autism were poor at choosing the correct pronunciation, typically using the most frequent pronunciation regardless of the preceding sentence context. So for example, in a sentence containing the phrase ". . . in Lucy's dress there was a big tear", the participants with autism would pronounce *tear* to rhyme with *beer*.

Another striking demonstration of weak central coherence, this time at the level of perception, was also provided by Happé (1996). She presented people with autism with visual illusions based on the distorting effect of context. For example, in the Ebbinghaus illusion, two identical circles are surrounded by either smaller circles or large circles. The one surrounded by smaller circles appears to be larger. Happé asked her subjects whether the two central circles were different or the same size. Ordinary 8-year-olds succumbed to most of the illusions, whereas children with autism of similar verbal mental age answered most questions correctly. When the to-be-judged items were artificially disembedded from the context by placing brightly coloured plastic strips over them, both ordinary and autistic participants performed well. Even at the perceptual level, it seems people with autism see the world more as a collection of details rather than a unified whole.

Savant ability

Weak central coherence might also explain why some people with autism possess savant skills. These amazing abilities in highly prescribed areas are fascinating and have proved difficult to explain. Autistic savants can show amazing abilities in calendrical calculations, areas of mathematics, drawing and painting, languages and music—while remaining in other respects profoundly autistic. Frith (2003) suggests that these abilities may have in common that they start with intense focus on small elements, which provides the building blocks for the savant talent.

She cites a drawing savant who begins with an unimportant detail and builds an entire drawing up from there, without sketching any overall plan as a nonautistic draughtsman might. Similarly, many people with autism have absolute pitch—the ability to identify and label musical notes. Very rare in the general population, people with autism may be more able to perceive individual notes in a pure fashion, free of the influence of other notes and sounds. This may form the basis of savant musical ability.

Although this is all speculative, there is some evidence that savant-like ability can be temporarily induced in normal people. Snyder, Bahramali, Hawker and Mitchell (2006) used a technique called repetitive transcranial magnetic stimulation (rTMS), in which a powerful electromagnetic field temporarily inhibits activity in part of the brain. They inhibited the left anterior temporal lobe of brave volunteers. The volunteers were asked to guess how many dots there were on a computer screen. Arrays of between 50 and 150 dots appeared for 1.5 seconds, much too briefly to count. There are some autistic savants who are able to judge numbers of items in this sort of situation very quickly and accurately (e.g., Sacks, 1986). The volunteers were quite poor at this before stimulation, and poor 1 hour after stimulation. However, they were significantly better just after rTMS, getting to within 5 of the correct number on a quarter of trials (participants, who may have thought they were guessing, tended to answer in multiples of 5). Snyder et al. speculate that they have effectively knocked out part of the brain concerned with meaning and concepts, which may normally inhibit the perception of detail. The participants may have temporarily been given conscious access to literal details.

This is speculative too, but the similarity to weak central coherence is clear. Further, it is also clear that (temporary) brain abnormality may allow at least one savant-like skill associated with detailed processing, and allow it immediately, without any learning or development. Weak central coherence theory has clear potential to explain, amongst other things, savant ability.

How does it all fit together?

Frith (1989) originally suggested that weak central coherence could account for theory of mind difficulties; social understanding plausibly requires the integration of a large amount of disparate information. Mental states serve to explain at a higher level a wide variety of behaviours. More recently, Frith (2003) and Happé (2000) have altered their position to one in which weak central coherence exists alongside a mindreading deficit, separate but interacting. In the general population there may be a continuum from strong to weak central coherence, and either end of the continuum would have information processing benefits of certain types, and corresponding weaknesses: "Autism occurs more often in families of physicists, engineers, and mathematicians" (Baron-Cohen et al., 1998). However, even weak central coherence would not result in autism unless accompanied by an additional theory of mind deficit, and the normal tendency towards strong central coherence might compensate for deficits in mindreading ability.

The empirical reason for relaxing the claims regarding weak central coherence is that there is patchy experimental evidence for a relationship between theory of mind and central coherence. For example, Happé (1994) found that performance of people with autism on theory of mind tasks was unrelated to their superior performance on the Block Design test. Happé (1997) showed that people with autism who passed false belief tasks were better at reading homographs in context, although not as good as normal controls, and those who passed second-order tasks were no better than those who only passed first-order tasks. Pellicano, Maybery, Durkin and Maley (2006) compared a group of 40 people with high-functioning autism on tests of central coherence, theory of mind and executive function. They found that good performance on central coherence tests in general was not strongly related to either theory of mind or executive function performance. (Comparisons of theory of mind and executive function were not reported.) One of the few demonstrations of a relationship was given by Jarrold, Butler, Cottington and Jimenez (2000). They compared a theory of mind battery with tests of central coherence with ordinary and autistic participants. In both groups, they found a strong relationship. However, this relationship was only apparent if mental age was partialled out; otherwise the two abilities were completely unrelated. Particularly in the case of normal 5-year-olds, it seems peculiar that mental age would vary in such a way as to mask this relationship, which makes these findings hard to interpret. Overall, existing evidence suggests any relationship between central coherence and theory of mind is at best very weak.

Conclusion

Autism resists explanation. The symptoms of the disorder themselves show weak central coherence. Theorists, on the other hand, have a drive for strong central coherence. This manifests itself in attempts to explain all the symptoms of autism in terms of a single cognitive deficit: such as theory of mind impairment, executive function impairments or weak central coherence. It also leads to a lack of attention to detail, especially details that do not fit the favoured theory well. The debate seems intractable so long as we assume that a single cognitive account is appropriate. Each of the current cognitive theories has its merits. Theory of mind and executive function accounts are very difficult to tease apart because if one were correct, it would give rise to the other: If autism results from a lack of theory of mind, that would probably lead to executive dysfunction, so signs of executive function could be indirect support for the theory of mind hypothesis; alternatively, if autism is primarily a consequence of executive dysfunction, this could result in an impaired theory of mind, so specific theory of mind deficits could be support for the executive dysfunction hypothesis. Weak central coherence theory stands somewhat apart from these two. It does not necessarily explain well the core symptoms of autism, but seems to capture nicely the quality of autistic thought.

However, as discussed earlier, a single cognitive theory is not necessarily appropriate. A single physical cause, whether one of genetics or of brain dysfunction, could give rise to multiple cognitive deficits, perhaps partially overlapping or interacting. At present this seems to be favoured by many theorists. Frith and Happé have couched weak central coherence and theory of mind impairment as separate deficits for some time. Happé et al. (2006) and Pellicano et al. (2006) think this may be the case with all three areas of impairment, if not also within each area. Ultimately, this question will probably be resolved by finding causal factors for autism at the physical level. Research into the genetic basis is promising: see Happé et al. (2006) for a brief review. The causal relationship between theory of mind and executive dysfunction may also be illuminated by work on the general population. The relationship of these two factors in normal development is as yet far from resolved.

Chapter 11

Coda

M Y AIM HAS BEEN to review research and theory concerning children's developing theory of mind. The
field has achieved a level of maturity and depth that makes
such a review worthwhile. Nevertheless, theory of mind is
very much a work in progress, and remains a fast-moving
field. For that reason, I do not propose an extensive general
conclusion beyond the specific summaries and conclusions
at the end of each chapter. Instead, I close the book with a
brief informal discussion.

One thing that I think is established beyond doubt
is that children start to understand belief from around
the age of 4 years. This gives them a new grasp of human
behaviour that is readily apparent both inside and outside
the laboratory. I began my research career convinced that
the false belief task underestimates children (Freeman,
Lewis & Doherty, 1991). However, after enough time
spent on your knees in preschools and nurseries playing
with dolls and boxes, it is difficult to avoid the conclusion
that 3-year-olds genuinely do not understand belief.

The false belief task has received a disproportionate
amount of attention. Nevertheless, it is a good diagnostic
test of a more general insight into the mind. Once children
can predict and explain false beliefs, they can also reason
about knowledge and ignorance, distinguish appearance

and reality, and realize how things look to other people. This is the bedrock on which understanding of more complex mental states is built. Children's basic understanding gradually becomes more sophisticated. They soon realize that limited perceptual access, such as seeing a small indistinguishable part of an object, is not always enough to know what something is, and that the five senses deliver distinct information. The ability to reason about mental states that concern other mental states develops slightly later. It is not until children are about 6 years that they can reason about one person's belief about another person's belief. At around the same time, they understand that emotions are not directly based on the objective state of the world, but on a person's beliefs about it. More complex mental state reasoning continues to develop into adulthood.

Of the three theories considered in Chapter 3, Theory Theory seems to fit the developmental data best. Simulation Theory is so intuitively plausible, however, that it is difficult to avoid the conclusion that we simulate others sometimes. This is particularly so for emotion. When we imagine ourselves in an emotive situation, we really feel a little of the emotion in question. Simulation also seems potentially useful for insight into very complex situations for which working through the machinations of a theory might be too difficult. Jane Austen was probably a superb simulator. I have nothing against Modularity Theory in principle, although as yet there is little specific evidence for it.

In particular I favour Perner's representational theory of theory of mind. This is not simply because he was my PhD supervisor. It is a well-known fact that pets frequently resemble their owners, and a similar phenomenon seems to occur between students and their supervisors. However that may be, I favour the theory for the more specific reason that my data demanded it. I designed my PhD research to be an honest test of Perner's theory. A natural prediction from the theory was that children should understand mental representation and linguistic representation at the same time. My way of testing this is described in Chapter 5. As it happened, the predictions were borne out, so I am inclined to think the theory is broadly correct. Recently Marina Wimmer and I have extended the method used for measuring understanding of linguistic representation to pictorial representation, in the form of ambiguous figures, and found similar findings.

The fact that mental and nonmental representation are understood at the same time is worth emphasizing. What develops at 4 years is not limited to an understanding of belief, and not even limited to an understanding of mental states. Instead, something quite general is developing. This fact should be taken into account when theorizing. Simulation Theory and Modularity Theory, for example, are construed entirely in terms of understanding of mental states, and provide no ready explanation for children's understanding extending beyond the mental.

It may even be appropriate to view the development at 4 years as broader still. The enthusiasm for research on executive functions stemmed initially from the idea that executive development might provide a straightforward explanation of theory of mind development. This proved anything but the case. It now seems likely that development of both theory of mind and executive function ability is complex and interrelated. There are certainly plausible causal effects in each direction, which experiments have been as yet unable to disentangle. It may be appropriate to view the development of executive function and theory of mind as aspects of a single phenomenon.

Theory of mind does not arise on its own. It arises alongside an understanding of nonmental representation, particularly a reflective understanding of language. This type of metalinguistic awareness has long been associated with the ability to control, monitor and plan linguistic processing: executive function ability, in other words. Both theory of mind and metalinguistic awareness are related to each other and to executive function ability in a seemingly complex and interdependent way. What happens around the age of 4 years can therefore be described as the rapid development of a general ability to reflect on and control one's own thought and linguistic processes. Recognizing the breadth of the phenomenon may help elucidate it.

Recent demonstrations of early implicit sensitivity to false beliefs suggest that something precedes explicit false belief understanding. There is too much counter-evidence from research on false belief understanding, executive function and language to argue that infants already have a functioning representational theory of mind. However, these new data suggest many interesting possibilities.

A suspicion of mine is that the relationship between implicit and explicit theories of mind may prove similar to the relationship between infant gaze following and preschool explicit judgements of gaze. As discussed in Chapter 7, children are sensitive to others' gaze from early infancy. By about 18 months old, infants have a sophisticated ability to follow gaze, even taking into account occluding barriers. However, children cannot make explicit judgements of eye direction until they are about 3 years old. Furthermore, children's ability to make *fine* judgements of gaze direction has only begun to develop at 3 years. This suggests that explicit understanding of attention does not arise out of children's excellent gaze-following ability.

Something similar may be the case with early sensitivity to others' beliefs. Hypothetically, humans have an innate ability to monitor aspects of what others are attending to and thinking about—a theory of mind and attention module, if you like. The output of this module would be used to direct our own attention to appropriate aspects of the environment. This would be extremely useful. However, these outputs may be either very rudimentary (the ability probably evolved only recently, after all) or in a form that is not readily available to the rest of the cognitive system. It proves its worth in early childhood, but is eventually superseded by an explicit theory of mind. The explicit form may well have only become possible with the advent of language, both in development and evolution.

Studies concerning the role of language in theory of mind development have produced some of the most interesting recent findings. In particular, it appears that mothers foster their children's theory of mind development. They do this by tailoring their use of mental state language to a level slightly above the child's competence, but within their zone of proximal development. Parenting style, mind-mindedness and interactions with other family members also play a role. We should remember that theory of mind develops in a social and cultural context. After all, it forms the basis of our social and cultural lives.

This is emphasized by the strange condition of autism, which is marked by difficulties with most of the developments discussed in this book. People with autism have impairments in theory of mind, joint attention, executive functions, language and a marked lack of pretend play. Viewing autism through the lens of theory of mind has led to a much deeper understanding of the syndrome. The theory of mind hypothesis has done its job well.

For the time being, that is all I wanted to say.

Notes

Chapter 2

1 Infancy is used throughout to mean from birth to 2 years. This is typical in the literature. Two-year-olds are referred to as toddlers; three- to four-year-olds are referred to as preschoolers.

2 A general problem with meta-analyses concerns publication bias. If a research group carries out an experiment looking at early competence, they are far more likely to pursue the line of research if they find good performance in young children. They are then more likely to write up and submit the research for publication. In turn, studies that show an effect are more likely to be accepted for publication. Thus, in fields where most researchers have preconceived ideas about the existence or direction of effects, there is a tendency for the literature to reflect these ideas even when there may be as many, or more, unpublished or discontinued studies demonstrating the opposite. For example, a recent meta-analysis on psychokinesis suggests that publication bias may account for observed effects (Bosch, Steinkamp & Boller, 2006). Most research into psychokinesis is carried out because the researchers believe in the phenomenon. A similar effect probably applies to theory of mind research; it is tempting to impute even young children with sophisticated social understanding. The false belief task is easy to carry out, requiring no specialized equipment or training. Thousands of people have done so, and even if the early competence hypothesis is incorrect, 5% of these would have found effects that satisfy the 5% significance criterion used for most psychological research. Meta-analyses are usually largely restricted to published data, and should therefore be interpreted with a degree of caution.

Chapter 3

1 Perner's account mainly deals with the development of children's *representational* understanding of mental states; he is not necessarily committed to all theory of mind being theory-like, and is reasonably sympathetic to some mindreading processes conforming to

Simulation Theory, often seen as the antithesis of Theory Theory. He might well object to being called a theory theorist.

2 Perner initially used "sense", following Frege (1892). Frege noted that the phrases "the morning star" and the "evening star" both refer to the planet Venus. However, although they refer to the same object, they clearly differ in meaning. The shared meaning Frege called the referent (Venus); the difference in meaning he called the sense. "Sense" however has specific philosophical connotations. Perner now uses "perspective". This term approximates its normal meaning: Any two views (or thoughts, or descriptions) of the same situation involve a difference in perspective.

3 A minority of philosophers claim that this kind of belief–desire psychology is not an accurate account of the way the mind works (e.g., Churchland, 1981). However, there is no alternative account on offer. Fodor has this to say: "If commonsense intentional psychology really were to collapse, that would be, beyond comparison, the greatest intellectual catastrophe in the history of our species; if we're that wrong about the mind, then that's the wrongest we've ever been about anything . . . We'll be in deep, deep trouble if we have to give it up" (Fodor, 1987, p. xii)

Chapter 4

1 Intuitively, I am inclined to think that 3-year-olds take most questions at face value. They are unaware they are being tested; experimenters take great pains to frame experiments as fun games. This kind of criticism does seem valid for older children, however, who, familiar with teacher's questions, are more anxious about giving wrong answers.

2 By varying the amount of information available in the portion, it is possible to vary the difficulty of the task. Even adults would probably have difficulty in the limiting case where there is almost but not quite enough information for the average person to accurately guess what the object is. This would be especially difficult if the adult had not initially seen just the portion and been unable to determine what it was. The difficulty of any particular version of the droodle task is therefore variable depending on the size and informativeness of the visible portion. This may explain why different research groups have found the task of varying difficulty.

Chapter 5

1 Even adults sometimes make mistakes about this. Recently, watching a film, I noticed my friend craning her neck trying to see what was behind one of the actors on screen.

2 Which is a normal way to speak of pictures. Magritte's painting, *The Treachery of Images* ("Ceci n'est pas une pipe") is subversive for this reason. The painting of a pipe, despite what we might say, is quite clearly not a pipe.

3 DeLoache also suggests that children find the model task hard because models have a dual identity: as objects in their own right, and as representations of something else. This is very plausible, and may result from the amount and type of experience children have with the different media: They have a lot of experience with pictures, including pictures of familiar people and specific objects; they have little experience with models, especially not with models of familiar people or specific objects. Neither do most adults. This may explain why pictures seem to us "transparent": Looking at a photograph of a familiar person, we see the person rather than the picture. If presented with a miniature model of a

familiar person, we might acknowledge the likeness, but it would not seem to *be* them in the same way that a picture does. This lack of transparency probably contributes to the difficulty of the model task.

4 This was a new puppet. The original Puppet was killed in action in 1994.

5 Expecting a preschool child to stare fixedly at something for a whole minute is naïvely optimistic. Marina Wimmer (2007) has been developing alternative methods of assessing children's ability to reverse.

Chapter 6

1 Strictly speaking, the contents of pretence are not so much false as not necessarily true. For example, in a pretend tea party, the proposition "this cup is full of tea" is usually false. Once the tea has been drunk, or some meddlesome teddy has poured it over a monkey, the proposition "this cup is empty" is true, but remains the content of pretence. In this instance, it just happens to coincide with reality.

2 In discussions of this experiment, the Jane's rabbit story is always used as the exemplar. In Perner et al.'s original report, the authors more fully describe the other story, in which children were shown a naked cardboard cut-out boy doll, complete with a penis. The doll was then dressed up as a girl. In one condition another doll had seen the transformation; in the other condition the second doll first encountered the boy in feminine form. This is the only developmental experiment I am aware of to combine nudity and transvestism. This is probably why commentators usually discuss the rabbit story.

Chapter 7

1 Farroni, Mansfield, Lai and Johnson (2003) subsequently attempted to show that the effect is due to an eye-direction detector after all. Using 4- to 5-month-old infants, who are much less subject to sticky fixation, they found that if the face was inverted the cuing effect did not occur. This might indicate that cuing is not simply due to motion. However, infants tended to move their eyes in the direction of the pupil shift before the face disappeared. This is likely to have produced "inhibition of return", a short-term inhibition of attention to recently attended locations, which would counteract the cuing effect. Their second finding can also be explained by inhibition of return: The eyes of an upright face shifted to one side then back to the centre. Infants were slower to locate the object when it appeared in the cued location, but they again tended to follow the gaze shift to the side before the face had disappeared.

2 Note the added cue of movement. Although full details are not provided, the clown's eyes would have appeared much larger than life. The clown's head and shoulders filled the screen, which was 32 inches (81 cm), and children were seated 12 inches (30 cm) from the screen.

3 The arm of the pointing man is a lot bigger than the eyes in the Looking-where task. In another experiment, we made stimuli with a much smaller pointing man; his arm was exactly the same length as the diameter of one of the eyes in the Looking-where stimuli. Performance on this version of the Point-direction task was just as good as the standard one.

Chapter 8

1 This type might also be considered an expression theory. If children have yet to develop a framework in which their mental state concepts can be employed, it is an emergence theory. If they have the framework but cannot use it (except under ideal conditions, perhaps), it is an expression theory.

2 The task is preceded by a lengthy 15 trial pretest with opaque boxes. This is intended to teach children that they get the chocolate if they point to the empty box. However, since they have no control in this phase, it may instead induce a sense of helplessness that contributes to perseveration later by demotivating them to alter the obvious response.

3 Simpson et al.'s novel task did not have the initial opaque boxes phase; their standard Windows task did. If the warm-up does induce a sense of helplessness, this may contribute to the different performance on the two tasks.

4 This bias may be situation-specific. Experiments that support the Mutual Exclusivity bias tend to require children to use two words for the same thing in the same situation. Counterevidence comes from the fact that children know and use many overlapping words (Clark, 1997). The two sets of findings can be resolved if it is assumed that children may use multiple terms for objects so long as different uses occur in different situations. They have difficulty using more than one term in a single situation (which would require redescription).

Chapter 10

1 Phrases like "autistic child" and particularly "autist" are now typically avoided. "Child with autism" or "person(s) with autism" are the preferred terms. Although they are unwieldy, they emphasize the person over the disorder.

Glossary

Executive functions

A loosely defined set of mental processes relating to self-control of thought, attention or action. Typically there are considered to be three types:

(1) Inhibition, generally of habitual or automatic responses.
(2) Effective use of working memory—holding information in mind and updating it as and when appropriate.
(3) Shifting between different sets of responses, according to what kind of response is currently appropriate.

False belief task

Considered to be the diagnostic test of "theory of mind". Here "theory of mind" is informally taken to require the ability to predict action on the basis of a character's belief, rather than on the basis of the real state of affairs. In order to distinguish between these two possibilities, the belief in question needs to be false. There are two commonly used types:

213

(1) *The unexpected transfer task* (a.k.a. transfer task, Maxi task, Sally–
Ann task)
A character typically places an object somewhere, and it is moved
while the character is absent. Children are asked where the character
will look: the original or current location of the object. This type of
task was devised by Wimmer and Perner (1983), based on a suggestion
by Dennett (1978).

(2) *The unexpected contents task* (a.k.a. contents task, Smarties task,
deceptive box task)
The child is shown a box which contains something other than the
presumable contents. Classically a Smarties chocolate tube is found to
contain pencils. Children are asked what they initially thought was
inside (own belief question) and what someone else will think is inside
when first seeing it (other belief question). This type of task was
devised by Hogrefe, Wimmer and Perner (1986).

Homonym
Each of two words with the same pronunciation but different meanings, such as
"bat" (flying mammal) and "bat" (sports equipment).

Metarepresentation
The process of "representing the representational relation itself" (Pylyshyn,
1978), or representing a representation as a representation (Perner, 1991). This
concept has proved difficult to understand, probably because of multiple uses of
a five-syllable word referring to different things in one sentence. Metarepresentation is necessary to understand false belief. It is also necessary to understand
synonymy or homonymy.

Modularity Theory
The claim that theory of mind reasoning is carried out by one or more specialized
neural systems. These are typically taken to be innate. Theory of mind development conforms to the maturation of these modules.

Propositional attitudes
Data structures for representing mental states. They have four parts:

(1) *The agent*: The person who holds the belief or desire.
(2) *The proposition*: The content of the belief or desire.
(3) *The attitude*: The kind of mental state we are talking about. Adults
recognize many kinds of attitude: think, believe, know, doubt, desire,
hope, fear, and so on.
(4) *The anchor*: The bit of the real world the proposition is about (tech-

nically speaking, according to which the proposition is to be evaluated).

Propositional attitudes can also be used to represent statements and other forms of communication.

Second-order tasks
Theory of mind tasks which test understanding of other people's mental states concerning other mental states. For example, understanding of one person's false belief about another person's belief. Another example concerns belief-based emotions: the understanding that emotions are based on what a person believes to be the case, irrespective of what is actually the case.

Sentential complements
Propositions embedded in a description of a mental state or communication description. They follow the "that" in statements like "Maxi thinks that his chocolate is in the cupboard" or "Sally says that her marble was here a moment ago".

Simulation Theory
The claim that we carry out theory of mind reasoning by using our own decision-making apparatus as a model of another person's. We imagine ourselves in the other person's position, and ask what we would think, feel or do, in those circumstances. Successful simulation would require differences between ourselves and the other person to be taken account of: different initial knowledge, information, beliefs, desires, character traits, and so on.

Synonym
A word or phrase that means the same as another word or phrase in the same language.

Theory Theory
The claim that theory of mind is theory-like: Mental state concepts such as belief and desire are linked to each other and to perception and action by a set of rules.

References

Aksu-Koç, A. A. (1988). *The acquisition of aspects and modality*. Cambridge: Cambridge University Press.

American Psychiatric Association. (1994). *Diagnostic and statistical manual of disorders, 4th edition*. Washington, DC: Author.

Anderson, J. R., & Doherty, M. J. (1997). Preschoolers' perception of other people's looking: Photographs and drawings. *Perception, 26*, 333–343.

Anderson, J. R., & Mitchell, R. W. (1999). Macqques, but not lemurs, co-orient visually with humans. *Folia Primatalogica, 70*, 17–22.

Anderson, J. R., Montant, M., & Schmitt, D. (1996). Rhesus monkeys fail to use gaze direction as an experimenter-given cue in an object-choice task. *Behavioural Processes, 37*, 47–55.

Anderson, J. R., Sallaberry, P., & Barbier, H. (1995). Use of experimenter-given cues during object-choice tasks by capuchin monkeys. *Animal Behaviour, 49*, 201–208.

Asperger, H. (1944). Die "Autistischen Psychopathen" im Kindesalter. *Archiv für Psychiatrie und Nervenkrankheiten, 117*, 76–136. Reprinted in Frith, U. (1991). *Autism and Asperger's Syndrome*. Cambridge: Cambridge University Press.

Astington, J., & Jenkins, J. (1995). Theory of mind development and social understanding. *Cognition and Emotion, 9*, 151–165.

Astington, J., & Jenkins, J. (1999). A longitudinal study of the relation between language and theory-of-mind development. *Developmental Psychology, 35*, 1311–1320.

Austen, J. (1813). *Pride and prejudice*. Whitehall, London: T. Egerton.

Avis, J., & Harris, P. (1991). Belief–desire reasoning among Baka children: Evidence for a universal conception of mind. *Child Development, 62*, 460–467.

Bailey, A., Le Couteur, A., Gottesman, I., Bolton, P., Simonoff, E., Yuzda, E., et al. (1995). Autism as a strongly genetic disorder: Evidence from a British twin study. *Psychological Medicine, 25*, 63–77.

Baillargeon, R. (1987). Object permanence in 3.5- and 4.5-month-old infants. *Developmental Psychology, 23*, 655–664.

Baron-Cohen, S. (1989a). Are autistic children behaviourists? An examination of their mental-physical, and appearance-reality distinctions. *Journal of Autism and Developmental Disorders, 19*, 579–600.

Baron-Cohen, S. (1989b). The autistic child's theory of mind: A case of specific developmental delay. *Journal of Child Psychology and Psychiatry, 30*, 285–289.

Baron-Cohen, S. (1995). *Mindblindness: An essay on autism and theory of mind*. Oxford: MIT Press.

Baron-Cohen, S. (2002). The extreme male brain theory of autism. *Trends in Cognitive Sciences, 6*, 248–254.

Baron-Cohen, S., Bolton, P., Wheelwright, S., Short, L., Mead, G., Smith, A., et al. (1998). Autism occurs more often in families of physicists, engineers, and mathematicians. *Autism, 2*, 296–301.

Baron-Cohen, S., & Cross, P. (1992). Reading the eyes: Evidence for the role of perception in the development of a theory of mind. *Mind & Language, 6*, 173–186.

Baron-Cohen, S., & Hammer, J. (1997). Parents of children with Asperger syndrome: What is the cognitive phenotype? *Journal of Cognitive Neuroscience, 9*, 548–554.

Baron-Cohen, S., Leslie, A. M., & Frith, U. (1985). Does the autistic child have a theory of mind? *Cognition, 21*, 37–46.

Baron-Cohen, S., Wheelwright, S., Stott, C., Bolton, P., & Goodyer, I. (1997). Is there a link between engineering and autism? *Autism, 1*, 153–163.

Bartsch, K., & Wellman, H. (1989). Young children's attribution of action to beliefs and desires. *Child Development, 60*, 946–964.

Beilin, H., & Pearlman, E. G. (1991). Children's iconic realism—object versus property realism. *Advances in Child Development and Behavior, 23*, 73–111.

Berg, E. A. (1948). A simple objective treatment for measuring flexibility in thinking. *Journal of General Psychology, 39*, 15–22.

Berguno, G., & Bowler, D. (2004). Understanding pretence and understanding action. *British Journal of Developmental Psychology, 22*, 531–544.

Bettelheim, B. (1967). *The empty fortress: Infantile autism and the birth of the self*. New York: Free Press.

Blades, M., & Cooke, Z. (1994). Young children's ability to understand a model as a spatial representation. *Journal of Genetic Psychology, 155*, 201–218.

Bosch, H., Steinkamp, F., & Boller, E. (2006). Examining psychokinesis: The interaction of human intention with random number generators—a meta-analysis. *Psychological Bulletin, 132*, 497–523.

Boucher, J. (1996). What could possibly explain autism? In P. Carruthers & P. Smith (Eds.), *Theories of theories of mind* (pp. 223–241). Cambridge: Cambridge University Press.

Brennan, S. E., & Clark, H. H. (1996). Conceptual pacts and lexical choice in conversation. *Journal of Experimental Psychology: Learning, Memory and Cognition, 22,* 1482–1493.

Bretherton, I., & Beeghly, M. (1982). Talking about internal states: The acquisition of an explicit theory of mind. *Developmental Psychology, 18,* 906–921.

Briskman, J., Happé, F., & Frith, U. (2001). Exploring the cognitive phenotype of autism: Weak "central coherence" in parents and siblings of children with autism: II. Real-life skills and preferences. *Journal of Child Psychology and Psychiatry, 42,* 309–316.

Brooks, P. J., Hanauer, J. B., Padowska, B., & Rosman, H. (2003). The role of selective attention in preschoolers' rule use in a novel dimensional card sort. *Cognitive Development, 18,* 195–215.

Bruce, V., Campbell, R. N., Doherty-Sneddon, G., Import, A., Langton, S., McAuley, S., et al. (2000). Testing face processing skills in children. *British Journal of Developmental Psychology, 18,* 319–333.

Burns, S. M., & Brainerd, C. J. (1979). Effects of constructive and dramatic play on perspective taking in very young children. *Developmental Psychology, 15,* 512–521.

Butler, S. C., Caron, A. J., & Brooks, R. (2000). Infant understanding of the referential nature of looking. *Journal of Cognition and Development, 1,* 359–377.

Call, J., & Tomasello, M. (1999). A nonverbal theory of mind test. The performance of children and apes. *Child Development, 70,* 381–395.

Callaghan, T., Rochat, P., Lillard, A., Claux, M. L., Odden, H., Itakura, S., et al. (2005). Synchrony in the onset of mental-state reasoning: Evidence from five cultures. *Psychological Science, 16,* 378–384.

Carlson, S. M., Mandell, D. J., & Williams, L. (2004). Executive function and theory of mind: Stability and prediction from ages 2 to 3. *Developmental Psychology, 40,* 1105–1122.

Carlson, S. M., & Moses, L. J. (2001). Individual differences in inhibitory control and children's theory of mind. *Child Development, 72,* 1032–1053.

Carlson, S. M., Moses, L. J., & Breton, C. (2002). How specific is the relation between executive function and theory of mind? Contributions of inhibitory control and working memory. *Infant and Child Development, 11,* 73–92.

Carruthers, P. (1996). Autism as mind-blindness: An elaboration and partial defence. In P. Carruthers & P. Smith (Eds.), *Theories of theories of mind* (pp. 257–273). Cambridge: Cambridge University Press.

Cassidy, K. W. (1995, April). *Use of a desire heuristic in a theory of mind task.* Paper presented at the biennial meeting of the Society for Research in Child Development, Indianapolis, IN.

Cassidy, K. W. (1998). Three- and 4-year-old children's ability to use desire- and belief-based reasoning. *Cognition, 66,* B1–B11.

Chandler, M., Fritz, A. S., & Hala, S. (1989). Small-scale deceit: Deception as a marker of two-, three-, and four-year-olds' early theories of mind. *Child Development, 60,* 1263–1277.

Chandler, M. J., & Helm, D. (1984). Developmental-changes in the contribution of shared experience to social role-taking competence. *International Journal of Behavioral Development, 7,* 145–156.

Charman, T., Ruffman, T., & Clements, W. (2002). Is there a gender difference in false-belief development? *Social Development, 11,* 1–10.

Chen, F. C., & Li, W. H. (2001). Genomic divergences between humans and other hominoids and the effective population size of the common ancestor of humans and chimpanzees. *American Journal of Human Genetics, 68,* 444–456.

Chen, M. J., & Lin, Z. X. (1994). Chinese preschoolers' difficulty with theory-of-mind tests. *Bulletin of the Hong Kong Psychological Society, 32/33,* 34–36.

Chen, R. T., & DeStefano, F. (1998). Vaccine adverse effects: Causal or coincidental? *The Lancet, 351,* 611–612.

Chess, S. (1977). Follow-up report on autism in congenital rubella. *Journal of Autism and Childhood Schizophrenia, 7,* 69–81.

Churchland, P. M. (1981). Eliminative materialism and the propositional attitudes. *Journal of Philosophy, 78,* 67–90.

Clark, E. V. (1978). Awareness of language: Some evidence from what children say and do. In A. Sinclair, R. J. Jarvella, & W. J. M. Levelt (Eds.), *The child's conception of language* (pp. 17–43). Berlin: Springer-Verlag.

Clark, E. V. (1988). On the logic of contrast. *Journal of Child Language, 15,* 317–335.

Clark, E. V. (1997). Conceptual perspective and lexical choice in acquisition. *Cognition, 64,* 1–37.

Clark, E. V., & Anderson, E. S. (1979, March). *Spontaneous repairs: Awareness in the process of acquiring language.* Paper presented at symposium on Reflections on Metacognition, Society for Research in Child Development, San Francisco, CA.

Clements, W. A., & Perner, J. (1994). Implicit understanding of belief. *Cognitive Development, 9,* 377–395.

Colvert, E., Custance, D., & Swettenham, J. (2002). Rule-based reasoning and theory of mind in autism: A commentary on the work of Zelazo, Jacques, Burack and Frye. *Infant and Child Development, 11,* 197–200.

Connolly, J. A., & Doyle, A. (1984). Relation of social fantasy play to social competence in preschoolers. *Developmental Psychology, 20,* 797–806.

Corkum, V., & Moore, C. (1995). Development of joint visual attention in infants. In C. Moore & P. Dunham (Eds.), *Joint attention: Its origins and role in development* (pp. 61–84). Hove, UK: Lawrence Erlbaum Associates.

Custer, W. L. (1996). A comparison of young children's understanding of contradictory representations in pretense, memory, and belief. *Child Development, 67,* 678–688.

Cutting, A. L., & Dunn, J. (1999). Theory of mind, emotion understanding, language, and family background: Individual differences and interrelations. *Child Development, 70,* 853–865.

Davis, H. L., & Pratt, C. (1995). The development of children's theory of mind: The working memory explanation. *Australian Journal of Psychology, 47,* 25–31.

Deák, G. O., Ray, S. D., & Brenneman, K. (2003). Children's perseverative appearance-reality errors are related to emerging language skills. *Child Development, 74,* 944–964.

DeLoache, J. S. (1987). Rapid change in the symbolic functioning of very young children. *Science, 238,* 1556–1557.

DeLoache, J. S., & Burns, N. M. (1994). Early understanding of the representational function of pictures. *Cognition, 52,* 83–110.

DeLoache, J. S., Pierroutsakos, S. L., Uttal, D. H., Rosengren, K. S., & Gottlieb, A. (1998). Grasping the nature of pictures. *Psychological Science, 9,* 205–210.

Dennett, D. C. (1978). Beliefs about beliefs. *Behavioral and Brain Sciences, 1,* 568–570.

D'Entremont, B., Hains, S. M. J., & Muir, D. W. (1997). A demonstration of gaze following in 3- to 6-month-olds. *Infant Behavior and Development, 20,* 569–572.

de Villiers, J. G., & de Villiers, P. A. (2000). Linguistic determination and the understanding of false beliefs. In P. Mitchell & K. J. Riggs (Eds.), *Children's reasoning and the mind* (pp. 191–228). Hove, UK: Psychology Press.

de Villiers, J. G., & Pyers, J. E. (2002). Complements to cognition: A longitudinal study of the relationship between complex syntax and false-belief-understanding. *Cognitive Development, 17,* 1037–1060.

Diamond, A., & Kirkham, N. (2005). Not quite as grown-up as we like to think: Parallels between cognition in childhood and adulthood. *Psychological Science, 16,* 291–297.

Dockrell, J., & Campbell, R. (1986). Lexical acquisition strategies in the preschool child. In S. A. Kuczaj & M. D. Barrett (Eds.), *The development of word meaning* (pp. 121–154). New York: Springer-Verlag.

Doherty, M. J. (1999). Selecting the wrong processor: A critique of Leslie's theory of mind mechanism-selection processor theory. *Developmental Science, 2,* 81–85.

Doherty, M. J. (2000). Children's understanding of homonymy: Metalinguistic awareness and false belief. *Journal of Child Language, 27,* 367–392.

Doherty, M. J. (2006). The development of mentalistic gaze understanding. *Infant and Child Development, 15,* 179–186.

Doherty, M. J., & Anderson, J. R. (1999). A new look at gaze: Preschool children's understanding of eye-direction. *Cognitive Development, 14,* 549–571.

Doherty, M. J., Anderson, J. R., & Howieson, L. (2007). *The rapid development of explicit gaze judgment ability at 3 years.* Manuscript submitted for publication, University of Stirling.

Doherty, M. J., & Kikuno, H. (2005). *Japanese children's theory of mind: Delayed or different?* Paper presented at the XIIth European Conference on Developmental Psychology La Laguna, Tenerife, Spain.

Doherty, M., & Perner, J. (1998). Metalinguistic awareness and theory of mind: Just two words for the same thing? *Cognitive Development, 13,* 279–305.

Doherty, M. J., & Wimmer, M. C. (2005). Children's understanding of ambiguous figures: Which cognitive developments are necessary to experience reversal? *Cognitive Development, 20,* 407–421.

Donaldson, M. (1978). *Children's minds.* London: Fontana.

Dow, G. A., & Pick, H. L. (1992). Young children's use of models and photographs as spatial representations. *Cognitive Development, 7,* 351–363.

Dunn, J., Brown J., & Beardsall, L. (1991a). Family talk about emotions, and children's later understanding of others' emotions. *Developmental Psychology, 27,* 448–455.

Dunn, J., Brown, J., Slomkowski, C., Tesla, C., & Youngblade, L. (1991b). Young children's understanding of other people's feelings and beliefs: Individual differences and their antecedents. *Child Development, 62,* 1352–1366.

Dunphy-Lelii, S., & Wellman, H. M. (2004). Infants' understanding of occlusion of others' line-of-sight: Implications for an emerging theory of mind. *European Journal of Developmental Psychology, 1,* 49–66.

Dyer, J. R., Shatz, M., & Wellman, H. M. (2000). Young children's storybooks as a source of mental state information. *Cognitive Development, 15,* 17–37.

Emery, N. J. (2000). The eyes have it: The neuroethology, function and evolution of social gaze. *Neuroscience and Biobehavioral Reviews, 24,* 581–604.

Emery, N. J., Lorincz, E. N., Perrett, D. I., Oram, M. W., & Baker, C. I. (1997). Gaze following and joint attention in rhesus monkeys (*Macaca mulatto*). *Journal of Comparative Psychology, 111,* 286–293.

Farroni, T., Csibra, G., Simion, F., & Johnson, M. H. (2002). Eye contact detection in humans from birth. *Proceedings of the National Academy of Sciences, 99,* 9602–9605.

Farroni, T., Johnson, M. H., Brockbank, M., & Simion, F. (2000). Infants' use of gaze direction to cue attention: The importance of perceived motion. *Visual Cognition, 7,* 705–718.

Farroni, T., Mansfield, E. M., Lai, C., & Johnson, M. H. (2003). Infants perceiving and acting on the eyes: Tests of an evolutionary hypothesis. *Journal of Experimental Child Psychology, 85,* 199–212.

Flavell, J. (1974). The development of inferences about others. In T. Mischel (Ed.), *Understanding other persons* (pp. 66–116). Oxford: Blackwell.

Flavell, J. H., Flavell, E. R., & Green, F. L. (1983). Development of the appearance–reality distinction. *Cognitive Psychology, 15,* 95–120.

Flavell, J. H., Miller, P. H., & Miller, S. A. (1993). *Cognitive development.* Englewood Cliffs, NJ: Prentice Hall.

Fodor, J. A. (1983). *The modularity of mind: An essay on faculty psychology.* Cambridge, MA: MIT Press.

Fodor, J. A. (1987). *Psychosemantics.* Cambridge, MA: MIT Press.

Fodor, J. A. (1992). A theory of the child's theory of mind. *Cognition, 44,* 283–296.

Fombonne, E. (2003). The prevalence of autism. *Journal of the American Medical Association, 289,* 87–89.

Fombonne, E., & Chakrabati, S. (2001). No evidence for a new variant of measles-mumps-rubella-induced autism. *Pediatrics, 108,* e56.

Freeman, N. H., Lewis, C., & Doherty, M. (1991). Preschoolers grasp of a desire for knowledge in false belief prediction: Practical intelligence and verbal report. *British Journal of Developmental Psychology, 9,* 139–157.

Frege, G. (1892). Über Sinn und Bedeutung. *Zeitschrift für Philosophie und Philosophische Kritik, 100,* 25–50.

Frith, U. (1989). *Autism: Explaining the enigma* (1st ed.). Oxford: Blackwell.

Frith, U. (2003). *Autism: Explaining the enigma* (2nd ed.). Oxford: Blackwell.

Frye, D., Zelazo, P. D., & Palfai, T. (1995). Theory of mind and rule-based reasoning. *Cognitive Development, 10,* 483–527.

Gerstadt, C. L., Hong, Y. J., & Diamond, A. (1994). The relationship between cognition and action: Performance of children 3½–7 years old on a stroop-like day–night test. *Cognition*, *53*, 129–153.

Golinkoff, R. M., Hirsh-Pasek, K., Bailey, L. M., & Wenger, N. R. (1992). Young-children and adults use lexical principles to learn new nouns. *Developmental Psychology*, *28*, 99–108.

Gombert, J. E. (1990/1992). *Metalinguistic development*. London: Harvester Wheatsheaf.

Goméz, J. C. (1996). Non-human primate theories of (non-human primate) minds: Some issues concerning the origins of mind-reading. In P. Carruthers & P. Smith (Eds.), *Theories of theories of mind* (pp. 330–343). Cambridge: Cambridge University Press.

Goméz, R. L., & Gerken, L. (2000). Infant artificial language learning and language acquisition. *Trends in Cognitive Sciences*, *4*, 178–186.

Gopnik, A., & Astington, J. W. (1988). Children's understanding of representational change and its relation to the understanding of false belief and the appearance–reality distinction. *Child Development*, *59*, 26–37.

Gopnik, A., & Graf, P. (1988). Knowing how you know—young children's ability to identify and remember the sources of their beliefs. *Child Development*, *59*, 1366–1371.

Gopnik, A., & Meltzoff, A. N. (1984). Semantic and cognitive development in 15- to 21-month-old children. *Journal of Child Language*, *11*, 495–513.

Gopnik, A., & Rosati, A. (2001). Duck or rabbit? Reversing ambiguous figures and understanding ambiguous representations. *Developmental Science*, *4*, 175–183.

Gopnik, A., Slaughter, V., & Meltzoff, A. (1994). Changing your views: How understanding visual perception can lead to a new theory of mind. In C. Lewis & P. Mitchell (Eds.), *Children's early understanding of mind: Origins and development* (pp. 157–181). Hove, UK: Lawrence Erlbaum Associates Ltd.

Gopnik, A., & Wellman, H. M. (1992). Why the child's theory of mind really is a theory. *Mind & Language*, *7*, 145–171.

Gopnik, A., & Wellman, H. M. (1994). The theory theory. In L. Hirschfeld & S. Gelman (Eds.), *Domain specificity in cognition and culture* (pp. 257–293). New York: Cambridge University Press.

Gordon, A. C. L., & Olson, D. R. (1998). The relation between acquisition of a theory of mind and the capacity to hold in mind. *Journal of Experimental Child Psychology*, *68*, 70–83.

Gordon, R. (1986). Folk psychology as simulation. *Mind & Language*, *1*, 158–171.

Gratch, G. (1972). A study of the relative dominance of vision and touch in six-month-old infants. *Child Development*, *43*, 615–623.

Grice, H. P. (1957). Meaning. *The Philosophical Review*, *66*, 377–388.

Haddon, M. (2003). *The curious incident of the dog in the night-time*. London: Doubleday.

Hadwin, J., & Perner, J. (1991). Pleased and surprised: Children's cognitive theory of emotion. *British Journal of Developmental Psychology*, *9*, 215–234.

Hakes, D. T. (1980). *The development of metalinguistic abilities in children*. New York: Springer-Verlag.

Hala, S., & Russell, J. (2001). Executive control within strategic deception: A window on early cognitive development? *Journal of Experimental Child Psychology*, *80*, 112–141.

Hansen, M. B., & Markman, E. M. (2005). Appearance questions can be misleading: A discourse-based account of the appearance–reality problem. *Cognitive Psychology, 50*, 233–263.

Happé, F. G. E. (1994). An advanced test of theory of mind—understanding of story characters thoughts and feelings by able autistic, mentally-handicapped, and normal-children and adults. *Journal of Autism and Developmental Disorders, 24*, 129–154.

Happé, F. G. E. (1995). The role of age and verbal ability in the theory of mind task: Performance of subjects with autism. *Child Development, 66*, 843–855.

Happé, F. G. E. (1996). Studying weak central coherence at low levels: Children with autism do not succumb to visual illusions. A research note. *Journal of Child Psychology and Psychiatry and Allied Disciplines, 37*, 873–877.

Happé, F. G. E. (1997). Central coherence and theory of mind in autism: Reading homographs in context. *British Journal of Developmental Psychology, 15*, 1–12.

Happé, F. (2000). Parts and wholes, meaning and minds: Central coherence and its relation to theory of mind. In S. Baron-Cohen, H. Tager-Flusberg, & D. J. Cohen (Eds.), *Understanding other minds. Perspectives from developmental cognitive neuroscience* (2nd ed., pp. 203–221). Oxford: Oxford University Press.

Happé, F., Ronald, A., & Plomin, R. (2006). Time to give up on a single explanation for autism. *Nature Neuroscience, 9*, 1218–1220.

Hare, B., Call, J., Agnetta, M., & Tomasello, M. (2000). Chimpanzees know what conspecifics do and do not see. *Animal Behaviour, 59*, 771–778.

Hare, B., Call, J., & Tomasello, M. (2001). Do chimpanzees know what conspecifics know? *Animal Behaviour, 61*, 139–151.

Harms, T., & Clifford, R. (1980). *Early Childhood Environmental Rating Scale*. New York: Teachers College Press, Columbia University.

Harris, P. L. (1992) From simulation to folk psychology: The case for development. *Mind & Language, 7*, 120–144.

Harris, P. L., Brown, E., Marriot, C., Whittall, S., & Harmer, S. (1991). Monsters, ghosts and witches: Testing the limits of the fantasy–reality distinction in younger children. *British Journal of Developmental Psychology, 9*, 105–123.

Harris, P. L., Johnson, C. N., Hutton, D., Andrews, G., & Cooke, T. (1989). Young children's theory of mind and emotion. *Cognition and Emotion, 3*, 379–400.

Harris, P. L., & Kavanaugh, R. D. (1993). Young children's understanding of pretense. *Monographs of the Society for Research in Child Development, 58*, 1–107.

Harris, P. L., Lillard, A., & Perner, J. (1994). Commentary: Triangulating pretence and belief. In C. Lewis & P. Mitchell (Eds.), *Children's early understanding of mind: Origins and development* (pp. 427–455). Hove, UK: Lawrence Erlbaum Associates Ltd.

Heal, J. (1986). Replication and functionalism. In J. Butterfield (Ed.), *Language, mind, and logic* (pp. 135–150). Cambridge: Cambridge University Press.

Heider, F., & Simmel, M. (1944) An experimental study of apparent behavior. *American Journal of Psychology, 57*, 243–249.

Hermelin, B. (2001). *Bright splinters of the mind: A personal story of research with autistic savants*. London: Kingsley.

Hickling, A. K., Wellman, H. M., & Gottfried, G. M. (1997). Preschoolers' understanding of others' mental attitudes towards pretend happenings. *British Journal of Developmental Psychology, 15*, 339–354.

Hill, E. L. (2004). Executive dysfunction in autism. *Trends in Cognitive Sciences, 8*, 26–32.

Hobolth, A., Christensen, O. F., Mailund, T., & Schierup, M. H. (2007). Genomic relationships and speciation times of human, chimpanzee, and gorilla inferred from a coalescent hidden Markov model. *PLoS Genetics, 3*, 294–304.

Hogrefe, G. J., Wimmer, H., & Perner, J. (1986). Ignorance versus false belief: A developmental lag in attribution of epistemic states. *Child Development, 57*, 567–582.

Holbourn, A. H. S. (1943). Mechanics of head injuries. *The Lancet, 2*, 438–441.

Holmes, H. A., Black, C., & Miller, S. A. (1996). A cross-task comparison of false belief understanding in a head start population. *Journal of Experimental Child Psychology, 63*, 263–285.

Hood, B. M., Willen, J. D., & Driver, J. (1998). Adult's eyes trigger shifts of visual attention in human infants. *Psychological Science, 9*, 131–134.

Houston-Price, C., & Nakai, S. (2004). Distinguishing novelty and familiarity effects in infant preference procedures. *Infant and Child Development, 13*, 341–348.

Howes, C., & Matheson, C. C. (1992). Sequences in the development of competent play with peers: Social and social pretend play. *Developmental Psychology, 28*, 961–974.

Howes, C., Ungerer, O., & Seidner, L. B. (1989). Social pretend play in toddlers: Parallels with social play and with solitary pretend. *Child Development, 60*, 77–84.

Hresko, W. P., Reid, D. K., & Hammill, D. D. (1981). *Test of early language development* Austin, TX: Pro-Ed.

Hresko, W. P., Reid, D. K., & Hammill, D. D. (1999). *Test of early language development* (3rd ed.). Austin, TX: Pro-Ed.

Hughes, C. (1998). Finding your marbles: Does preschoolers' strategic behavior predict later understanding of mind? *Developmental Psychology, 34*, 1326–1339.

Hughes, C., Jaffee, S. R., Happé, F., Taylor, A., Caspi, A., & Moffitt, T. E. (2005). Origins of individual differences in theory of mind: From nature to nurture. *Child Development, 76*, 356–370.

Hughes, C., & Russell, J. (1993). Autistic children's difficulty with mental disengagement from an object: Its implications for theories of autism. *Developmental Psychology, 29*, 498–510.

Humphrey, N. K. (1983). *Consciousness regained*. Oxford: Oxford University Press.

Itakura, S., & Tanaka, M. (1998). Use of experimenter-given gaze cues during object-choice tasks by chimpanzees (*Pan troglodytes*), an orangutan (*Pongo pygmaeus*), and human infants (*Homo sapiens*). *Journal of Comparative Psychology, 112*, 119–126.

Jarrold, C., Butler, D., Cottington, E., & Jimenez, F. (2000). Linking theory of mind and central coherence bias in autism and in the general population. *Developmental Psychology, 36*, 126–138.

Jarrold, C., Carruthers, P., Smith, P. K., & Boucher, J. (1994). Pretend play: Is it metarepresentational? *Mind & Language, 9*, 445–468.

Jarrold, C., & Routh, D. A. (1998). Is there really a link between engineering and autism? *Autism, 2*, 281–289.

Jaynes, J. (1976). *The origin of consciousness in the breakdown of the bicameral mind*. Boston, MA: Houghton Mifflin.

Joliffe, T., Lansdown, R., & Robinson, C. (1992). Autism: A personal account. *Communication, 26*, 12–19.

Jones, L. B., Rothbart, M. K., & Posner, M. I. (2003). Development of executive attention in preschool children. *Developmental Science, 6*, 498–504.

Kanner, L. (1943). Autistic disturbances of affective contact. *Nervous Child, 2*, 217–250.

Kavanaugh, R. D., & Harris, P. L. (1994). Imagining the outcome of pretend transformations: Assessing the competence of normal children and children with autism. *Developmental Psychology, 30*, 847–854.

Kirkham, N. J., Cruess, L., & Diamond, A. (2003). Helping children apply their knowledge to their behaviour on a dimension-switching task. *Developmental Science, 6*, 449–476.

Klin, A., Pauls, D., Schultz, R., & Volkmar, F. (2005). Three diagnostic approaches to Asperger Syndrome: Implications for research. *Journal of Autism and Developmental Disorders, 35*, 221–234.

Kloo, D., Aichorn, M., & Perner, J. (2007). *The case of object cognition: Opposite set-shifting effects in children from those in adults.* Unpublished manuscript, University of Salzburg.

Kloo, D., Dabernig, S., & Perner, J. (2007, March). *Reversal shifts vs. extra-dimensional shifts in preschoolers: Evidence against a selective attention account.* Poster presented at the biennial meeting of the Society for Research in Child Development, Boston, MA.

Kloo, D., & Perner, J. (2003). Training transfer between card sorting and false belief understanding: Helping children apply conflicting descriptions. *Child Development, 74*, 1823–1839.

Kloo, D., & Perner, J. (2005). Disentangling dimensions in the dimensional change card-sorting task. *Developmental Science, 8*, 44–56.

Knickmeyer, R., Baron-Cohen, S., Raggatt, P., & Taylor, K. (2005). Foetal testosterone, social relationships, and restricted interests in children. *Journal of Child Psychology and Psychiatry, 46*, 198–210.

Kobayashi, H., & Kohshima, S. (2001). Unique morphology of the human eye and its adaptive meaning: Comparative studies on external morphology of the primate eye. *Journal of Human Evolution, 40*, 419–453.

Lang, B., & Perner, J. (2002). Understanding of intention and false belief and the development of self-control. *British Journal of Developmental Psychology, 20*, 67–77.

Lee, K., Eskritt, M., Symons, L. A., & Muir, D. (1998). Children's use of triadic eye gaze information for "mind reading." *Developmental Psychology, 34*, 525–539.

Lee, K., Olson, D. R., & Torrance, N. (1999). Chinese children's understanding of false beliefs: The role of language. *Journal of Child Language, 26*, 1–21.

Leslie, A. M. (1987). Pretense and representation: The origins of "theory of mind." *Psychological Review, 94*, 412–426.

Leslie, A. M. (1988). Some implications of pretence for mechanisms underlying the child's theory of mind. In J. W. Astington, P. L. Harris, & D. R. Olson (Eds.), *Developing theories of mind* (pp. 19–46). Cambridge: Cambridge University Press.

Leslie, A. M. (1991). The theory of mind impairment in autism: Evidence for a modular mechanism of development? In A. Whiten (Ed.), *Natural theories of mind: Evolution, development and simulation of everyday mindreading* (pp. 63–78). Oxford: Blackwell.

Leslie, A. M. (1994). Pretending and believing: Issues in theory of ToMM. *Cognition, 50*, 211–238.

Leslie, A. M. (2005). Developmental parallels in understanding minds and bodies. *Trends in Cognitive Sciences, 9,* 459–462.

Leslie, A. M., Friedman, O., & German, T. P. (2004). Core mechanisms in "theory of mind." *Trends in Cognitive Sciences, 8,* 528–533.

Leslie, A. M., & Frith, U. (1988). Autistic children's understanding of seeing, knowing and believing. *British Journal of Developmental Psychology, 4,* 315–324.

Leslie, A. M., German, T. P., & Polizzi, P. (2005). Belief–desire reasoning as a process of selection. *Cognitive Psychology, 50,* 45–85.

Leslie, A. M., & Roth, D. (1993). What autism teaches us about metarepresentation. In S. Baron-Cohen, H. Tager-Flusberg, & D. J. Cohen (Eds.), *Understanding other minds: Perspectives from autism* (pp. 83–111). New York: Oxford University Press.

Leslie, A. M., & Thaiss, L. (1992). Domain specificity in conceptual development: Neuro-psychological evidence from autism. *Cognition, 43,* 225–251.

Levinson, B. (Director). (1988). *Rainman* [Motion picture]. United States: Universal Artists.

Lewis, C. N., & Freeman, N. H. (1992). *Dissociation of inferences about beliefs and pictures in preschoolers.* Unpublished manuscript, Departments of Psychology, Universities of Lancaster and Bristol.

Lewis, C. N., Freeman, N. H., Kyriakidou, C., Maridaki-Kassotaki, K., & Berridge, D. M. (1996). Social influences on false belief access: Specific sibling influences or general apprenticeship? *Child Development, 67,* 2930–2947.

Lewis, C. N., & Osborne, A. (1990). Three-year-olds' problems with false belief: Conceptual deficit or linguistic artifact? *Child Development, 61,* 1514–1519.

Lewis, M., Stanger, C., & Sullivan, M. W. (1989). Deception in 3-year-olds. *Developmental Psychology, 25,* 439–443.

Lewis, V., & Boucher, J. (1988). Spontaneous, instructed, and elicited play in relatively able autistic children. *British Journal of Developmental Psychology, 6,* 325–339.

Lichtermann, L. (1991). *Young children's understanding of desires.* Unpublished under-graduate dissertation, University of Sussex.

Light, P., & Nix, C. (1983). Own view versus good view in a perspective-taking task. *Child Development, 54,* 480–483.

Lillard, A. (1993). Young children's conceptualization of pretense: Action or mental repre-sentational state? *Child Development, 64,* 372–386.

Lillard, A. (1998). Ethnopsychologies: Cultural variations in theories of mind. *Psychological Bulletin, 123,* 3–32.

Lillard, A. (2001). Pretend play as twin earth: A social-cognitive analysis. *Developmental Review, 21,* 495–531.

Lohmann, H., & Tomasello, M. (2003). The role of language in the development of false-belief understanding: A training study. *Child Development, 74,* 1130–1144.

Long, G. M., & Toppino, T. C. (2004). Enduring interest in perceptual ambiguity: Alterna-ting views of reversible figures. *Psychological Bulletin, 130,* 748–768.

Lotter, V. (1966). Epidemiology of autistic conditions in young children. I. Prevalence. *Social Psychiatry, 1,* 124–137.

MacLeod, C. M. (1991). Half a century of research on the Stroop Effect: An integrative review. *Psychological Bulletin, 109,* 163–203.

MacWhinney, B., & Snow, C. (1985). The child language data exchange system. *Journal of Child Language, 12*, 271–296.

MacWhinney, B., & Snow, C. (1990). The child language data exchange system: An update. *Journal of Child Language, 17*, 457–472.

Markman, E. M. (1989). *Categorization and naming in children: Problems of induction.* Cambridge, MA: MIT Press.

Markman, E. M., & Wachtel, G. F. (1988). Children's use of mutual exclusivity to constrain the meanings of words. *Cognitive Psychology, 20*, 121–157.

Marshall, J. C., & Morton, J. (1978). On the mechanics of EMMA. In A. Sinclair, R. J. Jarvella, & W. J. M. Levelt (Eds.), *The child's conception of language* (pp. 225–239). Berlin: Springer-Verlag.

Masangkay, Z. S., McCluskey, K. A., McIntyre, C. W., Sims-Knight, J., Vaughn, B. E., & Flavell, J. H. (1974). The early development of inferences about the visual percepts of others. *Child Development, 45*, 349–372.

Meins, E., Fernyhough, C., Wainwright, R., Das Gupta, M., Fradley, E., & Tuckey, M. (2002). Maternal mind-mindedness and attachment security as predictors of theory of mind understanding. *Child Development, 73*, 1715–1726.

Merriman, W. E., & Bowman, L. L. (1989). The mutual exclusivity bias in children's word learning. *Monographs of the Society for Research in Child Development, 54*, 1–129.

Milgram, S. (1963). Behavioral study of obedience. *Journal of Abnormal and Social Psychology, 67*, 371–378.

Milligan, K., Astington, J. W., & Dack, L. A. (2007). Language and theory of mind: Meta-analysis of the relation between language ability and false-belief understanding. *Child Development, 78*, 622–646.

Milne, A. A. (1926). *Winnie-the-Pooh*. London: Methuen.

Mitchell, P. (1996). *Acquiring a conception of mind: A review of psychological research and theory*. Hove, UK: Psychology Press.

Mitchell, P., & Lacohée, H. (1991). Children's early understanding of false belief. *Cognition, 39*, 107–127.

Miyake, A., Friedman, N. P., Emerson, M. J., Witzki, A. H., Howerter, A., & Wager, T. D. (2000). The unity and diversity of executive functions and their contributions to complex "frontal lobe" tasks: A latent variable analysis. *Cognitive Psychology, 41*, 49–100.

Moll, H., & Tomasello, M. (2006). Level 1 perspective-taking at 24 months of age. *British Journal of Developmental Psychology, 24*, 603–613.

Moore, C. (2006). Commentary on The Development of Mentalistic Gaze Understanding. Understanding the directedness of gaze: Three ways of doing it. *Infant and Child Development, 15*, 191–193.

Moore, C., & Corkum, V. (1998). The origins of joint visual attention in infants. *Developmental Psychology, 34*, 28–38.

Moore, C., Jarrold, C., Russell, J., Lumb, A., Sapp, F., & MacCallum, F. (1995). Conflicting desire and the child's theory of mind. *Cognitive Development, 10*, 467–482.

Moore, C., Pure, K., & Furrow, D. (1990). Children's understanding of the modal expression of speaker certainty and uncertainty and its relation to the development of a representational theory of mind. *Child Development, 61*, 722–730.

Morris, M. W., & Peng, K. (1994). Culture and cause: American and Chinese attributions for social and physical events. *Journal of Personality and Social Psychology, 67*, 949–971.

Morton, A. (1980). *Frames of mind: Constraints on the common-sense conception of the mental.* Oxford: Clarendon Press.

Moses, L. J. (2001). Executive accounts of theory-of-mind development. *Child Development, 72*, 688–690.

Moses, L. J. (2005). Executive functioning and children's theories of mind. In B. F. Malle & S. D. Hodges (Eds.), *Other minds: How humans bridge the divide between self and others* (pp. 11–25). New York: Guilford Press.

Moses, L. J., & Flavell, J. H. (1990). Inferring false beliefs from actions and reactions. *Child Development, 61*, 929–945.

Muller, U., Zelazo, P. D., & Imrisek, S. (2005). Executive function and children's understanding of false belief: How specific is the relation? *Cognitive Development, 20*, 173–189.

Munakata, Y., & Yerys, B. E. (2001). All together now: When dissociations between knowledge and action disappear. *Psychological Science, 12*, 335–337.

Murphy, M., Bolton, P. F., Pickles, A., Fombonne, E., Piven, J., & Rutter, M. (2000). Personality traits of the relatives of autistic probands. *Psychological Medicine, 30*, 1411–1424.

Myowa-Yamakoshi, M., Tomonaga, M., Tanaka, M., & Matsuzawa, T. (2003). Preference for human direct gaze in infant chimpanzees (*Pan troglodytes*). *Cognition, 89*, B53–B64.

Naito, M., & Koyama, K. (2006). The development of false-belief understanding in Japanese children: Delay and difference? *International Journal of Behavioral Development, 30*, 290–304.

Newcombe, N., & Huttenlocher, J. (2000). *Making space: The development of spatial representation and reasoning.* Cambridge, MA: MIT Press.

Nichols, S., & Stich, S. (2003). *Mindreading: An integrated account of pretense, self-awareness and understanding other minds.* Oxford: Oxford University Press.

Nisbett, R. E., & Miyamoto, Y. (2005). The influence of culture: Holistic versus analytic perception. *Trends in Cognitive Sciences, 9*, 467–473.

Nisbett, R. E., & Ross, L. (1980). *Human inference: Strategies and shortcomings of social judgment.* Englewood Cliffs, NJ: Prentice Hall.

Norman, D. A., & Shallice, T. (1986). Attention to action: Wilted and automatic control of behavior. In R. J. Davidson, G. E. Schwarts, & D. Shapiro (Eds.), *Conciousness and self-regulation: Advances in research and theory* (Vol. 4, pp. 1–18). New York: Plenum Press.

O'Neill, D. K. (1996). Two-year-old children's sensitivity to a parent's knowledge state when making requests. *Child Development, 67*, 659–677.

O'Neill, D. K., Astington, J. W., & Flavell, J. H. (1992). Young children's understanding of the role that sensory experiences play in knowledge acquisition. *Child Development, 63*, 474–490.

O'Neill, D. K., & Chong, S. C. F. (2001). Preschool children's difficulty understanding the types of information obtained through the five senses. *Child Development, 72*, 803–815.

Onishi, K. H., & Baillargeon, R. (2005). Do 15-month-old infants understand false beliefs? *Science, 308,* 255–258.

Ozonoff, S., Pennington, B. F., & Rogers, S. J. (1991). Executive functioning deficits in high-functioning autistic individuals: Relationship to theory of mind. *Journal of Child Psychology and Psychiatry, 32,* 1081–1105.

Pellicano, E. A., Maybery, M. T., Durkin, K. A., & Maley, A. N. (2006). Multiple cognitive capabilities/deficits in children with an autism spectrum disorder: "Weak" central coherence and its relationship to theory of mind and executive control. *Development and Psychopathology, 18,* 77–98.

Perner, J. (1988). Developing semantics for theories of mind: From propositional attitudes to mental representation. In J. W. Astington, P. L. Harris, & D. R. Olson (Eds.), *Developing theories of mind* (pp. 141–172). New York: Cambridge University Press.

Perner, J. (1991). *Understanding the representational mind.* Cambridge, MA: MIT Press.

Perner, J. (1995). The many faces of belief: Reflections on Fodor's and the child's theory of mind. *Cognition, 57,* 241–269.

Perner, J. (2000). RUM, PUM, and the perspectival relativity of sortals. In J. W. Astington (Ed.), *Minds in the making: Essays in honor of David R. Olson* (pp. 212–232). Oxford: Blackwell.

Perner, J., Baker, S., & Hutton, D. (1994a). Prelief: The conceptual origins of belief and pretence. In C. Lewis & P. Mitchell (Eds.), *Children's early understanding of mind: Origins and development* (pp. 427–455). Hove, UK: Lawrence Erlbaum Associates Ltd.

Perner, J., Frith, U., Leslie, A. M., & Leekam, S. R. (1989). Exploration of the autistic child's theory of mind: Knowledge, belief, and communication. *Child Development, 60,* 689–700.

Perner, J., & Howes, D. (1992). "He thinks he knows": And more developmental evidence against the simulation (role-taking) theory. *Mind & Language, 7,* 72–86.

Perner, J., & Kühberger, A. (2006). Framing and the theory-simulation controversy: Predicting people's decisions. In R. Viale, D. Andler, & L. Hirschfeld (Eds.), *Biological and cultural bases of human inference* (pp. 161–176). New York: Erlbaum.

Perner, J., & Lang, B. (2000). Theory of mind and executive function: Is there a developmental relationship? In S. Baron-Cohen, H. Tager-Flusberg, & D. J. Cohen (Eds.), *Understanding other minds: Perspectives from developmental cognitive neuroscience* (pp. 150–181). Oxford: Oxford University Press.

Perner, J., & Lang, B. (2002). What causes 3-year-olds' difficulty on the dimensional change card sorting task? *Infant and Child Development, 11,* 93–105.

Perner, J., Lang, B., & Kloo, D. (2002a). Theory of mind and self-control: More than a common problem of inhibition. *Child Development, 73,* 752–767.

Perner, J., Leekam, S. R., Myers, D., Davis, S., & Odgers, N. (1998). *Misrepresentation and referential confusion: Children's difficulty with false beliefs and outdated photographs.* Retrieved December 19, 2007, from http://cogprints.org/708/

Perner, J., Leekam, S. R., & Wimmer, H. (1987). Three-year-olds' difficulty with false belief: The case for a conceptual deficit. *British Journal of Developmental Psychology, 5,* 125–137.

Perner, J., & Ruffman, T. (2005). Infants' insight into the mind: how deep? *Science, 308,* 214–216.

Perner, J., Ruffman, T., & Leekam, S. R. (1994b). Theory of mind is contagious: You catch it from your sibs. *Child Development, 65*, 1228–1238.

Perner, J., Sprung, M., Zauner, P., & Haider, H. (2003). Want that is understood well before say that, think that, and false belief: A test of de Villiers' linguistic determinism on German speaking children. *Child Development, 74*, 179–188.

Perner, J., Stummer, S., & Lang, B. (1999). Executive functions and theory of mind: Cognitive complexity or functional dependence? In P. D. Zelazo, J. W. Astington, & D. R. Olson (Eds). *Developing theories of intention: Social understanding and self-control* (pp. 133–152). Mahwah, NJ: Lawrence Erlbaum Associates, Inc.

Perner, J., Stummer, S., Sprung, M., & Doherty, M. (2002b). Theory of mind finds its Piagetian perspective: Why alternative naming comes with understanding belief. *Cognitive Development, 17*, 1451–1472.

Perner, J., & Wimmer, H. (1985). John thinks that Mary thinks that: Attribution of 2nd-order beliefs by 5-year-old to 10-year-old children. *Journal of Experimental Child Psychology, 39*, 437–471.

Perner, J., Zauner, P., & Sprung, M. (2005). What does "that" have to do with point of view? The case of conflicting desires and "want" in German. In J. Astington & J. A. Baird (Eds.), *Why language matters for theory of mind* (pp. 220–244). Oxford: Oxford University Press.

Peskin, J. (1992). Ruse and representations: On children's ability to conceal information. *Developmental Psychology, 28*, 84–89.

Peskin, J., & Ardino, V. (2003). Representing the mental world in children's social behavior: Playing hide-and-seek and keeping a secret. *Social Development, 12*, 496–512.

Peskin, J., & Astington, J. W. (2004). The effects of adding metacognitive language to story texts. *Cognitive Development, 19*, 253–273.

Peterson, C. M., & Siegal, M. (1999). Representing inner worlds: Theory of mind in autistic, deaf and normal hearing children. *Psychological Science, 10*, 126–129.

Peterson, C. M., & Siegal, M. (2000). Insights into theory of mind from deafness and autism. *Mind & Language, 15*, 123–145.

Pillow, B. H. (1989). Early understanding of perception as a source of knowledge. *Journal of Experimental Child Psychology, 47*, 116–129.

Povinelli, D. J., Bierschwale, D. T., & Čech, C. G. (1999). Comprehension of seeing as a referential act in young children, but not juvenile chimpanzees. *British Journal of Developmental Psychology, 17*, 37–60.

Povinelli, D. J., & Eddy, T. J. (1996a). Chimpanzees: Joint visual attention. *Psychological Science, 7*, 129–135.

Povinelli, D. J., & Eddy, T. J. (1996b). What young chimpanzees know about seeing. *Monographs of the Society for Research in Child Development, 61* (3, Serial No. 247).

Povinelli, D. J., & Vonk, J. (2003). Chimpanzee minds: Suspiciously human? *Trends in Cognitive Science, 7*, 157–160.

Povinelli, D. J., & Vonk, J. (2004). We don't need a microscope to explore the chimpanzee's mind. *Mind & Language, 19*, 1–28.

Pratt, C., & Bryant, P. (1990). Young children understand that looking leads to knowing (so long as they are looking into a single barrel). *Child Development, 61*, 973–982.

Premack, D., & Woodruff, G. (1978). Does the chimpanzee have a theory of mind? *Behavioral and Brain Sciences, 1,* 515–526.

Pylyshyn, Z. W. (1978). When is attribution of beliefs justified? *Behavioral and Brain Sciences, 1,* 592–593.

Rakoczy, H., Warneken, F., & Tomasello, M. (2007). "This way!", "No! That way!"—3-year-olds know that two people can have mutually incompatible desires. *Cognitive Development, 22,* 47–68.

Repacholi, B. M., & Gopnik, A. (1997). Early reasoning about desires: Evidence from 14- and 18-month-olds. *Developmental Psychology, 33,* 12–21.

Rice, C., Koinis, D., Sullivan, K., Tager-Flusberg, H., & Winner, E. (1997). When 3-year-olds pass the appearance–reality test. *Developmental Psychology, 33,* 54–61.

Rieffe, C., Meerum Terwogt, M., & Cowan, R. (2005). Children's understanding of mental states as causes of emotions. *Infant and Child Development, 14,* 259–272.

Rivera, S. M., Wakeley, A., & Langer, J. (1999). The drawbridge phenomenon representational reasoning or perceptual preference? *Developmental Psychology, 35,* 427–435.

Robinson, E. J., & Mitchell, P. (1995). Masking of children's early understanding of the representational mind: Backwards explanation versus prediction. *Child Development, 66,* 1022–1039.

Rock, I., Gopnik, A., & Hall, S. (1994). Do young children reverse ambiguous figures? *Perception, 23,* 635–644.

Ross, H. S., & Lollis, S. P. (1987). Communication within infant social games. *Developmental Psychology, 23,* 241–248.

Ruffman, T. (1996). Do children understand the mind by means of simulation or a theory? Evidence from their understanding of inference. *Mind & Language, 11,* 388–414.

Ruffman, T. (2000). Nonverbal theory of mind: Is it important, is it implicit, is it simulation, is it relevant to autism? In J. W. Astington (Ed.), *Minds in the making: Essays in honor of David R. Olson* (pp. 250–266). Oxford: Blackwell.

Ruffman, T., Garnham, W., Import, A., & Connolly, D. (2001). Does eye gaze indicate implicit knowledge of false belief? Charting transitions in knowledge. *Journal of Experimental Child Psychology, 80,* 201–224.

Ruffman, T., & Keenan, T. R. (1996). The belief-based emotion of surprise: The case for a lag in understanding relative to false belief. *Developmental Psychology, 32,* 40–49.

Ruffman, T., Olson, D. R., & Astington, J. W. (1991). Children's understanding of visual ambiguity. *British Journal of Developmental Psychology, 9,* 89–102.

Ruffman, T., & Perner, J. (2005). Do infants really understand false belief? Response to Leslie. *Trends in Cognitive Sciences, 9,* 462–463.

Ruffman, T., Perner, J., Naito, M., Parkin, L., & Clements, W. A. (1998). Older (but not younger) siblings facilitate false belief understanding. *Developmental Psychology, 34,* 161–174.

Ruffman, T., Perner, J., & Parkin, L. (1999). How parenting style affects false-belief understanding. *Social Development, 8,* 395–411.

Ruffman, T., Slade, L., & Crowe, E. (2002). The relation between children's and mothers' mental state language and theory-of-mind understanding. *Child Development, 73,* 734–751.

Ruffman, T., Slade, L., Rowlandson, K., Rumsey, C., & Garnham, A. (2003). How language relates to belief, desire, and emotion understanding. *Cognitive Development, 18,* 139–158.

Russell, J. (1996). *Agency: Its role in mental development.* Hove, UK: Psychology Press.

Russell, J., Hala, S., & Hill, E. (2003). The automated windows task: The performance of preschool children, children with autism, and children with moderate learning difficulties. *Cognitive Development, 18,* 111–137.

Russell, J., Jarrold, C., & Potel, D. (1994). What makes strategic deception difficult for children: The deception or the strategy? *British Journal of Developmental Psychology, 12,* 301–314.

Russell, J., Mauthner, N., Sharpe, S., & Tidswell, T. (1991). The windows task as a measure of strategic deception in preschoolers and autistic subjects. *British Journal of Developmental Psychology, 9,* 331–349.

Russell, P. A., Hosie, J. A., Gray, C. D., Scott, C., Hunter, N., Banks, J. S., et al. (1998). The development of theory of mind in deaf children. *Journal of Child Psychology and Psychiatry, 39,* 903–910.

Rutherford, M. D., & Rogers, S. J. (2003). Cognitive underpinnings of pretend play in autism. *Journal of Autism and Developmental Disorders, 33,* 289–302.

Rutter, M. (1966). Behavioural and cognitive characteristics of a series of psychotic children. In J. K. Wing (Ed.), *Early childhood autism* (pp. 51–81). Oxford: Pergamon Press.

Rutter, M. (2005). Aetiology of autism: Findings and questions. *Journal of Intellectual Disability Research, 49,* 231–238.

Rutter, M., Andersen-Wood, L., Beckett, C., Bredenkamp, D., Castle, J., Groothues, C., et al. (1999). Quasi-autistic patterns following severe early global privation. *Journal of Child Psychology and Psychiatry, 40,* 537–549.

Sacks, O. (1986). *The man who mistook his wife for a hat.* London: Picador.

Samuels, C. (1985). Attention to eye contact opportunity and facial motion by 3 month old infants. *Journal of Experimental Child Psychology, 40,* 105–114.

Savage-Rumbaugh, S., & McDonald, K. (1988). Deception and social manipulation in symbol-using apes. In R. W. Byrne & A. Whiten (Eds.), *Machievellian intelligence: Social expertise and the evolution of intellect in monkeys, apes, and humans* (pp. 224–237). Oxford: Oxford University Press.

Saxe, R. (2005). Against simulation: The argument from error. *Trends in Cognitive Sciences, 9,* 174–179.

Scaife, M., & Bruner, J. S. (1975). The capacity for joint visual attention in the infant. *Nature, 253,* 265–266.

Schick, B., de Villiers, P., de Villiers, J., & Hoffmeister, P. (2007). Language and theory of mind: A study of deaf children. *Child Development, 78,* 376–396.

Scholl, B. J., & Leslie, A. M. (2001). Minds, modules, and meta-analysis. *Child Development, 72,* 696–701.

Segal, G. (1996). The modularity of theory of mind. In P. Carruthers & P. Smith (Eds.), *Theories of theories of mind* (pp. 141–157). Cambridge: Cambridge University Press.

Shah, A., & Frith, U. (1993). Why do autistic individuals show superior performance on the block design task? *Journal of Child Psychology and Psychiatry, 34,* 1351–1364.

Shatz, M., Diesendruck, G., Martinez-Beck, I., & Akar, D. (2003). The influence of language and socioeconomic status on children's understanding of false belief. *Developmental Psychology, 39*, 717–729.

Siegal, M., & Beattie, K. (1991). Where to look first for children's knowledge of false beliefs. *Cognition, 38*, 1–12.

Siegal, M., & Peterson, C. C. (1994). Children's theory of mind and the conversational territory of cognitive development. In C. Lewis & P. Mitchell (Eds.), *Children's early understanding of mind: Origins and development* (pp. 427–455). Hove, UK: Lawrence Erlbaum Associates Ltd.

Simpson, A., Riggs, K. J., & Simon, M. (2004). What makes the windows task difficult for young children: Rule inference or rule use? *Journal of Experimental Child Psychology, 87*(2), 155–170.

Slaughter, V. (1998). Children's understanding of pictorial and mental representations. *Child Development, 69*, 321–332.

Smith, L. B., & Thelen, E. (2003). Development as a dynamic system. *Trends in Cognitive Sciences, 7*, 343–348.

Snyder, A., Bahramali, H., Hawker, T., & Mitchell, D. J. (2006). Savant-like numerosity skills revealed in normal people by magnetic pulses. *Perception, 35*, 837–845.

Sodian, B., Taylor, C., Harris, P. L., & Perner, J. (1991). Early deception and the child's theory of mind: False trails and genuine markers. *Child Development, 62*, 468–483.

Sodian, B., & Wimmer, H. (1987). Children's understanding of inference as a source of knowledge. *Child Development, 58*, 424–433.

Southgate, V., Senju, A., & Csibra, G. (2007). Action anticipation through attribution of false belief by 2-year-olds. *Psychological Science, 18*, 587–592.

Stern, W., & Stern, C. (1999). *Recollection, testimony, and lying in early childhood.* (J. Lamiell, Trans.). Washington, DC: APA. (Original work published 1909)

Stich, S., & Nichols, S. (1992). Folk psychology: Simulation or tacit theory. *Mind & Language, 6*, 29–65.

Stouthamer-Loeber, M. (1991). Young children's verbal misrepresentations of reality. In K. J. Rotenberg (Ed.), *Children's interpersonal trust: Sensitivity to lying, deception, and promise violations* (pp. 20–42). Berlin: Springer-Verlag.

Stroop, J. R. (1935). Studies of interference in serial verbal reactions. *Journal of Experimental Psychology, 18*, 643–662.

Stuss, D. T. (1992). Biological and psychological development of executive functions. *Brain & Cognition, 20*, 8–23.

Sullivan, K., Zaitchik, D., & Tager-Flusberg, H. (1994). Preschoolers can attribute 2nd-order beliefs. *Developmental Psychology, 30*, 395–402.

Surian, L., Baron-Cohen, S., & Van der Lely, H. (1996). Are children with autism deaf to Gricean maxims? *Cognitive Neuropsychology, 1*, 55–71.

Tager-Flusberg, H. (1991). Semantic processing in the free recall of autistic children: Further evidence for a cognitive deficit. *British Journal of Developmental Psychology, 9*, 417–430.

Tager-Flusberg, H. (1992). Autistic children's talk about psychological states: Deficits in the early acquisition of a theory of mind. *Child Development, 63*, 161–172.

Tardif, T., Wellman, H. M., & Cheung, K. M. (2004). False belief understanding in Cantonese-speaking children. *Journal of Child Language, 31*, 779–800.

Taumoepeau, M., & Ruffman, T. (2006). Mother and infant talk about mental states relates to desire language and emotion understanding. *Child Development, 77,* 465–481.

Taumoepeau, M., & Ruffman, T. (in press). Stepping stones to others' minds. *Child Development.*

Taylor, M. (1988). The development of children's understanding of the seeing–knowing distinction. In J. W. Astington, P. L. Harris, & D. R. Olson (Eds.), *Developing theories of mind* (pp. 207–225). New York: Cambridge University Press.

Taylor, M., & Carlson, S. M. (1997). The relation between individual differences in fantasy and theory of mind. *Child Development, 68,* 436–455.

Thatcher, R. W. (1992). Cyclic cortical reorganization during early childhood. *Brain & Cognition, 20,* 24–50.

Thayer, S. (1977). Children's detection of on-face and off-face gazes. *Developmental Psychology, 13,* 673–674.

Tomasello, M., Call, J., & Hare, B. (2003). Chimpanzees understand psychological states—the question is which ones and to what extent. *Trends in Cognitive Science, 7,* 153–156.

Towse, J. N., Redbond, J., Houston-Price, C. M. T., & Cook, S. (2000). Understanding the dimensional change card sort: Perspectives from task success and failure. *Cognitive Development, 15,* 347–365.

Tunmer, W. E., & Herriman, M. L. (1984). The development of metalinguistic awareness: A conceptual overview. In W. E. Tunmer, C. Pratt, & M. L. Herriman (Eds.), *Metalinguistic awareness in children* (pp. 1–22). New York: Springer-Verlag.

Turner, M. (1997). Towards an executive dysfunction account of repetitive behaviour in autism. In J. Russell (Ed.), *Autism as an executive disorder* (pp. 57–99). Oxford: Oxford University Press.

Van Kleeck, A. (1982). The emergence of linguistic awareness: A cognitive framework. *Merrill-Palmer Quarterly, 28,* 237–265.

Vecera, S. P., & Johnson, M. H. (1995). Gaze detection and the cortical processing of faces: Evidence from infants and adults. *Visual Cognition, 2,* 59–87.

Vinden, P. (1996). Junín Quecha children's understanding of mind. *Child Development, 67,* 1707–1716.

Vinden, P. (1999). Children's understanding of mind and emotion: A multi-culture study. *Cognition and Emotion, 13,* 19–48.

Vinden, P. (2002). Understanding minds and evidence for belief: A study of Mofu children in Cameroon. *Journal of International Behavioral Development, 26,* 445–452.

Vinden, P., & Astington, J. W. (2000). Culture and understanding other minds. In S. Baron-Cohen, H. Tager-Flusberg, & D. Cohen (Eds.), *Understanding other minds: Perspectives from developmental cognitive neuroscience* (pp. 503–520). Oxford: Oxford University Press.

Vygotsky, L. S. (1978). *Mind in society: The development of higher psychological processes.* Cambridge, MA: Harvard University Press.

Wakefield, A. J., Murch, S. H., Anthony, A., Linnell, J., Casson, D. M., Malik, M., et al. (1998). Ilcal-lymphoid-nodular hyperplasia, non-specific colitis and pervasive developmental disorder in children. *The Lancet, 351,* 637–641.

235

Wellman, H. M. (1990). *The child's theory of mind*. Cambridge, MA: MIT Press.

Wellman, H. M. (1993). Early understanding of mind: The normal case. In S. Baron-Cohen, H. Tager-Flusberg, & D. Cohen (Eds.), *Understanding other minds: Perspectives from autism* (pp. 10–39). Oxford: Oxford University Press.

Wellman, H. M., & Bartsch, K. (1994). Before belief: Children's early psychological theory. In C. Lewis & P. Mitchell (Eds.), *Children's early understanding of mind: Origins and development* (pp. 331–354). Hove, UK: Lawrence Erlbaum Associates Ltd.

Wellman, H. M., Cross, D., & Watson, J. (2001). Meta-analysis of theory-of-mind development: The truth about false belief. *Child Development, 72,* 655–684.

Wellman, H. M., & Estes, D. (1986). Early understanding of mental entities: A re-examination of childhood realism. *Child Development, 57,* 910–923.

Whiten, A., & Byrne, R. W. (1991). The emergence of metarepresentation in human ontogeny and primate phylogeny. In A. Whiten (Ed.), *Natural theories of mind* (pp. 67–281). Oxford: Blackwell.

Wimmer, H., Hogrefe, G. J., & Perner, J. (1988). Children's understanding of informational access as source of knowledge. *Child Development, 59,* 386–396.

Wimmer, H., & Perner, J. (1983). Beliefs about beliefs: Representation and constraining function of wrong beliefs in young children's understanding of deception. *Cognition, 13,* 103–128.

Wimmer, H., & Weichbold, V. (1994). Children's theory of mind: Fodor's heuristics examined. *Cognition, 53,* 45–57.

Wimmer, H., & Mayringer, H. (1998). False belief understanding in young children: Explanations do not develop before predictions. *International Journal of Behavioral Development, 22,* 403–422.

Wimmer, M. (2007). *Children's perception and understanding of ambiguous figures.* Unpublished doctoral thesis, Department of Psychology, University of Stirling.

Wing, L., & Gould, J. (1979). Severe impairments of social interaction and associated abnormalities in children: Epidemiology and classification. *Journal of Autism and Developmental Disorders, 9,* 11–29.

Wing, L., & Potter, D. (2002). The epidemiology of autistic spectrum disorder: Is the prevalence rising? *Mental Retardation and Developmental Disabilities Research Reviews, 8,* 151–161.

Woodward, A. L. (2003). Infants' developing understanding of the link between looker and object. *Developmental Science, 6,* 297–311.

Woolfe, T., Want, S. C., & Siegal, M. (2002). Signposts to development: Theory of mind in deaf children. *Child Development, 73,* 768–778.

World Health Organization. (1993). *International Classification of Diseases, 10th Edition (ICD-10).* Geneva: Author.

Youngblade, L. M., & Dunn, J. (1995). Individual differences in young children's pretend play with mother and sibling: Links to relationships and understanding of other people's feelings and beliefs. *Child Development, 66,* 1472–1492.

Yuill, N., Perner, J., Pearson, A., Peerbhoy, D., & Ende, J. van den (1996). Children's changing understanding of wicked desires: From objective to subjective and moral. *British Journal of Developmental Psychology, 14,* 457–475.

Zaitchik, D. (1990). When representations conflict with reality: The preschooler's problem with false beliefs and "false" photographs. *Cognition, 35,* 41–68.

Zelazo, P. D., & Frye, D. (1997). Cognitive complexity and control: A theory of the development of deliberate reasoning and intentional action. In M. Stamenov (Ed.), *Language structure, discourse, and the access to conciousness* (pp. 113–153). Amsterdam: John Benjamins.

Zelazo, P. D., Frye, D., & Rapus, T. (1996). An age-related dissociation between knowing rules and using them. *Cognitive Development, 11,* 37–63.

Author index

Subject index